Plato's Tough Guys and Their Attachment to Justice

Plato's Tough Guys and Their Attachment to Justice

Peter J. Hansen

LEXINGTON BOOKS
Lanham • Boulder • New York • London

Published by Lexington Books
An imprint of The Rowman & Littlefield Publishing Group, Inc.
4501 Forbes Boulevard, Suite 200, Lanham, Maryland 20706
www.rowman.com

6 Tinworth Street, London SE11 5AL

Copyright © 2019 by The Rowman & Littlefield Publishing Group, Inc.

All rights reserved. No part of this book may be reproduced in any form or by any electronic or mechanical means, including information storage and retrieval systems, without written permission from the publisher, except by a reviewer who may quote passages in a review.

British Library Cataloguing in Publication Information Available

ISBN 9781498590976 (cloth)
ISBN 9781498590990 (pbk)

Library of Congress Control Number: 2019949649

To Kathryn, with love and admiration

Contents

Acknowledgments	ix
Introduction	xi
1 Reading Plato	1
2 Thrasymachus' Attack on Justice	11
3 Socrates Refutes Thrasymachus	37
4 Callicles' Attack on Justice	59
5 Socrates Questions Callicles	89
6 Callicles Retreats	119
7 Socrates Concludes	141
8 Other Tough Guys	157
Conclusion	179
Bibliography	181
Index	185
About the Author	189

Acknowledgments

This book grew out of a dissertation which I wrote with the Committee on Social Thought at the University of Chicago. I owe an exceptional debt of thanks to my dissertation committee chairman, Nathan Tarcov, for the patience he showed me over the years, as well as for many incisive and insightful comments on my work. I am grateful also to my other dissertation committee members, David Bolotin and Ralph Lerner.

I worked especially closely on the dissertation with David Bolotin, and over many years I have learned a great deal from his courses, his conversation, and his published work. David is the best teacher I have known at conveying something of the delicate task of interpreting Plato.

I have been very fortunate to have other extraordinary teachers as well, including Christopher Bruell, John Harper, David Leibowitz, Harvey Mansfield, Clifford Orwin, Lad Sessions, and the late Allan Bloom and Werner Dannhauser.

I am grateful to my wife, Kathryn Hansen, for many things large and small, including encouraging and helping me to turn my dissertation into this book. Kathryn is my best friend and my chief intellectual companion, with whom I share reading groups and thoughts about everything. (We usually agree, but when we don't, she's usually right.) She is also a wonderfully warm and loving woman, and I am extremely fortunate to be sharing life with her.

Manuel Lopez has been my closest male friend for many years. His distinctive and penetrating way of viewing the world has added so much to mine. His insights often sparkle in their brilliance and quickness. He is also a singularly loyal and warm friend.

I have enjoyed and benefited from thought-provoking conversations with other friends and colleagues, including Nasser Behnegar, Malcolm Brownlee, Tom Cleveland, Daniel Doneson, Jonathan Hand, Marjorie Kasch, Steven Lenzner, Craig Lerner, Renee Lettow Lerner, Rory Schacter, Anna Schmidt, Devin Stauffer, and Bernhardt Trout.

I am grateful to those who read and commented on parts of this book while I was working on it: Kathryn Hansen, Craig Lerner, Manuel Lopez, Heinrich Meier, Nathan Tarcov, and especially David Bolotin. The anonymous reviewer for Lexington Books made helpful comments on the structure of the book and on many details.

I want to stress, however, that the interpretations and thoughts presented in the book are my own, and may not—in some cases certainly do not—reflect the (widely divergent) thought of the people I have mentioned.

I wrote this book above all because I needed to examine the questions the book discusses. As a young man, I thought I had answered these questions; but in early middle age, I found myself compelled to raise the questions again, more fully and openly, and in some ways to revise my earlier answers. I found in Plato a better guide in this inquiry than I had any reason to hope for. I derived exceptional enrichment and satisfaction from working on this book. I hope my readers find it enriching as well.

Introduction

Scholars and non-scholars alike assume that people pursue what they think is good for them, though not necessarily effectively or rationally. Put another way, we assume that self-interest is the basis of our actions. This assumption is shared by utilitarianism, libertarianism, "rational choice" theories, and, perhaps most importantly, by liberalism itself, from its origins in Thomas Hobbes and John Locke to its more recent manifestations in John Rawls and others.

But is this assumption true? Do people simply seek what they perceive to be their own good? What if our deepest motive is not so much the pursuit of a concrete good, but something more elusive and questionable? What if we need to devote ourselves even more than we need to pursue our own good, or if the only way in which we ultimately feel we are truly pursuing our good is through devoting ourselves to something other and higher than ourselves? Might we then need to reconsider how we look at ourselves?

But why would we consider such a view? What could be a more reasonable starting point than the assumption that people pursue their own good? One salient problem with this assumption is that few of the people who make it truly seem to live by it. One might consider the example of Thomas Hobbes, who famously teaches that "without a common Power to keep them all in awe," men live in a state of war where life is "solitary, poore, nasty, brutish, and short."[1] This leads Hobbes to identify "the first, and Fundamental Law of Nature" as "to seek Peace, and follow it."[2] He speaks often in praise of fear, the "Passion to be reckoned upon,"[3] the one most able to produce peace, which is the greatest political good. Despite his praise of fear and his urging men to avoid danger, however, Hobbes' own writings were so bold as to endanger his own life.[4] The great political or social good of establishing his principles seems to have been more important to him than actually living by those principles.

Hobbes is not alone in evincing tension between his principles and the way he lives his own life. Many or most thinkers whose work is based upon the assumption of human selfishness hope to contribute to a common good or a social good. Robert Nozick, for example, begins his *Anarchy, State, and Utopia* with the assertion, "Individuals have rights."[5] He argues for a "minimal state" which is just because it protects people without violating their rights, and is moreover "inspiring." One might ask, though, why a thinker who begins with rights rather than duties is so concerned with the rights and the good of others. The primacy of rights over duties implies that man's central concern is and should be his own good,[6] but if this is so, why focus on the rights of others? One might say that only if the rights of all are secure, are the rights of any secure; but this consideration does not seem to be the source of Nozick's attachment to his minimal state theory, as he shows most clearly in arguing that it is a "framework of utopia."[7] He asks if the minimal state can "thrill the heart or inspire people to struggle or sacrifice."[8] But if the just or good political order must inspire people to sacrifice, then surely it should be built upon some foundation other than their private rights or selfish good.

Ronald Dworkin is another recent thinker who focuses on rights. He differs from Nozick on many points, but of Dworkin too one might ask, if the most important political fact is rights, shouldn't one's primary concern be one's *own* rights? Dworkin identifies fundamental rights as "moral rights," which it is morally incumbent upon others (and the government) to respect or at least take seriously.[9] At times Dworkin suggests that we should respect the rights of others so that ours too will be respected, or that our rights are simply our most fundamental interests.[10] However, he also clearly thinks that morality demands we respect the rights of others as an end, for their sake not ours.[11] But what makes rights worthy of this sort of sacrifice or devotion? According to Dworkin, someone "may have the right to do something that is the wrong thing for him to do, as might be the case with gambling."[12] He is not alone in thinking that rights include a right to do what is wrong; but one must ask in what sense we can have a moral, not merely prudential, obligation to respect and protect somebody's ability to do something foolish and harmful.[13] Dworkin seems (unwittingly) torn in how he views rights, and the human beings who have them. His view of justice and virtue doesn't quite jibe with his basic orientation toward rights rather than duties or obligations.

The work of psychologists Daniel Kahneman and Amos Tversky has raised interesting questions about the widespread assumption that people are "generally rational" at pursuing their good.[14] Kahneman and Tversky have spawned a sub-field of economics called behavioral economics which examines ways in which people are *not* rational at pursuing their good. What is not examined (so far), however, is the assumption that people pursue their own good; but this assumption seems questionable in the case of scholars themselves. Is a scholar's work in behavioral economics, or in the rival field of rational choice theory, motivated simply by self-interest? Or is the scholar motivated by concern for truth, or by the belief that truth will serve society or the common good? Or by some complicated combination of these factors? Of course one can define a person's interest as whatever he wishes to pursue; but this seems to distort committed scholarly work and many other phenomena, e.g., a soldier risking his life in battle. We might ask of the scholar, does he wish to enjoy a private good, akin to eating, or is he responding to something more like a calling or a duty?[15]

If one believes that human beings are selfish actors, shouldn't one's own life be chiefly directed toward amassing as much as possible of whatever one considers good for oneself? This does not really seem to be what makes most scholars and thinkers tick. Since Hobbes' time, the world has seen an ever-increasing number of scientifically minded people who deny older understandings of human directedness toward God or other people, but who make great efforts and sometimes take great chances to promote a good larger than their own.

For most of human history, people have not understood themselves simply in terms of their own interest or benefit. In more devout ages, selfishness was considered a temptation and a sin, while our true or essential nature was thought to be directed toward love of God and neighbor. Even now remnants of this view remain, and not only among those who are particularly devout. The founders of liberalism, notably Hobbes, directly confronted this view,[16] and achieved tremendous political success in doing so. However, this doesn't prove that their understanding of human beings was correct, only that it mitigated political conflict arising from disagreements about ultimate beliefs. Clearly something has been gained, but perhaps something has been lost too; perhaps our view of human beings as self-interested reflects not a superior, scientific attitude, but a failure of self-knowledge, a parochial assumption which can seem plausible to us only because we are blinded by the beliefs of the time in which we live and on which our governments are founded.

Demanding that people be devoted to God and their neighbors may well have tended to produce a certain hypocrisy.[17] Our age, however, with its emphasis on rights and self-interest, may tend to produce a lack of self-awareness about our more generous or larger impulses. One might consider, for example, Winston Churchill's discussion of the Oxford Union debaters who in 1933 "passed their ever-shameful resolution, 'That this House will in no circumstances fight for its King and country,'" but who later on the battlefield proved themselves "the finest generation ever bred in Britain"[18]; George Eliot's description in *Daniel Deronda* of a humorous "mixture of kindliness and the desire to justify it in the light of a calculation"[19]; and Alexis de Tocqueville's statement that Americans

> are pleased to explain, with the aid of self-interest well-understood, almost all the actions of their life; they show complacently how the enlightened love of themselves leads them ceaselessly to aid each other and disposes them to sacrifice willingly a part of their time and their wealth to the good of the State. I think that in this it often comes to them not at all to do themselves justice; for one sometimes sees in the United States, as elsewhere, the citizens abandon themselves to the disinterested and unreflective fervors which are natural to man; but the Americans scarcely avow that they yield to movements of this kind; they like better to do honor to their philosophy than to themselves.[20]

Perhaps the true view of human nature lies between these two extremes—but how? Should we simply split the difference and say people are partly self-interested and partly altruistic? Or is the true view more complicated, and more interesting?

Arguably the best way to consider general questions about human nature is to examine particular human beings. A person who denies all altruistic or self-sacrificing impulses, and criticizes those who (claim to) feel such impulses, would be especially interesting in terms of the questions I have raised. Somebody who claims to be altruistic might be hypocritical, but we have less reason to suspect this of somebody who claims to be selfish. Moreover, people who champion selfishness sometimes claim that they expose or reveal what the rest of us are genuinely like, though we are too afraid or self-deluded to admit it.[21]

While we sometimes encounter outspoken immoralists in movies, however, we generally don't in real life in contemporary America. Despite the prevalence of the general theory that people are selfish, most people seem to be at least partly concerned for something beyond their private good, or at least they claim they are. One partial exception is followers of the novelist and thinker Ayn Rand, self-styled Objectivists, who champion selfishness, which Rand considers a virtue.[22] Strikingly, though, the heroic characters in Rand's novels are also explicitly devoted to "values" or principles, and will undergo not merely privation but torture in defense of them.[23]

Greek antiquity offers a better place to look for outspoken and consistent immoralists. Even though no regime in ancient Greece was explicitly based upon selfish principles, it was nonetheless more common in Plato's Athens to repudiate justice than it is now, and to consider at least some of the implications of doing so.[24] Plato offers famous and, in my view, unequalled portraits of two outspoken immoralists, Thrasymachus in his *Republic* and Callicles in his *Gorgias*. Both offer articulate and passionate attacks upon justice, at least as normally understood, and champion thoroughgoing selfishness.

At first glance examining Thrasymachus and Callicles seems unlikely to challenge the view that self-interest is a sufficient framework within which to understand human nature. As we shall see, however, if we follow the subtleties of Plato's presentation, we find that both men display a kind of devotion to their selfish principles, and more broadly a peculiar combination of contempt for justice and unselfconscious attachment to it. They offer surprising and dramatic support for the proposition that human beings are not simply self-interested; we might even consider them extreme cases which suggest that in fact nobody is simply selfish. Plato therefore suggests a very different view of human beings from the one widespread in our time. Moreover, as we shall see, the surprising attachment to justice that Thrasymachus and Callicles display, an attachment of which they themselves are only dimly aware, is in many respects akin to the attachment to justice that most of us feel. By portraying these men, Plato enables us to better understand ourselves, our own attachment to justice, and justice itself.

Of course Thrasymachus and Callicles could be idiosyncratic, or Plato's understanding of this type of man could be flawed, or both. It therefore seems worthwhile to consider other outstanding portrayals of tough guys or immoralists as well. In Chapter 8 I shall examine three of the most famous such characters in modern literature: Shakespeare's Richard III, Dostoevsky's Raskolnikov in *Crime and Punishment*, and Gide's Michel in *The Immoralist*. Different though these authors are from Plato and from each other, I shall argue that their portraits of tough guys invite conclusions similar to those suggested by Plato.

Before turning to Thrasymachus and Callicles, I shall discuss my approach to reading Plato, and contrast it with those of some other scholars. One must read with care in order to understand Plato, and I think it will be helpful for me to give some indication of what I mean by reading with care. In particular, I shall argue, the *ad hominem* character of much of what Plato writes, though frequently acknowledged, has not been sufficiently digested by scholars who have examined Thrasymachus and Callicles.

Some recent scholars have suggested that Thrasymachus and Callicles are attached to justice despite their attacks on it. Regarding Thrasymachus, I am referring to Devin Stauffer's "Thrasymachus' Attachment to Justice?"; David Leibowitz's "Thrasymachus's Blush"; and the discussion of Thrasymachus in Thomas L. Pangle and Timothy W. Burns's *The Key Texts of Political Philosophy*. Regarding Callicles, I am referring to Stauffer's *The Unity of Plato's Gorgias*.[25] All of these are thoughtful treatments, each with its own strengths; but as I shall argue below, none of them fully presents the attachment to justice of the character being considered. In particular, the moral character of Thrasymachus' attraction to artisanship, and of Callicles' attraction to virtue, aren't sufficiently recognized. Without careful attention to these attractions, one cannot appreciate the depth of either man's attachment to justice, or the kinship between their attachment to justice and that of most other human beings. Since these scholars' interpretations demand careful attention to the characters being analyzed, I shall consider them in my chapters on Thrasymachus and Callicles, not in the earlier chapter on reading Plato.

Some definitions are in order. I will return to the large question of defining justice, but except when I indicate otherwise, what I mean by justice is the common good or, where I am speaking of a person being just, devotion to the common good. (Of course the phrase "common good" itself invites questions, some of which I will consider later.) By "tough guy" or "immoralist" I mean somebody who rejects justice understood this way, and embraces injustice. I do not mean somebody who is neutral about justice (if there is any such person), nor somebody who is ambivalent, who has reservations about justice but does not reject or repudiate it.

Neither "tough guy" nor "immoralist" is a perfect term for Thrasymachus or Callicles, but I do not know of a better one. ("Cynic" isn't right because Thrasymachus and Callicles aren't cynics, if by cynic one means someone who denies the existence of human excellence or happiness.) The phrase "tough guy" tends to suggest someone who actually engages in violence, rather than merely praising others who do so. Shakespeare's Richard III qualifies as a tough guy, but it's debatable whether Thrasymachus and Callicles do. On the other hand, the word "immoralist" has an intellectual, apolitical flavor which is alien to both men, particularly Callicles. Moreover, the word suggests rejection of something Plato doesn't precisely discuss: morality or moral virtue. However, rejection of morality is obviously close to, if not exactly the same as, rejection of justice. Neither term is perfect, but in the absence of a superior alternative, I will use them both.

NOTES

1. Thomas Hobbes, *Leviathan* (Cambridge: Cambridge University Press, 1997), 88–89.
2. Hobbes, *Leviathan*, 92.
3. Hobbes, *Leviathan*, 99.
4. Following the publication of *Leviathan* in 1651, Hobbes was endangered by the hostility of fellow English exiles in France, and returned to England to live under the Commonwealth. In 1666, after the Restoration, the House of Commons introduced a bill which attacked atheism and profanity. The committee to which the bill was referred was specifically empowered to receive information about two authors, one of whom was Hobbes (http://www.british-history.ac.uk/report.aspx?compid=26780).
5. Robert Nozick, *Anarchy, State, and Utopia* (New York: Basic Books, 1974), ix.
6. Cf. Hobbes, *Leviathan*, 91: "The Right of Nature, which Writers commonly call *Jus Naturale*, is the Liberty each man hath, to use his own power, as he will himselfe, for the preservation of his own Nature."
7. Nozick, *Anarchy, State, and Utopia*, 332.
8. Nozick, *Anarchy, State, and Utopia*, 297.

9. Ronald Dworkin, *Taking Rights Seriously* (Cambridge, MA: Harvard University Press, 1978), 184.

10. Dworkin, *Taking Rights Seriously*, 176: "The basic idea of a rights-based theory is that distinct individuals have interests that they are entitled to protect if they so wish."

11. Dworkin, *Taking Rights Seriously*, 205: "The institution of rights is therefore crucial, because it represents the majority's promise to the minorities that their dignity and equality will be respected." In other words, respecting the rights of others is important not so much for ensuring that ours too will be respected, but in service of another aim or duty, respecting people's dignity.

12. Dworkin, *Taking Rights Seriously*, 188.

13. Cf. Plato, *The Republic*, 331c, where Socrates asks Cephalus whether it is just to return weapons one has borrowed from a friend who has since gone insane. The Greek text I am using is Plato, *Opera*, Tomus IV, edited by Ioannes Burnet (New York: Oxford University Press, 1978). Henceforth citations from *The Republic* will be given with their Stephanus numbers in parentheses. All translations from *The Republic* are my own, but I have consulted the translation provided by Allan Bloom in Bloom, *The Republic of Plato* (New York: Basic Books, 1991).

14. Daniel Kahneman, *Thinking, Fast and Slow* (New York: Farrar, Straus and Giroux, 2011), 8.

15. Cf. Friedrich Nietzsche, *Beyond Good and Evil*, translated by Walter Kaufmann (New York: Random House, 1966), aphorism 6. "If one would examine how the abstrusest metaphysical claims of a philosopher really came about, it is always well (and wise) to ask first: at what morality does all this (does *he*) aim?" Italics in the original.

16. Cf. Hobbes, *Leviathan*, 70.

17. Cf. Thomas Babington Macaulay, *The History of England from the Accession of James II* (London: The Folio Press, 1985), Volume I, Chapter II, 125–26. Discussing the power of Puritans during England's Commonwealth in the seventeenth century, Macaulay observes that "when a sect becomes powerful, when its favour is the road to riches and dignities, worldly and ambitious men crowd into it, talk its language, conform strictly to its ritual, mimic its peculiarities, and frequently go beyond its honest members in all the outward indications of zeal. No discernment, no watchfulness, on the part of ecclesiastical rulers, can prevent the intrusion of such false brethren."

18. Winston S. Churchill, *The Gathering Storm* (New York: Houghton Mifflin Company, 1948), 77.

19. George Eliot, *Daniel Deronda* (New York: Oxford University Press, 1988), 339.

20. Alexis de Tocqueville, *De la Democratie en Amerique* (Paris: Garnier-Flammarion, 1981), Volume II, 502. The translation is mine.

21. Cf. Plato, *Republic*, 344c, 360c–d.

22. Ayn Rand, *The Virtue of Selfishness* (New York: New American Library, 1964), 34.

23. Ayn Rand, *Atlas Shrugged* (New York: New American Library, 1996), 1047.

24. Cf. Thucydides, *The Peloponnesian War*, translated by Richard Crawley (New York: Random House, 1982), II.63, V.105; Leo Strauss, *Natural Right and History* (Chicago: The University of Chicago Press, 1953), 93–109. Consider also the lines of Pindar partially quoted by Plato's character Callicles in his *Gorgias*, a fuller version of which is provided in E.R. Dodds, *Plato: Gorgias: A Revised Text with Introduction and Commentary* (Oxford: Oxford University Press, 2001), 270.

25. Devin Stauffer, "Thrasymachus' Attachment to Justice?" *Polis* 26 (2009): 1–10; David Leibowitz, "Thrasymachus's Blush" in *Recovering Reason: Essays in Honor of Thomas L. Pangle*, edited by Timothy Burns (Lanham, MD: Rowman & Littlefield, 2010); Thomas L. Pangle and Timothy W. Burns, *The Key Texts of Political Philosophy: An Introduction* (New York: Cambridge University Press, 2015); and Stauffer, *The Unity of Plato's Gorgias* (New York: Cambridge University Press, 2006).

Chapter One

Reading Plato

In this chapter I shall discuss my approach to reading Plato. I shall describe what has been lacking, in my view, in other scholarly treatments of Thrasymachus and Callicles. I shall indicate how my approach differs from the ones I criticize; however, I think my approach will become compelling, will come to life I might say, only in the context of interpreting particular passages, which I shall do in later chapters.

In examining the portions of the *Republic* and the *Gorgias* in which Socrates talks with Thrasymachus and Callicles, I shall focus less on justice itself (though this must be considered in examining these conversations) than on what these men say about it. In discussing Thrasymachus and Callicles, I shall draw attention to contradictions in their views. By this I do not mean that neither man offers a clear position. I mean that there are contradictions within their views that render those views ultimately untenable. It is not that they give us nothing to analyze or hold onto; it is rather that what they give proves incoherent upon closer examination. In particular each man's repudiation of justice (at least as commonly understood) sits alongside a belief in and dependence upon justice, especially in the sense of an order to the universe in which some people deserve good things and others deserve bad ones, and also in the sense of devotion to something larger than oneself. Although these two meanings of justice are logically separable to some extent, Plato suggests that they support each other and belong together.

Some scholars argue that Thrasymachus and Callicles are inconsistent or muddled.[1] In her interpretation of the *Republic*, Julia Annas gives a detailed presentation of such a view of Thrasymachus. She says Thrasymachus is driven by Socrates "from a muddled and misleading formulation of what he holds to a clearer and more defensible statement."[2] She is speaking of Thrasymachus' shift from the position that justice is the "advantage of the stronger" or whatever the law dictates, meaning that it has no enduring content, to the position that justice is "someone else's good," meaning that it has an enduring content which he considers undesirable. She characterizes this shift as a move from "conventionalism" to "immoralism."

Clearly there is such a shift. Thrasymachus' initial definition of justice is a form of mockery. He knows that people think justice involves concern for others, and his definition is meant to cast that concern in a ridiculous light. If justice is indeed "nothing other than the advantage of the stronger" (338c), then it's foolish to concern oneself with it, beyond considering how one must behave to avoid trouble.[3] Thrasymachus' former position therefore presupposes and points to his latter position, which is his serious position (as Socrates himself suggests at 349a6), and which he initially sees no need to state in so many words. I shall discuss this reading more fully in the next chapter. Annas, however, seems to find Thrasymachus "muddled" because she does not grasp the link between his two definitions, or appreciate that Thrasymachus is speaking for an audience which he assumes to possess a certain subtlety and wit.

Mistaking Thrasymachus' mockery for confusion, Annas fails to see much of what is at stake in the subsequent conversation. She comments that "there is not much to say about the two pieces of argument that go from 341a–342e and from 345e–347e. They are both attempts to force Thrasymachus to make clear exactly what his position is."[4] This is an uninspiring summary of passages in which Thrasymachus forcefully states his views, and Socrates points to interesting tensions in those views. Annas says the following about the point where Thrasymachus spurns the suggestion of his ally Cleitophon and introduces his definition of the ruler as one who "does not err" (341a).

> This is a very counter-intuitive position, and Thrasymachus is probably only forced into saying this about skills in general because he finds it plausible to hold as a position about the stronger in any situation. He is thinking of the obviously true point that the man who has the upper hand cannot afford to make mistakes.... But this flouts all our beliefs about doctors, rulers, etc., and it is clear that he has essentially given up the idea that the stronger can be equated with the ruler.[5]

It would be hard to imagine a reading of this passage more different than the one I shall offer. I take this to be the moment of the conversation most revealing of Thrasymachus (even more than the moment at which he blushes at 350d). I shall argue that Thrasymachus' definition of the ruler as an error-free craftsman brings us to the heart of his beliefs and concerns—as his vehemence about it suggests. By demanding that the word "stronger" mean not merely the one with political power, but the one who, in addition to having political power, does not err, or is wise, Thrasymachus introduces a notion of human excellence, and reveals that this notion is of more concern to him than describing actual political rule.

I also question Annas's statement that Thrasymachus' position here is "very counter-intuitive." Is it true that it "flouts all our beliefs" to deny that a doctor is truly a doctor while making mistakes? It seems to me that this constitutes part of what we ordinarily mean when we speak of doctors and other artisans. Annas avoids Thrasymachus' other examples of the calculator and the grammarian, which particularly lend themselves to his "error-free" definition (340d).

On one important point, however, I agree with Annas. Contrary to the criticism Socrates offers of his discussion with Thrasymachus at 354b, the discussion in fact implicitly considers the question of what justice is alongside the question of whether it is truly good (or, as Annas puts it, whether it "pays"). "The whole of the *Republic* is in fact based on the idea that the two questions belong together."[6] However, Annas does not indicate what seems to me the most profound meaning of this joint treatment. The two questions meet in the following single question: Is justice something that benefits us, or not? This question lurks behind the entire *Republic*, most obviously during Book II when Glaucon and Adeimantus restate and amplify the objections to justice originally presented by Thrasymachus.

Plato shows, I shall argue, that people want the answer to this question to be both no and yes. We feel that justice entails concern for the good of others rather than our own; yet we also somehow believe it is good for us as well. Those who believe in justice most strongly tend to be attracted precisely to the sacrifices or demands that it entails. However, such people are shocked and repelled by the view that justice is bad. The question of the goodness of justice is difficult to resolve because we do not quite *want* to resolve it, or even to grasp it adequately. Our uncertainty or dividedness about this question makes it impossible for us to adequately address the question of what justice is.

I suspect some readers are drawn to the view that Thrasymachus and Callicles are muddled because it seems to minimize the challenge to justice that these men pose. However, it also invites the question of why Plato bothers with them. As I shall argue, the view that Thrasymachus and Callicles are muddled cannot withstand a careful reading of Plato's dialogues. There is indeed confusion in the views of both men, but I shall try to show that it is a characteristically human confusion, a confusion that points to serious and difficult concerns and questions. Plato invites us to confront the challenge to justice that Thrasymachus and Callicles offer. I believe he thinks we cannot truly understand justice unless we do so.

One way some readers approach Plato is to analyze the arguments offered in the dialogues with scarcely a glance at the people making them, and then take the victorious position presented by Socrates as the true Platonic position. This approach is inadequate on many grounds, including the unavoidably *ad hominem* character of the Socratic elenchus. As Gregory Vlastos and others have pointed out, Socrates' procedure consists of showing that one belief of his interlocutor contradicts another belief of that same interlocutor. It is to say the least unclear that such a procedure can reliably establish a positive teaching. As Christina Tarnopolsky asks, "How does the Socratic elenchus move from revealing inconsistencies within an interlocutor's beliefs to establishing certain Socratic theses to be true?"[7]

A reader might reply that Plato creates interlocutors who enable him to bring forth his own or Socrates' true views. However, this does not adequately account for Plato's use of the dialogue form. Instead of writing essays, Plato creates rich and interesting characters like Thrasymachus and Callicles. At the very least he wants to show how these characters respond to things Socrates says. Moreover, treating Socrates' interlocutors as mere props who help him to express Platonic views does not account for the inadequacy of many of the arguments Socrates makes, or the frequent contradictions among those arguments.

Vlastos offers an interesting suggestion for how the Socratic elenchus might reach something like truth. "Since Socrates does expect to discover truth by this method, he must be making an exceedingly bold assumption which he never states . . . that side by side with all their false beliefs, his interlocutors always carry truth somewhere or other in their belief system; hence if Socrates pokes around in their belief system he can expect to turn up *true beliefs entailing the negation of each of their false ones.*"[8] Vlastos adds that since this method depends critically upon an unproven assumption, it cannot yield certainty.

This suggestion still fails to account for the inadequacy of many Socratic arguments. I shall argue that much of what Socrates says when conversing with Thrasymachus and Callicles, especially his more questionable arguments, is meant to cast light on those interlocutors and what they themselves believe. However, I agree with Vlastos that these interlocutors don't wholly hold their untenable beliefs. After all, it is only natural to doubt what is false.

If we accept that the Socratic elenchus takes as its starting point the beliefs of Socrates' interlocutors, then we have no reason to conclude that a given belief of an interlocutor is true simply because Socrates does not challenge it. To take one important example, in the *Gorgias* Socrates suggests, and Callicles agrees, that good things and their opposites are not found simultaneously in the same person. This forms the basis of a refutation of Callicles' hedonism. But is it true? In explaining what he means by this, Socrates says, "For of course (δήπου) a person is not at the same time both healthy and sick, nor is he at the same time released from both health and sickness."[9] But death releases us from health and sickness at the same time. I believe Plato means the attentive reader to think of death here. Moreover, since we are beings who die, isn't our very being precisely a mixture of health and sickness? We could not live if we were not healthy in myriad ways; yet as mortal beings we are heading toward death, or decaying.

I interpret this passage not as demonstrating the inadequacy of Callicles' hedonism (which Socrates does more effectively elsewhere), but as pointing to an unrealistic belief that Callicles holds in the possibility of an unmixed good for human beings. Whether or not my interpretation is correct (I shall make my case when we come to Callicles), it is different than the interpretations that Vlastos and others present.[10] In my view Socrates is intentionally offering a bad argument which casts light on Callicles precisely because he embraces it.

It is perhaps controversial to suggest that Plato's Socrates intentionally offers bad arguments; but it is not controversial to discuss Socratic irony, which is evidently a related phenomenon. As Vlastos points out, "the intention to deceive, so alien to our word for irony, is normal in its Greek ancestor *eironeia, eiron, eironeuomai.*"[11] (One might question the assertion that the intention to deceive is *wholly* alien to our word irony; but the point is nonetheless well taken.) Vlastos traces the transition of the term, noting that Quintilian defined the Latin word *ironia* as "that figure of speech or trope 'in which something contrary to what is said is to be understood.'"[12] By Quintilian's time, the term had lost its "disreputable past" and become a form of "mockery innocent of deceit."[13]

Vlastos makes the provocative suggestion that while we "lack the massive linguistic data" needed to track the term's transition, "we can say *who* made it happen: Socrates." He rightly observes that Socrates was "a previously unknown, unimagined type of personality, so arresting to his contemporaries and so memorable for ever after, that the time would come, centuries after his death, when educated people would hardly be able to think of *ironia* without bringing Socrates to mind." He plausibly speculates that "as this happened the meaning of the word altered. The image of Socrates as the paradigmatic *eiron* effected a change in the previous connotation of the word. Through the eventual influence of the after-image of its Socratic incarnation, the use which had been marginal in the classical period became its central, its normal and normative use: *eironeia* became *ironia.*"[14]

This is an intriguing hypothesis; however, I do not share Vlastos's confidence that the popular "after-image" of Socratic irony is correct. Without any clear support apart from this "after-image," Vlastos asserts that Socratic irony is "as innocent of intentional deceit as a child's feigning that the play chips are money."[15] He also notes, however, that in the *Republic* Thrasymachus "is charging that Socrates lies."[16] Thrasymachus presents deceptive irony as a quality for which Socrates is renowned.

Vlastos seems to take it for granted that a decent man like Socrates must not have been a deceiver. This is hard to reconcile with Socrates' presentation of the noble lie in the *Republic*, or even with what he says to Cephalus about deceiving a friend who has gone mad (331c). Vlastos might respond with his claim that the *Republic* shows a Platonized Socrates, not the true Socrates we see in earlier dialogues such as the *Crito* and the *Apology*.[17] However, Vlastos himself presents Book I of the *Republic*, where Socrates' conversation with Cephalus of course appears, as belonging to "Plato's earlier period."[18]

I myself am more concerned with trying to understand the dialogues than trying to date them. Since dating the dialogues is a concern of many scholars and since it suggests a different method of interpretation than the one I shall use (particularly in the face of apparent contradictions among things Plato's Socrates says), I shall briefly explain my position. While some philosophers tell us that their thought has evolved and that their earlier writings are less significant or final than their later ones, Plato says no such thing. We know nothing from Plato about the order of composition of the dialogues; we have only what later scholars have surmised.

To be sure, the fact that there are tensions or contradictions among things Socrates says in different dialogues gives plausibility to the notion that Plato's thought evolved. However, there are also tensions or contradictions among things Socrates says in single dialogues. To take an example from the *Gorgias*, at 521d Socrates makes the surprising claim that he alone among his contemporaries practices politics, while at 527d he says that he and Callicles must practice virtue in common before they consider applying themselves to political affairs. To take an example from the *Republic*, at 345c–d Socrates makes the even more surprising claim that the shepherd's art consists of providing what is best for sheep rather than men, while at 370d–e he presents shepherds as providing the city with hides and wool. Therefore we cannot use the presence of apparent contradictions to indicate that Plato has changed his mind, unless we take him to be a sloppy thinker or author or both. I believe we must start from the assumption that Plato repudiates none of his dialogues, and we must examine the dramatic context when we confront apparent contradictions. (For example, I shall argue in Chapter Two that Plato's Socrates does not really endorse or believe what he says about the shepherd at 345c–d; rather he is drawing out an implication of what Thrasymachus has said.)

Vlastos discusses what he calls "complex irony," meaning that Socrates says things which both are and are not true. "What is said both is and isn't what is meant: its surface content is meant to be true in one sense, false in another. Thus when Socrates says he is a 'procurer' [in Xenophon's *Symposium*] he does not, and yet does, mean what he says. He obviously does not in the common, vulgar, sense of the word. But nonetheless he does in another sense."[19] This is a helpful way of characterizing much of what Socrates says, including some of his most famous statements. However, I doubt that Vlastos is right that Socrates never intends his complex ironies to be misunderstood by (at least some of) his interlocutors. Vlastos says that Socrates allows this to happen but does not encourage it.[20] This is already a suggestive correction or amplification of his presentation of Socratic truth-telling.

Vlastos offers some enlightening suggestions, but he also makes unwarranted assumptions that undermine his ability to see where Plato is leading us. He still treats the dialogues too much like essays, in which Socrates or Plato is arguing for his true views, and not enough like dramatic works, in which a character or a problem is being shown to the reader.

Some scholars approach the dialogues as dramatic works but still do not seem to grasp what makes our tough guys tick or how Plato is showing them to us. In his discussion of the conversation between Socrates and Thrasymachus, Leo Strauss makes some important points about justice with force, economy, and lucidity. However, his interpretation is not as successful in showing Thrasymachus' concerns or his attachment to justice. At times the interpretation veers in a peculiar direction. Strauss maintains that Thrasymachus "plays the city" by saying that justice is the advantage of the stronger, meaning whatever the rulers decree.[21] This seems true to a certain extent; however, to say nothing of the turn that Thrasymachus' argument takes beginning at 340c, it does not reflect the way cities present themselves. They claim that their laws are based on justice, not that justice is nothing other than whatever they happen to decree. At the very least Thrasymachus rips away the veil with which rulers seek to adorn their power.

In discussing Thrasymachus' definition of the ruler as one who "does not err" (341a), Strauss writes, "Since he is or rather plays the city, his choice of the alternative which proves fatal to him was inevitable. If the just is to remain the legal, if there is to be no appeal from the laws and the rulers, the rulers must be infallible; if the laws are bad for the subjects, the laws will lose all respectability if they are not at least good for the rulers."[22] This observation is peculiar. (Perhaps it is intended to be humorous.) Laws that are understood to be "bad for the subjects" are naturally resented by those subjects and have little "respectability" whether or not they are good for the rulers. There is surely room for "appeal" from such laws. Perhaps Strauss means to recapitulate the muddled thinking of Thrasymachus under the pressure of the argument (though this doesn't explain his use of the word "inevitable"); if so, however, I don't think he gets it right. Thrasymachus' attention here is less on the subjects than on the ruler, and on what the ruler is "according to precise speech" (340e1–2). Moreover, Thrasymachus would not subsequently hold so fiercely to his definition of the ruler as one who does not err if it simply served as an ineffective response at one difficult moment in the conversation.

Strauss also says that Thrasymachus "made his fatal choice with a view to his own advantage." As "a famous teacher of rhetoric," Thrasymachus has an interest in showing that "prudence is of the utmost importance for ruling." This latter point seems reasonable, but it doesn't support the suggestion that Thrasymachus speaks here with a view to his own advantage as a teacher of rhetoric. From that point of view, he might do better to say that rulers pursue their own good but need the assistance of his art in order to do so effectively. A ruler who pursues his own good without erring would not need Thrasymachus' help.[23]

Thrasymachus' definition of the ruler as an error-free artisan clearly has something to do with his view of himself as an artisan; however, I shall argue that he gives this definition not because "to praise art is conducive to Thrasymachus' private good"[24] but because of his allegiance to art or skill. Thrasymachus is evidently impressed by the power of rulers on the one hand, and by the skill of craftsmen on the other. He is reluctant to think that the great power of rulers has no intrinsic connection to skill or ability or virtue. To think this would be to view the world as disconcertingly chaotic. It is much more satisfying to what we might call his moral sense to define the true ruler as a kind of craftsman.

Allan Bloom observes about the point at which Thrasymachus identifies the ruler as one who does not err, "The ruler is hence a man who seeks his own advantage. . . . If he fails to attain it, he is a failure as a ruler and a man."[25] This summary doesn't bring out Thrasymachus' *admiration* of craftsmen and of the error-free ruler, which (I shall argue) is critical for understanding him. He is refuted by Socrates in part because he views artisanship, and skillful ruling, both as ends in themselves and as means of satisfying one's desires. While Bloom makes some valuable observations, he doesn't seem to grasp the way Plato is showing Thrasymachus to us.

I have learned much from some of the scholars I have mentioned here, especially Leo Strauss and my former teacher Allan Bloom, but I do not think any of them gets Thrasymachus or Callicles quite right. I shall approach these characters in a somewhat different way. While most of the scholars I have mentioned carefully analyze what Socrates and his interlocutors say, I believe they do not sufficiently consider what Socrates says in terms of what it reveals about his interlocutors. As indicated above, I take the dubious arguments and questions that Socrates offers, and that his interlocutors accept or even embrace, not as revealing Socrates' own views, nor as tricks by which he refutes his interlocutors, but rather as keys to the beliefs and concerns of those interlocutors. I shall try to show that Socrates' dubious arguments and questions, and the responses that Thrasymachus and Callicles offer, expose the deep but unselfconscious attachment to justice that both men feel, even as they vehemently attack it. Moreover, I shall argue that understanding Thrasymachus and Callicles can teach us about our own attachment to justice, and ultimately about justice itself.

NOTES

1. See, for example, J. P. Maguire, "Thrasymachus . . . or Plato?" *Phronesis* 16 (1971): 142–63. Maguire attempts to distinguish the historical Thrasymachus from Plato's Thrasymachus, and attributes inconsistency to the latter. (I myself shall examine the character Plato presents, rather than attempting to discover or reconstitute the historical Thrasymachus.)
2. Julia Annas, *An Introduction to Plato's Republic* (New York: Oxford University Press, 1992), 37.
3. The phrase "nothing other than" (οὐκ ἄλλο τι ἤ) at 338c2 indicates that Thrasymachus knows he is defying what people generally say.
4. Annas, *An Introduction to Plato's Republic*, 49.
5. Annas, *An Introduction to Plato's Republic*, 43.
6. Annas, *An Introduction to Plato's Republic*, 39.
7. Christina Tarnopolsky, "Shame and Moral Truth in Plato's *Gorgias*: The Refutation of Gorgias and Callicles" (paper presented to the University of Chicago Political Theory Workshop, April 3, 2000, available online), 9.
8. Gregory Vlastos, *Socrates: Ironist and Moral Philosopher* (Ithaca: Cornell University Press, 1991), 113–14. In this book, italics in citations appear in the work cited unless otherwise indicated.
9. Plato, *Gorgias*, 495e. The Greek text I am using is E.R. Dodds, *Plato: Gorgias: A Revised Text with Introduction and Commentary* (Oxford: Oxford University Press, 2001). Henceforth citations from the *Gorgias* will be given with their Stephanus numbers in parentheses. The translations from the *Gorgias* are mine, but I have made use of the translation provided by James H. Nichols Jr. in Plato, *Gorgias* (Ithaca: Cornell University Press, 1998).
10. Cf. Vlastos, *Socrates: Ironist and Moral Philosopher*, 204–5, and Christina H. Tarnopolsky, *Prudes, Perverts, and Tyrants: Plato's Gorgias and the Politics of Shame* (Princeton: Princeton University Press, 2010), 82. Dodds helpfully points out tensions between this argument against hedonism and Socratic statements in other dialogues. Nonetheless, he accepts it as establishing the "non-identity of two concepts (Pleasure and Good) by the non-identity of their marks (capacity in one case, incapacity in the other, for coexistence with its contrary)" (Dodds, *Plato: Gorgias*, 309–10).
11. Vlastos, *Socrates: Ironist and Moral Philosopher*, 23.
12. Vlastos, *Socrates: Ironist and Moral Philosopher*, 21.
13. Vlastos, *Socrates: Ironist and Moral Philosopher*, 28.
14. Vlastos, *Socrates: Ironist and Moral Philosopher*, 29.
15. Vlastos, *Socrates: Ironist and Moral Philosopher*, 29.
16. Vlastos, *Socrates: Ironist and Moral Philosopher*, 24.
17. Vlastos, *Socrates: Ironist and Moral Philosopher*, 45–50.
18. Vlastos, *Socrates: Ironist and Moral Philosopher*, 46.
19. Vlastos, *Socrates: Ironist and Moral Philosopher*, 31.
20. Vlastos, *Socrates: Ironist and Moral Philosopher*, 42.
21. Strauss, *The City and Man* (Chicago: The University of Chicago Press, 1964), 78.
22. Strauss, *The City and Man*, 79–80.
23. I shall use masculine singular pronouns when referring to unspecific individuals. I am no less eager to appeal to female than to male readers, but the two people I shall closely examine are men, and I prefer uniformity on stylistic grounds.
24. Strauss, *The City and Man*, 80.
25. Bloom, *The Republic of Plato*, 330.

Chapter Two

Thrasymachus' Attack on Justice

DEFINING JUSTICE

I turn to Thrasymachus with an eye to the questions raised in the Introduction. Every reader of Plato's *Republic* knows that Thrasymachus attacks justice and that Socrates defends it; but it isn't easy to say exactly what the defense consists of. Many readers share the reaction of Glaucon, who thinks that while Thrasymachus has been silenced, his attack on justice has not truly been refuted (358b). I shall try to show that Thrasymachus is refuted in what one might consider a peculiarly effective manner: Socrates shows that Thrasymachus himself does not truly accept his own attack on justice, but is rather deeply attached to justice, albeit unwittingly.[1]

Thrasymachus enters the conversation with the demand that Socrates (and, to a lesser extent, Polemarchus) behave more seriously in considering what justice is. He accuses Socrates of gratifying his love of honor by refuting what others say without venturing to risk being refuted himself, and he demands that Socrates instead state his own opinion about justice. (He assumes Socrates has an opinion.) One might say that Thrasymachus, the champion of injustice, enters the conversation with the demand that Socrates be more just.[2] He also demands that Socrates not give as an answer that justice is "the needful, nor the helpful, nor the profitable, nor the gainful, nor the beneficial . . . as I will not accept it if you say such nonsensical things" (336c–d).

We might wonder what makes Thrasymachus expect these rather Socratic answers, since this seems to be the first substantial conversation they have had. (I infer this from Thrasymachus' evident surprise at much of what Socrates says. By the time the conversation ends, he has gained some appreciation of how unusual a character Socrates is, and it is unlikely that he would be as surprised if a second conversation were to occur.) In Plato's *Cleitophon*, Cleitophon recounts how Socrates' associates gave him similar answers when he asked what the just man produces.³ In that dialogue Cleitophon goes on to explain his dissatisfaction with these answers: They fail to distinguish justice from the arts, which also produce what is profitable, beneficial, and so forth, each in its own domain. In other words, they fail to define justice in particular.

This seems to be at least part of what Thrasymachus means in saying that such answers are "nonsensical" (ὕθλους). He may also have in mind that they do not reflect the most obvious feature of justice: that it is the good of others. Cleitophon appears in the *Republic* as an ally of Thrasymachus, and is even more determined than Thrasymachus to resist Socratic arguments, as we shall see below.⁴ It seems probable that at some point prior to the action of the *Republic*, Cleitophon has told Thrasymachus that Socrates (sometimes) defines justice in this manner that they both find unsatisfying (but note *Cleitophon* 410b1, where Socrates is said to have defined justice differently). It may be that Thrasymachus enters the conversation in the *Republic* hoping to show his student that he is superior to that student's previous teacher.

Socrates gives two responses to Thrasymachus' attack. First, he says that any mistake he and Polemarchus are making is an unwilling mistake. "Do not suppose that if we were seeking gold we would never willingly make way for one another in the search and destroy the chance of finding it, while when we are seeking justice, a thing more honorable than much gold, we would then foolishly yield to one another and not be eager that it appear as much as possible" (336e). This defense tends to suggest that any disregard of justice by anybody is involuntary (except perhaps if someone does not believe that justice is honorable or valuable, which would either be a mistake, or else a correct view, and either way hardly blameworthy). More broadly, the comment suggests that nobody knowingly disregards what is good, or that wrongdoing is involuntary. This does not allay Thrasymachus' suspicion that Socrates has an opinion about justice which he is keeping to himself. When Socrates adds that he and Polemarchus should be pitied rather than treated harshly by Thrasymachus, the latter not surprisingly responds by accusing him of irony.

Socrates then compares his situation to that of someone who is asked what twelve is, but forbidden to say two times six, or three times four, or six times two, or four times three. Socrates thus strongly suggests that he views justice as equivalent to the very things Thrasymachus has forbidden him to say; but he still does not offer a definition. After initially disparaging the comparison, Thrasymachus asks if Socrates is going to give one of the answers he forbade. Socrates replies merely that he wouldn't be surprised if that were his opinion upon consideration (337c). While Thrasymachus treats the various forbidden answers as distinct (though similar), and therefore asks if Socrates will give "one of these" (τούτων τι) answers, Socrates seems to treat them as different aspects or qualities of what is fundamentally one answer, akin to defining twelve as two times six or three times four. Therefore he says he would not be surprised if it should appear "thus" (οὕτω) to him (337c9).

Thrasymachus then turns from trying to get a definition of justice from Socrates to giving his own. He asks what Socrates would deserve to suffer if he were shown a better answer to the question. Socrates responds, "What else than the very thing which is fitting for the one who does not know to suffer? And surely it is fitting for him to learn from the one who knows" (337d). Socrates tacitly suggests that the just (what he deserves) is what is fitting.

This suggestion is consistent with the position that emerged during Socrates' exchange with Polemarchus, that it is not just to harm anybody (335d), even to punish wrongdoing. The just punishment for Socrates' (alleged) ignorance about justice is learning—a benefit. The question of whether it is just to harm or punish is not emphasized during the exchange with Thrasymachus, but it is related to a question they do examine, whether justice is good. Socrates' exchanges with Cephalus and Polemarchus essentially focus on the question of whether justice is good for others, while the exchange with Thrasymachus focuses on whether justice is good for the just man himself. If we wish to understand the exchange with Thrasymachus, it might help us to briefly consider the position that it is never just to harm anybody.

Many or most people disagree with this position, and think that harming those who have done injustice is in fact just. In light of the powerful considerations discussed by Socrates and Polemarchus, one might wonder why this is so. As Devin Stauffer asks, "does the belief that unjust men deserve to suffer, and the zeal to punish them, indicate a doubt of the ... belief ... that justice is good? For if one were utterly convinced that the just are better off than the unjust, wouldn't one be content with, or even pity, the situation of unjust men who (one would be convinced) are suffering already by being unjust?"[5] To be sure, not all punishment indicates doubt about the goodness of justice. As parents we punish our children for many kinds of misbehavior that we don't believe to be good. Such punishment is meant to educate; we seek to inculcate good habits in our children before they are fully capable of understanding the goodness of those habits. The short-term harm of punishment is meant to foster a long-term improvement in the one punished. This sort of punishment passes the test that Socrates and Polemarchus implicitly develop: It is good (or intended to be good) for the one punished. Socrates reaches some paradoxical conclusions about justice with Polemarchus by ignoring or even implicitly denying the possibility that harm or correction can be good in the long run for the one "harmed" (335b–c).

When we move from juvenile misdemeanors to adult crimes, however, it becomes harder to understand punishment in this light. It is particularly hard to see how being executed can be good for the one executed. Nonetheless, there is an obvious way in which even capital punishment improves people. While it is hard to see how it can improve the one executed, it is easy to see how it might improve those who remain behind. A world in which there is no reliable punishment for serious crimes is not merely a world of violent anarchy, but also a world in which people have serious doubts about the goodness of justice. An effective system of criminal punishment strengthens the belief that justice operates in the world. This belief in turn tends to strengthen people's attachment to justice, both in the sense of obeying the law, and in the sense of feeling concerned about the good of others. A confidence that crime does not pay allows us to move beyond a narrow concern with what pays. A confidence that the unjust generally suffer and the just generally flourish makes it seem that the world supports justice. This allows us to care more about justice, to demand more of ourselves, and to hope for more from being just. By contrast, regimes where criminality flourishes tend to produce young people whose concern for justice is attenuated.[6] As Socrates says later in the *Republic*, "it is necessary that the good judge be . . . a late learner of what injustice is" (409b).

The issue is not merely one of deterrence. Deterrence can make certain deeds unprofitable, but it says nothing about whether they are in themselves good or bad. Punishment goes further. The unjust must not merely be prevented or deterred; they must *pay*, for they have done *wrong*. Thrasymachus suggests that those who talk about justice simply wish to prevent bolder people from behaving unjustly (344c); but this clearly doesn't explain the motives of people like Polemarchus, Glaucon, and Adeimantus. These young men don't merely hope to avoid harm; they wish to be *good*.

We live in an age when the notion of punishment is often derided, and is no longer entirely respectable.[7] It offends both our democratic belief in equality (which resists sharp distinctions) and our putative enlightenment (which ensures that most educated people have encountered some logical critique of punishment). Punishment is also at odds with the Christian injunction to "turn the other cheek." Nonetheless, I think most people feel that punishment is just, even if they wouldn't say so. ("Whatever goes around, comes around" is a popular, slightly disguised formulation of this belief.) We remain deeply attached to the notion of punishment, for it expresses and confirms the goodness of justice in a way that mere deterrence cannot.

Nonetheless, the notion of "paying" for one's crimes seems to suggest a doubt that the crimes are really bad in themselves. One might object that this line of argument abstracts from the *harm* done by injustice. Someone who in no way envies a murderer might still feel that the murderer must pay for his crime, for the consequences will be grim if such acts are not very costly. Someone might, in other words, both pity the criminal and favor the punishment. It's not that the crime in itself is good, but that if unpunished it might *appear* good to other people who are tempted by lawlessness.

However, this merely redirects the conundrum we're considering. Perhaps there is a way of believing in both the goodness of justice and the necessity of punishment; but it grows out of an awareness that at least to some people, we must *make* justice good by *punishing* injustice. In other words, justice in itself is *not* necessarily good for everybody—or at least not everybody can appreciate its goodness. Although the just tend to live better lives than the unjust (at least in a relatively decent society), the goodness of justice in itself is ambiguous—as is already suggested by our sense that, whatever else it may be, justice is "someone else's good" (as Thrasymachus will soon say). By punishing, we not only deter those who must be deterred; we also encourage people to believe in the goodness of justice, and of being just. Perhaps paradoxically, this is the most effective way to prevent injustice.[8] A decent society operates for the most part not on the basis of fear of the bad things that may result from injustice, but on the basis of the desire to be a good or just person and the hope (more or less articulated) that this will bring one a good life. However tempting injustice may appear, few people are immune to the potentially greater charms of justice.

It might be useful at this point to distinguish two meanings or aspects of justice as commonly understood. Justice is both a virtue and a principle. It is putting something before oneself, and it is the thing, if we define it precisely, that a just person puts before himself. A just man might risk his life in defense of his country, for example. He might believe that his country is more important or higher than he is, or that he owes his country a debt for rearing and protecting him, or that his country embodies the common good, or all of these things; but the thing to which he subordinates himself is ultimately not so much his country as justice itself, the principle that the higher should take precedence over the lower, or the principle that one should pay one's debts, or the principle that the common good should take precedence over the individual good.[9] The first of these principles, which is arguably the deepest one or the one to which others ultimately appeal, is what Aristotle calls justice in distributions. This is the principle by which different people deserve or are worthy of the same or different things.[10] Our immoralists will give us the opportunity to consider whether the two meanings or aspects of justice I have identified are necessarily linked, in particular whether it is possible to believe in deserving or distributive justice as a principle without believing in justice or self-sacrifice as a virtue.

Thrasymachus eventually gives his own answer to the question of what justice is. He says that the just is "nothing other than the advantage of the stronger" (338c). This is apparently greeted with a brief silence, following which Thrasymachus says, "But why don't you praise me? But you won't be willing."

When Socrates asks him to explain what he means, Thrasymachus says that in each city the ruling group sets down laws for its own advantage, and these laws it declares to be just, so that everywhere justice is the advantage of the stronger. He implies that justice (τὸ δίκαιον) is merely a word with which rulers adorn their laws, laws which are made with an eye to their interest alone. The definition is a kind of joke, as Socrates will later suggest (349a). Those who rule do not need to call that which benefits them "just" in order to want to pursue it, and those who are ruled do not feel any happier about being exploited if they consider it to be "just" merely in this sense. This doesn't exactly mean that Thrasymachus rejects justice as he defines it; on the contrary, he thinks that he and most other people must obey the law, or defer to what the stronger have established, lest they invite serious trouble. The joke (or mockery) is in stating so baldly that there is nothing more to justice than that.[11]

Socrates notes that Thrasymachus too defines justice as the advantageous, though he adds "of the stronger" to it. Thrasymachus sees little significance in this comparison (339b1). However, Socrates repeats the comparison, this time emphasizing the difference rather than the similarity between the two definitions (339b). Apparently he sees some significance in the comparison. While Thrasymachus' definition is a kind of joke or mockery, intended to cast light on justice in a way that debunks it, the advantage of the stronger is a serious concern, at least for the stronger themselves. Thrasymachus does not take justice seriously (or thinks he doesn't); but he does take seriously the ability to pursue one's own advantage. His definition could be said to have two sides or aspects to it: the perspective of most people, for whom justice means being exploited; and the perspective of "the stronger," whose advantage is justice.[12] While Thrasymachus thinks primarily of the former aspect of the definition, Socrates turns to examining the latter, which clearly has something in common with the definitions of justice he himself was forbidden to give.

Socrates asks Thrasymachus if it is also just to obey the rulers. Thrasymachus says it is. Socrates then asks if rulers are infallible, or if they make mistakes. Thrasymachus answers that they make mistakes. Having answered this, and then having answered, as expected, that ruling correctly consists of commanding what is in one's own interest, Thrasymachus obviously will be forced to concede that rulers do not always command what is in their interest, and thus that the legal or just is not always the advantage of those who rule. Yet when Socrates draws out this conclusion, Thrasymachus is slow to see it, and slow to respond. Apparently he is accustomed to responding only to those who criticize his definition of justice on other grounds (339b–e).

RULER AND ARTISAN

Cleitophon interrupts to suggest the most obvious way of saving Thrasymachus' argument from contradicting itself: that the just is what the stronger *believes* to be his advantage.[13] Cleitophon is trying to help Thrasymachus, but Thrasymachus disdains his suggestion. He asks, "Do you think that I call stronger the one erring, when he errs?" (340c). This response is crucial for understanding Thrasymachus. By demanding that the word "stronger" (κρείττων) mean not merely the one with political power, but the one who, in addition to having political power, does not err, or performs flawlessly, Thrasymachus introduces a notion of human excellence, and reveals that this notion is of more concern to him than describing politics as it actually exists.[14] By asking if rulers are infallible, Socrates turns the discussion from the claim that justice is nothing other than the advantage of the stronger or the rulers, to an examination of rulers seeking their advantage; and Thrasymachus eagerly accepts this change of focus.[15]

Thrasymachus compares the proper definition of the stronger (κρείττων) to the proper definition of artisans, and insists that would-be artisans are not truly artisans insofar as they make mistakes. "Do you call the one who errs regarding those who are sick, with reference to this in which he errs, a doctor? Or the one who errs in calculation, at the time when he errs, with reference to this error, skilled in calculating? . . . But I suppose each of these, insofar as he is that which we call him, never errs. So according to precise speech . . . none of the craftsmen errs. For the one erring errs due to knowledge leaving [him], in which there is no craftsman" (340d–e).

This definition of the artisan has a certain logic, but is incomplete or partial. If we deny that anybody participates in a craft except when giving the best possible performance, then in some sense we eliminate the craftsmen (any of whom might err occasionally) and are left only with disembodied crafts. Moreover, in many or most crafts (though perhaps not calculation), it surely matters what the error is. We might properly refuse to call somebody a plumber who often breaks pipes, but not somebody who inadvertently installs one which contains a leak. Further, how are we to understand progress in a given art? As Stanley Rosen observes, "What is technically correct today may be recognized tomorrow as an error."[16] My guess is Thrasymachus would say that a practitioner who does the best job possible given the state of knowledge at his time (which may not be the same thing as the most common practice among practitioners in his time) would qualify as a true craftsman; but clearly this consideration qualifies the perfection he envisages. Thrasymachus is very interested in skill or perfection, and he emphasizes that aspect of being an artisan. However, he disregards other important aspects: doing a necessary job in the regime or society (which cannot wait upon an inhumanly perfect practitioner, or a technically perfect future), and earning a livelihood.

The absence of the latter aspect from his discussion is striking in light of his championing the pursuit of one's own advantage.

Returning to the ruler, Thrasymachus says that "no craftsman or wise man or ruler errs at the time when he is ruler" (340e). Accordingly he henceforth speaks of the ruler in the singular (ἄρχων), whereas earlier he, and Polemarchus and Cleitophon, spoke of "the rulers."[17] Obviously a large group of people is unlikely to be skilled in the way Thrasymachus now demands.

After defining the skill required of craftsmanship "according to precise speech," and stipulating that these are the terms in which he defines the ruler, Thrasymachus says briefly that the ruler "sets down (τίθεσθαι) the best thing for himself" (340e–341a). He is more interested in the ruler as one skilled at procuring his own good than as one benefiting from what he has procured. In other words, the skill that he defines as a mere means seems more important to him than the ostensible end, the advantage of the ruler.

Socrates approaches this difficulty from another angle. He asks if a doctor in the precise sense is one who makes money, or one who heals the sick. Thrasymachus answers that a doctor is a healer of the sick (341c). The difficulty in his position is quickly evident. Craftsmen (as Thrasymachus defines them) work for something other than their own benefit. The conversation has turned to craftsmanship due to Thrasymachus' insistence that the ruler is like a true craftsman who does not err in pursuing his own advantage. However, if ruling truly resembles the arts, then those who rule must aim at something other than their own benefit.[18]

Socrates then introduces an apparently extraneous line of questioning. He asks if the pilot is a ruler of sailors or a sailor. Thrasymachus answers, a ruler of sailors. Socrates says he supposes that it need not be taken into account that the pilot sails in the ship, nor is he called a sailor; he is called a pilot not because of sailing but because of ruling sailors. Thrasymachus agrees. Socrates asks if there is something advantageous "for each of these" (ἑκάστῳ τούτων), and whether the art of being a pilot is naturally directed toward providing for the advantage of "each" (341c–d). Thrasymachus answers affirmatively to both of these questions, but it is not altogether clear whether "each" means each of the sailors, or both the sailors and the pilot himself. The former reading is perhaps more natural; but there was no comparable ambiguity regarding whose benefit the doctor seeks.

Piloting is unlike the other examples Socrates uses in this section, medicine and horsemanship, because the pilot as such watches out for his *own* well-being. The pilot is on board the ship along with the sailors, and is in a sense a sailor himself, as Socrates has suggested (341d2). Socrates mentions the pilot again at 342e2, but there he does not suggest that he provides for his own advantage. I think this invites the careful reader to notice and consider the significance of the missing suggestion or ambiguity.

There is a natural common interest or coincidence of interest between a pilot and his sailors that does not exist between a doctor and his patients: If the ship sinks, the pilot dies. (This may be why Socrates does not mention money regarding the pilot as he did regarding the doctor. An external incentive is needed to make being a doctor worthwhile, but not necessarily to make being a pilot worthwhile, at least once he is on board the ship.[19]) Obviously the pilot in this way resembles a ruler. The ruler *as ruler* watches out for himself as well as those over whom he rules, or, to put it another way, the ruler as ruler watches out for himself as citizen along with the other citizens. Why does Socrates point to this here? He suggests that, as Thrasymachus thinks but not in the way he thinks, the true ruler does take care of himself. As he unsuccessfully argues for the complete selfishness of ruling, Thrasymachus neglects the limited degree of selfishness that actually characterizes it. (Nonetheless, a wise man might have better things to do than rule, at least if he can safely leave the job to somebody else [347c–d].)

Socrates asks if there is "any advantage" (τι συμφέρον) for each of the arts other than to be "most perfect" or "most complete" (μάλιστα τελέαν). Thrasymachus asks him to explain the question. Socrates says that because a body is "defective" (πονηρὸν), it needs medicine, which has been devised to provide "the advantageous things" (τὰ συμφέροντα) for it (341d–e). One might think this overstates the power of art to correct nature. Not all bodies are defective in a way that art can remedy.[20] (Mortality is a universal defect of bodies, and not one that art can remedy.) Nonetheless, Thrasymachus accepts what Socrates says. As we have already begun to see, he tends to overestimate the importance of art in human life.

Socrates then asks a series of questions which present three different ways of understanding whether or how the arts are defective. First, he asks if anything defective or bad (τις πονηρία) is in each art itself so that it needs another art which considers its advantage (τὸ συμφέρον), and whether that art in turn needs another art of the same kind, "and is this endless?" (342a) Second, he asks if each art considers its own advantage by itself. Third, he asks if each art needs "neither itself nor another [art] to look for the advantage for its defect (πονηρίαν); for neither defect (πονηρία) nor error (ἁμαρτία) is present to any art, nor does it belong to an art to seek the advantage of anything other than that of which it is the art." He adds to this that each art is "without harm and pure, each being right so long as it is precise, whole, the very thing which it is" (342b). Thrasymachus answers that it appears thus.

There are two (related) problems with this line of questioning. First, it abstracts from the artisans, whom Socrates does not mention. His odd initial question, whether there is "any advantage" for each of the arts other than to be "most perfect," prepares this omission (341d10–1). (Thrasymachus never actually answers this question.) It is only metaphorically, not in "precise speech," that one could say there is an "advantage" for an art, and it isn't entirely clear how the metaphor should be understood.[21] People are of course the ones who seek their advantage or their good; and there are many good things for an artisan apart from practicing or perfecting his art.[22] Similarly, Socrates' subsequent question about whether each art has any defect or need would be suitable as a question about artisans instead of arts.

Second, Socrates' emphasis upon each art's defect (πονηρία) and the advantage which remedies its defect conceals rather than elucidates the true nature of and relation among the arts. Socrates' third alternative mentioned above is the least defective one Socrates offers, since arts as such are not defective, and do not seek their own advantage; however, this does not mean they are independent of each other or "whole." As Aristotle says at the beginning of the *Nicomachean Ethics,* all arts aim at some good. Other arts are properly subordinate to the one that aims at the most comprehensive good. This art (which Aristotle tentatively identifies as politics) uses the other arts in a subordinate capacity.[23] While arts are not as such defective or bad, each one is dependent and bound up in hierarchic relations with other arts. (One might call this dependence a kind of defect or badness, but that seems to stretch or distort the meaning of πονηρία.) Thus politics dictates the ends of the art of war, which dictates the ends of the art of horsemanship, which dictates the ends of the art of bridle-making. To put it another way, bridle-making serves horsemanship, which serves the art of war, which serves politics. All other arts ultimately depend on a master art to dictate the ends of their activity, while it depends on them to help it achieve its aims. None of the three alternatives which Socrates offers includes any such hierarchy. The master art does not appear in the endless chain of defective arts depending in turn on other defective arts, nor among the defective arts each of which supplies its own defect, nor among the self-sufficient arts which have no mutual dependence.

Thrasymachus faces demanding questions here in rapid succession, and we can hardly fault him for failing to analyze the assumptions embedded in them. Nonetheless, it is striking that he doesn't suggest that art aims at our good, or that other arts are properly subordinate to a ruling art. He has acknowledged both of these points regarding piloting in particular (341d), but he does not think of them in the context of a general description of art. This reflects his high, perhaps excessive, respect for art.[24] In some way Thrasymachus feels that no art is essentially subordinate to another, or even to the ends of human beings; thus he agrees that each art is "pure . . . precise, whole, the very thing which it is" (342b). Of course he knows this is not true when he thinks of particular arts such as sailing and piloting; nonetheless, the fact that he chooses without objection the third of Socrates' three alternative descriptions suggests that when considering art in general, he thinks that any art is an end in itself. He may be particularly reluctant to see his own art, rhetoric, as subordinate to ruling, or anything else; but his attachment to rhetoric reflects his high regard for art in general.

If one believes that each art is an end, then it's hard to see what one could consider the aim or purpose of art other than taking care of (or managing) that over which it is set. (Some arts, such as calculation, manage but do not take care.[25]) Socrates later reiterates the view that each art takes care of "nothing other than that which it has been set over (τέτακται)," and applies it to shepherding (345d). The shepherd *qua* shepherd cares more about sheep than about human beings. Socrates makes it clear when he says this that he is applying Thrasymachus' view of art. Thrasymachus himself has introduced the example of the shepherd in order to ridicule this way of understanding art, but he does not offer another one (345b8–c2). He has nothing else to offer because in some way he genuinely views each art as an end, which implies the rest of what Socrates says.[26] Aristotle's discussion, by contrast, would indicate that the shepherd's art exists to benefit the people who wear the sheep's wool and eat the sheep's meat. The purpose of the art is to serve people, not to take care of sheep.

My interpretation of this point differs from that of Stauffer, whose work I admire and whose approach in some ways resembles mine, so I think it's worth examining the difference. My analysis of the assumptions embedded in the three alternatives Socrates offers here is essentially the same as Stauffer's. Stauffer observes that Thrasymachus accepts Socrates' articulation of the alternatives; however, he does not consider what that tells us about Thrasymachus, except to note that he is committed to "painting the arts in the best possible light."[27] Stauffer notes that Socrates "avoids mentioning or even pointing to" the arts' need for knowledge of the good as the proper basis for organizing their action, but he does not suggest that this avoidance reflects Thrasymachus' own view of art.[28] He therefore underestimates the degree to which the conversation is exposing Thrasymachus' views. Thrasymachus has shown that he is drawn to viewing the arts in terms of perfection rather than in terms of pursuit of the good (340d–341a). Socrates frames questions and possible answers which draw out related beliefs held (at least with part of his mind) by Thrasymachus. Socrates is not so much making an argument here as exposing and articulating views Thrasymachus himself holds. To be sure, Thrasymachus does not really think that the sole purpose of shepherding is taking care of sheep; but this is implied by his view that each art is an end in itself. And that view of art matters to him; it is not one he can easily set aside—which is why he doesn't in this conversation.

Stauffer presents Socrates' or Plato's purpose here as twofold: Socrates refutes Thrasymachus while showing something about justice to the careful reader.[29] This seems to me true but incomplete. Plato also exposes Thrasymachus' beliefs to the careful reader, notably his peculiar and contradictory beliefs about art, and the unselfconscious belief in justice to which they point. More generally, I believe that exposing to careful readers the contradictory and often unselfconscious beliefs of Socrates' interlocutors is the purpose informing much of what Plato writes. I believe this is an important reason, perhaps the most important reason, why he writes dialogues rather than treatises. He aims both to teach careful readers about the matters under discussion, and to show that people are deeply attached to incoherent and often unselfconscious opinions about those matters.[30] And these two aims are largely one. Plato teaches the careful reader about the matters under discussion through showing how people are attached to incoherent opinions about those matters. We learn about justice from learning about Thrasymachus' beliefs about justice, and vice versa. Moreover, in learning about justice and Thrasymachus' beliefs about justice, we learn about our own beliefs as well.

THRASYMACHUS' ADMIRATION OF THE ARTS

In his admiration of the arts, Thrasymachus tends to forget that they are worthwhile only insofar as they achieve the good of human beings. Thus he does not object to Socrates' neglect of pursuit of the good in his three alternative accounts of the arts' defectiveness or lack thereof, or to his neglect of artisans. Thrasymachus' initial strict definition of the artisan's knowledge (340d–341a) suggests that he carries in his mind's eye a favorable image of the artisan devoted to his art. This is probably why Socrates asks whether there is any "advantage" for the arts other than being perfect (341d). As noted above, it is artisans, not arts, who pursue their advantage; but Thrasymachus mingles the two, and feels that one is pursuing one's advantage when one seeks perfection in one's art. Thus he later admits only reluctantly that artisans need wages (346c).

Thrasymachus admires the skill of artisans, and feels it would be proper if that skill were something a human being could wholeheartedly pursue, without sacrificing his own good, or even while thereby ensuring its attainment. He doesn't really think people (other than rulers) can in fact do this; but he feels it would be fitting if they could. However, to feel that something would be proper or fitting is to feel, at least to some extent, that it should be or ought to be. And to feel that something should be is in some way to think that it is.

Perhaps this last statement requires defense or explication. To claim that the world "should" be a certain way is to claim at least this much: The world has a certain quality apart from what is immediately apparent which is not merely imaginary or arbitrary. Part of what the world is, is the way it "should" be. But what does it mean to say or think this? One might say one means merely that the world would be a better place if it were as it should be, or if people behaved as they ought. However, the world might also be a better place if delicious fruit grew on every tree, or if wishes were horses. When we talk about what should be, we mean something more substantial than that. One might say it is more substantial to talk about people behaving as they ought, since they have the ability to do so: All they need to do is choose what is good. However, if they are not already doing so, then they presumably don't share one's view of what is good—and why should they? We seem to feel there is reason for people to share our view of the good and behave accordingly, even when in fact they don't. To put it another way, we seem to feel that the world *is* at least to some extent as it should be, meaning either that it has some tendency to *become* what it should be, or that there is a part of the world we don't see (such as God or an afterlife) that ultimately confirms the goodness of behaving as one ought. In most if not all cases, the belief that the world "should" be a certain way implies a belief that some power, some god or moral order, wants it to be that way and draws it in that direction.

Now Thrasymachus does not explicitly speak of how people should behave. However, the enthusiasm he feels for the artisan's skill or excellence, and for those who pursue it, reminds us of the enthusiasm other people feel for justice and those who pursue justice. Moreover, like the just man, the artisan is concerned with something outside himself. Thrasymachus wants to think of art in selfish terms; but that doesn't really make sense. Even arts such as grammar and calculation (to use two of his examples) are concerned with something other than the artisan's advantage. Art as such is a generous or at least self-forgetting activity; one gives one's attention and thought to something.[31] And this giving of attention and thought, coupled with competence, is what Thrasymachus emphasizes in his discussion of art. He admires the artisan's skill but tends not to think of the artisan's human needs, or of the service he provides to others. He is excited by the artisan's devoting himself to his art, striving for a kind of perfection, and achieving it. Indeed, this is an inspiring image, when compared with the limitations and compromises that attend concentrating on ourselves and our own needs. But one might ask, are we really artisans? Is that life really our life?

Socrates asks Thrasymachus if medicine considers the advantage not of medicine, but of the body. This question resumes the thread of the exchange where Socrates left it before asking about the pilot. (Having asked about the doctor at 341c4–8, he asks now about the art of medicine at 342c1–3.) After Thrasymachus agrees that medicine considers the advantage of the body, Socrates offers a more surprising example: He asserts that horsemanship considers not the advantage of horsemanship, but of horses. This is further from the way we usually think of horsemanship, which is generally thought to serve people who use horses, than it is from the way we usually think of medicine. Socrates adds that no art considers its own advantage, for it has no need to do so, but rather the advantage of that "of which it is the art." Thrasymachus consents reluctantly: "It seems thus" (342c).

Thrasymachus doesn't really believe this definition of art, but he has no other definition to offer, in spite of or rather because of the great importance art has for him. That importance is bound up with, and even in part a consequence of, his being unclear about whether art is fundamentally a means to satisfying other needs, or an end, itself the worthwhile human activity. To put it another way, he is torn between viewing art as selfish (a way to satisfy one's needs) and as generous (a noble activity which characterizes good men), though the latter opinion is unselfconscious. Saying art is a means would make it limited and make untenable the great value or power it has for him; saying it is an end would seem odd since it isn't clear how art answers human needs except in limited ways consistent with viewing it as a means. A lack of clarity is therefore a necessary ingredient of the importance art has for him.

But perhaps this analysis slights a partial truth in Thrasymachus' position. He is not alone in admiring the arts, after all. There may be a way in which artisanship (or something akin to it) is properly viewed as an end: Most of us feel that the true human end or the best life must (at least in part) consist of some activity that demands our attention and effort and engages our faculties. Clearly Thrasymachus feels this way too. However, he isn't able to put it coherently because he also wants art to do more than serve our needs, even the need for something that demands and engages our faculties. He doesn't want art to be defined and confined by human needs; as we have seen, he wants each art to be master of its own realm, self-sufficient, even perfect. He wants art to be not so much a way of satisfying our needs as a noble activity to which we give ourselves. He feels (unselfconsciously) that in devoting ourselves to this high thing, we somehow transcend our needs and limits (and thereby address our deepest need). Since this doesn't really make sense, and obviously conflicts with his view of the rationality of selfishness and injustice, he is left with conflicting opinions about the place of art in our lives.

SHEEP, SHEPHERD, AND TYRANT

Socrates asks if the arts rule that of which they are the arts, to which Thrasymachus agrees with "very much toil and pain" (342c). (His reluctance here stems not from disagreement, but from seeing where the question leads.) When Socrates concludes that there is no ruler who considers his own benefit, Thrasymachus insults him.[32] He then delivers a long speech, which he begins by asserting that shepherds and cowherds actually work for the benefit of themselves and their masters, not for that of their flocks. True rulers regard the ruled the same way a man would regard sheep, so that what is just (or legal) is "really someone else's good," that of the man who is stronger and rules (343c).

Thrasymachus moves here from a sophistic definition of justice to a more sincere and substantial one. He presents the statement that justice is someone else's good as a clarification of his definition of justice as the advantage of the stronger, but it obviously contradicts that definition in the case of the ruler himself (for whom the advantage of the stronger is his own advantage, not someone else's). Apparently Thrasymachus does not think from the perspective of the ruler when presenting the two statements as consistent (343c). (The contradiction is repeated at 344c7–8 in such a way as to make it still clearer that he thinks from the perspective of the ruled.) For Thrasymachus the definition of the just as the advantage of the stronger was a mockery of the belief or hope that justice is something higher than that, as well as a description of how politics works; but more deeply, he, like most people, thinks that justice involves sacrificing for others, and he thinks he rejects it on that basis.[33] After his long speech, he and Socrates both set aside "the advantage of the stronger" and treat "someone else's good" or seeking the good of others as a working definition of justice.

Thrasymachus thinks that he, and most other people (344c), live in accord with a simple principle which one might summarize as follows. I live my own life and die my own death, and I feel my own pleasures and pains. Therefore I am concerned with my own life and death and pleasures and pains, not those of others. Thrasymachus thinks that only hypocrites and fools disagree with this reasoning. Indeed, one cannot deny it has a certain force. It resembles the prevalent view of human motives in our time, as I discussed in the Introduction. However, as Socrates shows, living by it proves to be more complicated than Thrasymachus thinks.

If there is a common good, even in the sense of a mere coincidence of goods, then it is possible to act so as to benefit both oneself and others. Thrasymachus implicitly denies that situations where there is a common good are fundamental enough that one can take one's bearings by them. He may underestimate the importance of such situations, but clearly he is right to this extent: If situations in which there is a common good do not cover every important contingency, then it seems prudent to be clear about which one puts first, the good of others or of oneself (or of a particular group of others, such as one's children). As Stauffer observes, "justice as devotion to the common good is necessary, in principle, only when there is no true common good in the strict sense."[34] Many people believe in a common good, yet shy away from posing the radical question of whom one puts first. (Of course there may be advantages to lack of clarity on that troubling question.) Such people believe in the goodness of justice (understood as seeking to benefit others, or at least not harm them), but their belief is mingled with uncertainty (hence the reluctance to look very closely).

Thrasymachus insists that art is selfish because he thinks selfishness is rational, but a truly selfish approach to art would view it as merely instrumental, to be used or set aside insofar as it satisfies one's desires or needs. Art is too important to Thrasymachus for him to treat it this way. Even here, he says that the shepherd and cowherd work for the good of their masters as well as their own (343b). Any art, indeed any work or job, tends to focus on something other than oneself. This is simply the nature of production as against consumption. Not only is there no avoiding this, but it is part of what impresses Thrasymachus about art. He could hardly be as impressed by mere consumption, even though consumption is more simply and unambiguously selfish than production.

Thrasymachus argues that injustice (according to his new definition) is more profitable than justice. He states that unjust men receive more from partnerships than just men do, that unjust men pay less in taxes, that unjust men get more when there are public distributions, and that unjust men profit and just men lose from holding public office. Thrasymachus says that just men incur the ill will of relatives and acquaintances by being unwilling to serve them against what is just (343e). He thereby actually alludes to a kind of common good (among relatives and acquaintances), one that is available to unjust men but not to just men. In calling such behavior unjust, he speaks more in the spirit of what we usually mean by justice than Socrates later does in saying such behavior is characterized by "a certain justice (τις . . . δικαιοσύνη)" (352c4).

The speech culminates in Thrasymachus' praise of tyranny, which he calls the "most complete injustice," and which makes the unjust one "most happy." Tyranny "takes away what belongs to others, what is sacred and profane and private and public, not bit by bit, but all at once" (344a). Those who do not succeed when attempting injustice endure the greatest reproaches, but when someone succeeds in doing complete injustice, "they are called happy and blessed (μακάριοι), not only by the citizens but also by as many others as hear that he has done the whole injustice. For those blaming injustice blame [it] fearing not to do injustice, but to suffer it" (344b–c).[35]

There are two striking features to this praise. One is that Thrasymachus says as much about how happy tyrants are *said* to be as about how happy they *are*. It seems his concern is largely to show the inconsistency and hypocrisy of people's condemnation of injustice, and the foolishness of anyone who is duped by that condemnation.

The second striking feature of this praise is that Thrasymachus says it. After all, he is not himself a tyrant, and he presumably has the same interest as those who reproach injustice because they fear suffering unjust deeds. It is true that he may work for tyrants, and may therefore to some degree share with them a common interest, but this speech is not what tyrants or other rulers want spoken about them. Neither is it generally what Athenians like to hear. While it is difficult to judge such things at a distance of 2,400 years, his praise of injustice and tyranny seems to reach an imprudent pitch. (It makes a striking contrast with the cautious speech of similarly situated foreigners in other dialogues, such as Gorgias and Protagoras. Even Polus seems tame by comparison.)

We encounter, therefore, the odd spectacle of a man acting against his interest by praising the pursuit of one's interest.[36] Thrasymachus wants to expose the hypocrisy of people's condemnation of injustice (344c3–4); but this desire is itself at odds with his espousal of injustice. His principles recommend hypocrisy for the weak, including himself![37] One might say his speech is doubly imprudent: He undermines the attempt of the many weak (of whom he is one) to defang the few strong, and in so doing he invites the wrath of the many weak against himself. Regarding the latter point, however, if Thrasymachus is right that the many themselves call tyrants "happy and blessed," then the hypocrisy he exposes is not very thoroughgoing, so he probably doesn't invite much wrath by exposing it. Nonetheless, both the many weak and the few strong have reason to conceal the aspect of political life that Thrasymachus emphasizes.

By espousing selfish principles with generous candor, Thrasymachus reveals that he does not really embrace those principles with his whole heart or mind.[38] He wants to show the men to whom he is speaking how things really are. (Of course Thrasymachus also wants to best Socrates in the argument, but this is not inconsistent with concern for the truth of what he is saying.) Moreover, he wants to give those whom he is talking about their due, whether by showing their virtue and happiness, or by exposing their inconsistency and hypocrisy. His candor about injustice suggests an impulse toward justice.[39]

Thrasymachus says that practicing "the most complete injustice" makes the tyrant "most happy." He enthusiastically describes the tyrant's expropriation of property. He mentions two other advantages of tyranny: power over the citizens, and being called "happy and blessed" by all men. However, he mentions the former primarily as a condition and guarantee of the tyrant's position, and the latter primarily as evidence that people believe tyrants to be happy (344a–c). The unlimited expropriation of the property of others seems to be the greatest advantage of tyranny in his mind. He thinks it demonstrates simultaneously the tyrant's injustice and his happiness. One who freely takes what he wants from others is incomparably happy. For Thrasymachus happiness is a relative position, a decisive superiority to others, not an internal state or activity.

The claim that all men call successful tyrants "happy and blessed (εὐδαίμονες καὶ μακάριοι)" is meant to demonstrate that people fear not doing injustice, but suffering it. This claim implies that people are insincere when denouncing less successfully unjust men; they call these men "disgraceful names" because they fear suffering unjust deeds. But how then does Thrasymachus know people are being sincere when they speak of tyrants? He suggests that a tyrant is so powerful that people have no hope of deterring his unjust deeds, so they have no reason to denounce him insincerely. However, by the same token, fear might cause the tyrant's subjects to flatter him by lying about how happy they think he is. Thrasymachus' confidence that people are sincere when speaking of the happiness of tyrants seems at least partly to reflect his *own* belief that tyrants are "happy and blessed."

His use of the word "blessed" (μακάριοι) is particularly striking (344b7). (The word is sometimes used simply to mean very happy, but in coupling it with εὐδαίμονες, Thrasymachus evidently wants to express more than that.) To be blessed is to be favored by gods. Perhaps many people Thrasymachus encounters say that tyrants are happy, but blessed? It seems unlikely that this is how a tyrant's subjects view him as he "takes away what belongs to [them] . . . not bit by bit, but all at once" and "enslaves" them (344a–b). Possibly some say this insincerely, out of fear; but this would seem to be going further than necessary. (Greek tyrants did not have the all-encompassing power of a Stalin or a Mao, and did not make equally extreme demands for flattery.[40]) Thrasymachus is exaggerating to some extent to support or dramatize his argument for the hypocrisy of people's criticism of injustice. However, conscious exaggeration alone does not account for his use of the word "blessed," since it seems too far from what people actually say to help his case. He apparently thinks it will help his case because he thinks many do at least partly consider tyrants blessed. Even this seems questionable, however. It seems likely that Thrasymachus thinks this because *he himself* feels in some way that tyrants are blessed.[41]

It is hard to say exactly what this means, since Thrasymachus probably does not believe in gods, or thinks he doesn't. With some part of his mind, however, he apparently feels tyrants are favored by gods, or godlike forces. (One might object that I am putting a lot of interpretive weight on one word. However, it is a surprising word for Thrasymachus to use, and therefore demands explanation. Moreover, my interpretation is consistent with the rest of what we see of him.) How is this possible? How can Thrasymachus believe (albeit unselfconsciously) that the greatest injustice is favored by gods?

I think the answer is along the following lines. As we have seen, Thrasymachus thinks selfishness is a fundamental fact of life, or even the fundamental fact of life. All men seek their own good; all men seek to enrich themselves.[42] One who freely expropriates what belongs to others lives the life that all men long for. He wins the only contest that matters; he demonstrates incontestably superior virtue. In some sense he lives in harmony with the fundamental principle of life, even the fundamental principle of the cosmos. Perhaps in return the cosmos, or the gods if there be gods who ordain the order of things, notice him and smile upon him. Perhaps he gains not merely what he takes from others, but what the cosmos or the gods give him for embodying and demonstrating their principle so finely. Perhaps for such a one it is not too much to hope even to transcend death. He lives in harmony with more-than-human forces. To Thrasymachus, this dwarfs this-worldly goods such as friendship or the satisfaction produced by an activity such as philosophy. (This is perhaps the core of the difference between him and Socrates.) The key step where a kind of piety emerges is in endowing the principle of life or the cosmos with an existence apart from its appearance in individual beings, so that one can be in harmony with it, rather than simply live it.

Of course these beliefs fall apart if they face the light of day. Thrasymachus must not notice that he believes gods reward the greatest injustice, or that his own defending injustice has a just quality to it, or that he views art as selfless. If he did, he would be at a loss—not simply because he would no longer know what he thinks, but more importantly because his hope of strengthening and perhaps transcending his fragile mortal life, a hope of which he is only dimly aware, would be undermined.[43] However, he does not, and probably cannot, notice these things. He is built to believe in the possibility of reaching beyond the limits he faces.

To be fair to Thrasymachus, he is not the only person whose beliefs won't bear the light of day. If one had to give a one-sentence summary of the Platonic corpus, one might simply say: Socrates shows that people's beliefs won't bear the light of day. Moreover, while Thrasymachus' beliefs seem contorted (with selfless selfishness and injustice as the basis of excellence and deserving), people's beliefs about justice are generally contorted. Thrasymachus squarely if not adequately faces human selfishness. Many people are more aware of their own belief in justice, but less aware of their own selfishness. Our nature drives us into fundamental contradictions. As mortal beings, we want something we don't believe we have; yet in some peculiar way we feel that maybe we can have it if we give so much that we might possibly deserve something wonderful in return; but we can only believe we are deserving if we don't notice that we give in order to receive; or possibly if we notice it and torment ourselves about it, without fully accepting why we are tormenting ourselves; and so forth. Such is the human drama. The distinctive characteristic of the immoralist is not to get off this treadmill (only the philosopher perhaps manages that), but to believe himself to be taking, not giving, while not noticing that he also believes himself to be giving, often to the very principle of taking.

Thrasymachus concludes from his discussion of tyrants that injustice, when it comes into being on a sufficient scale, is "stronger and freer and more masterful" than justice (344c5–6). However, it isn't clear that he looks very closely at actual tyrants. Even leaving aside the word "blessed," he arguably overstates their happiness as much as Socrates overstates their unhappiness in Book IX of the *Republic*. He does not mention the enmity that surrounds them, or their fear of assassination.[44] He may be exaggerating to some extent to make his point, but it is unlikely that his presentation of the tyrant's happiness is essentially insincere or ironic, since that would cast doubt on his allegiance to the principles for which he (generously but imprudently) argues.

On the other hand, as Seth Benardete notes, Thrasymachus "does not mention among the tyrant's advantages that he can kill or sleep with whomever he wants (360c1–2)."[45] (The latter advantage of course does not require the consent of the desired party.) In this way Thrasymachus arguably *understates* the advantages of tyranny. It may be that, not desiring these "advantages" himself, or sensing that they often turn out badly, he does not pay much attention to them as a common part of a life he is inclined to admire.[46] The tyrant is a kind of hero for Thrasymachus—from a distance. Thrasymachus is an intellectual, a teacher of rhetoric and of certain views about justice and the good life. Like some other intellectuals, he champions a way of life that represents the culmination and apparent vindication of his principles, without looking all that closely to see if the principles are in fact vindicated.

To Thrasymachus the tyrant represents the "most complete injustice." While he feels that the tyrant has other virtues (including technical ability, as we have seen), injustice is the one he stresses. It is the quality in which the tyrant surpasses all other men. Thrasymachus feels that injustice is worthy of being defended from hypocritical condemnation, worthy of happiness, and worthy even of devotion (I noted above the imprudence of his praise of injustice). Odd though it sounds to say so, Thrasymachus is to some extent devoted to injustice. He even vaguely feels that he deserves to be rewarded for his devotion to injustice, at least to the extent that he doesn't expect to pay a price for his candor on its behalf. His devotion to injustice is, in other words, an attachment to (a peculiar form of) justice.

Of course this devotion is necessarily unselfconscious and indirect, and therefore somewhat limited. Thrasymachus doesn't see himself as giving himself to injustice (let alone to justice), so he doesn't give himself as fully as a generous young man like Polemarchus gives himself to justice. On the other hand, since he confronts the problem of the apparent rationality of selfishness (inadequately, but still more fully than more conventional believers in justice), his attachment to justice is less clouded by doubts of its goodness than is true of Glaucon, for example, to say nothing of many who have not had Glaucon's advantages in life. Though it might sound paradoxical to say so, Thrasymachus takes (a peculiar form of) justice more for granted than Glaucon does. (Glaucon appears to take justice more seriously than any of Socrates' other interlocutors in the *Republic*; but that may be because he doubts its goodness more deeply.) A useful (though not infallible) indicator of the strength of a person's attachment to justice is the importance of admiration in his character.[47] Thrasymachus seems somewhat inclined to admiration, but does not seem to feel it with great intensity.

We might ask why Thrasymachus does not seek to become a tyrant. He has desires which could be more fully satisfied if he did. We can infer an eagerness for praise from his initial impatient demand for it (338c). This, and his emphasis on what is said about the happiness of tyrants, suggest that he would enjoy being famous. His general demeanor, and his insults of Socrates, suggest that he might have unsatisfied aggressive impulses; he would probably enjoy being able to tell others what to do and think. And he is obviously impressed by the tyrant's expropriation of the property of others.

However, he is not gripped by desire for money. Despite demanding money at the outset, he starts to leave without trying to collect any after his long speech (344d). As noted, he does not mention the erotic or murderous possibilities available to tyrants. More generally, he seems to be a fairly cheerful man, not one consumed by unsatisfied desires. This is suggested among other things by his staying and listening to the rest of the conversation in the *Republic* after being thoroughly refuted before many men he had hoped to impress. (He also participates briefly at 450a–b.) In the *Gorgias*, by contrast, Callicles, who is more of a gentleman than Thrasymachus and who has no professional need to impress others who are present, is nonetheless sullen after being refuted.

While Thrasymachus may envy tyrants in some respects, he clearly doesn't have the burning determination necessary for a man to undertake the difficult and perilous attempt to become a tyrant. He also probably feels he is more an intellectual than a man of action. He prides himself upon his art; he has acquired some money, and some renown; he is more or less content. Another factor is probably his candor, from which he evidently derives both enjoyment and self-respect. Although he does not seem to realize that he is more candid than his principles indicate he should be, he is aware that a tyrant must dissemble a great deal (note λάθρᾳ at 344a7). This is not to say that he despises the stealth employed by a tyrant; but he probably feels it is not for him.

A mild hostility to the *demos* is suggested by Thrasymachus' eagerness to expose the hypocrisy of most people's condemnation of injustice (344c). Moreover, his admiration for the skill of artisans likely entails hostility to the democratic tendency to downplay the significance of virtue. As we shall see, Callicles also has antidemocratic sympathies, despite being an Athenian politician. In Book II of the *Republic*, Glaucon describes the antidemocratic beliefs or presuppositions of immoralists (359a). This seems to be a tendency among immoralists, but it is milder in Thrasymachus than in Callicles. Thrasymachus is prouder of his art, and of thinking and speaking well (as he thinks), than concerned for the truth about justice. He is more complacent than Callicles or Glaucon, and perhaps a smaller man.

NOTES

1. As mentioned in the previous chapter, I intend to examine the character Plato presents, not the actual historical Thrasymachus (about whom we have a little but not much information apart from what appears in Plato). In addition to the *Republic*, I shall draw information from two other dialogues, *Phaedrus* and *Cleitophon*, where Thrasymachus is mentioned but does not appear.

2. Cf. Strauss, *The City and Man*, 77, and Stauffer, *Plato's Introduction to the Question of Justice*, 60. In *Phaedrus*, while discussing prominent rhetoricians, Socrates mentions Thrasymachus as one who is clever at "angering the many" and slandering people (Plato, *Phaedrus*, translated by James H. Nichols [Ithaca: Cornell University Press, 1998], 267c–d). Thrasymachus' apparent anger here may be feigned, or at least exaggerated.

3. Plato, *Cleitophon*, 409c, in Thomas L. Pangle, editor, *The Roots of Political Philosophy: Ten Forgotten Socratic Dialogues* (Ithaca: Cornell University Press, 1987).

4. Clearly both *Cleitophon* and the *Republic* occur after Cleitophon has grown dissatisfied with Socrates, but the *Republic* apparently occurs later dramatically, since in the *Cleitophon* both Socrates and Cleitophon speak of the latter's association with Thrasymachus as new or developing, which suggests it is not yet so firmly established as we see it in the *Republic*. (Consider Socrates' comment on Cleitophon's praise of Thrasymachus to Lysias at the beginning of *Cleitophon*, as well as Cleitophon's explanation at 410c that he is turning to Thrasymachus due to his dissatisfaction with Socrates.)

5. Stauffer, *Plato's Introduction to the Question of Justice*, 51.

6. I myself met many university students while I was traveling in Hungary in 1986, before the fall of Soviet-imposed communism. I was befriended by some who had refused to join the Communist Party, although they expected this refusal to entail serious consequences for the remainder of their lives, such as never owning a house. (They probably now all own houses, but things looked different at the time.) Even these young people, however, tended to look at the world through a cynical, semi-Marxist lens. They generally doubted the existence of generous motives in anyone with power or influence anywhere. They felt that the best one could do in life was to be honest in a quiet, private way—not a crazy view, but not one characteristic of the most generous youths. Although they had resisted the cynical, self-serving regime ruling their country, it had nonetheless influenced them, and clipped the wings of what might have been their highest aspirations.

7. Thus we call our prisons facilities for "correction," not "punishment," let alone "retribution." Punishment remains somewhat more respectable than retribution; however, punishment (unlike correction) necessarily includes retribution—not necessarily repaying the actual person to whom someone did an unjust deed, of course, but suffering some sort of comparable harm.

8. Cf. Walter Berns, *For Capital Punishment: Crime and the Morality of the Death Penalty* (New York: Basic Books, 1979), 138–39.

9. If one defines justice as subordinating oneself, one might think the virtue and the principle are the same. However, one needs to have some opinion regarding what should subordinate itself to what, or some principle of distributive justice which is distinct from the virtue of justice.

10. Aristotle, *Nicomachean Ethics*, 1131a25–28.

11. Devin Stauffer argues that Thrasymachus has a serious moral purpose here even though he doesn't fully realize it: to "expose the fraud of justice" (Stauffer, "Thrasymachus' Attachment to Justice?" *Polis* 26 [2009], 4). Stauffer makes an interesting case, but there are difficulties with it. Thrasymachus thinks people generally more or less agree with him about justice (344c), and he doesn't expect those who disagree to be convinced by what he says (349b). Thrasymachus wavers about whether there are in fact sincere believers in justice, as Stauffer notes, but he doesn't seem to think there are any believers in justice whom he will convince. A milder version of Stauffer's claim is probably valid: Thrasymachus seeks to articulate and proclaim, in a novel and clever manner, what people really think about justice.

12. Stauffer, *Plato's Introduction to the Question of Justice*, 69.

13. Cleitophon's proffered resolution of Thrasymachus' difficulty reflects his own dissatisfaction with Socratic questioning about justice, as I suggested above. As Cleitophon says in the

Cleitophon, he has grown weary of uncertainty about the meaning and, we may infer, the significance or goodness of justice. (Cf. Christopher Bruell, *On the Socratic Education* [Lanham, MD: Rowman & Littlefield], 196–99.) His turn to Thrasymachus prior to the action of the *Republic* reflects a readiness to accept and adhere to a simpler line: The just is merely the legal, or what the rulers lay down, believing it to be to their advantage. It probably comes as a surprise to him that Thrasymachus is unwilling to leave it at that. It is also worth noting that Cleitophon says in the *Cleitophon* that Socrates himself told him that it belonged to justice to harm enemies and do good to friends (410b), the very answer that Polemarchus offered earlier in Book I of the *Republic*, and that Socrates refuted (or led Polemarchus to refute).

14. The word κρείττων means "superior" as well as "stronger," so the turn Thrasymachus takes is somewhat less peculiar than it might seem to a reader of an English translation.

15. In the previous chapter I mentioned some other scholars' interpretations of this turn in the dialogue. David Leibowitz, and Thomas Pangle and Timothy Burns, offer interpretations which are closer to mine than the ones I discussed there (Leibowitz, "Thrasymachus's Blush," 121; Pangle and Burns, *The Key Texts of Political Philosophy: An Introduction*, 56). Leibowitz says that part of the reason Thrasymachus answers as he does is that he "has great respect for art or knowledge and great contempt for ignorance." As I shall discuss below, however, it seems to me Leibowitz does not sufficiently focus on this point in his subsequent interpretation. The interpretation I offer here is an expanded version of what I presented in "Thrasymachus and His Attachment to Justice," *Polis* 32 (2015), 344–68.

16. Stanley Rosen, *Plato's Republic: A Study* (New Haven: Yale University Press, 2005), 47.

17. All three men also earlier spoke of "the stronger" (κρείττονος in genitive singular), but they used it to mean one or more people.

18. The arts were treated very differently during the exchange between Socrates and Polemarchus, where Polemarchus had difficulty saying what justice produces in the manner of the arts (332d–333d), or, to put it another way, where justice was implicitly *contrasted* with art (Stauffer, *Plato's Introduction to the Question of Justice*, 72). Here the emphasis is upon the selflessness of art, which Thrasymachus can't help portraying even though he doesn't initially seem to notice it. (Thus at 340d he says the true doctor is the one who makes no mistakes *about the sick*, not the one who makes no mistakes about how he himself might benefit from treating the sick.)

19. Rosen notes that "nothing is said about moneymaking in connection with the pilot," unlike the doctor. However, he does not indicate the significance of this difference, adding that money "surely figures in the purposes of the pilot . . . as much as it does in those of the physician" (*Plato's Republic: A Study*, 46).

20. Cf. Pangle and Burns, *The Key Texts of Political Philosophy: An Introduction*, 57. Pangle and Burns note that Socrates indicates in the sequel that he is exaggerating the power of art by suggesting that art makes it possible for eyes to see and ears to hear (342a). Thrasymachus does not specifically agree to that suggestion; there Socrates is explaining the first of three possible ways of understanding the arts, and Thrasymachus will subsequently choose the third (342b). However, Socrates' suggestion about eyes and ears clarifies the meaning of his statement that a body needs medicine, to which Thrasymachus does agree.

21. Rosen carefully considers the question of arts seeking their own advantage (*Plato's Republic: A Study*, 45–46). However, he also asserts that Socrates "argues that the sole advantage of each of the arts is to be as perfect as possible" (46). He treats Socrates' questions (albeit leading questions in some cases) and Thrasymachus' answers as Socrates' arguments, rather than considering their significance for understanding Thrasymachus.

22. It is also unclear what Socrates means by an art being "most perfect." We might take this to refer either to improvement in how the art is generally practiced (e.g., the discovery of new methods), or to an individual artisan perfecting his skill. Socrates and Thrasymachus discuss only the latter meaning, but it seems further than the former from the art itself being "most perfect."

23. Aristotle, *Nicomachean Ethics* (Cambridge, MA: Harvard University Press, Loeb edition, 1982), 1094a1–b10.

24. Cf. Pangle and Burns, *The Key Texts of Political Philosophy: An Introduction*, 58.

25. Thrasymachus' way of viewing art would preclude viewing calculation as properly subordinate to an art that seeks a more comprehensive understanding such as science or philosophy.

26. Strauss comments that the example of the shepherd is "wisely chosen by Thrasymachus in order to destroy Socrates' argument" (*The City and Man*, 81). This is evidently how Thrasymachus views it, but it seems to me Thrasymachus' own position is being destroyed, as Socrates indicates. Strauss seems to underestimate the degree to which the conversation is exposing Thrasymachus' views. Pangle and Burns also fail to make clear that what Socrates says here about the shepherd follows from Thrasymachus' view of art. Instead (somewhat surprisingly) they ask: "For is it so obvious that shepherds do not, as shepherds, really care for the welfare of their sheep?" (*The Key Texts of Political Philosophy: An Introduction*, 60). As Socrates later indicates, the end of shepherding is the good of human beings, not of sheep (370d–e).

27. Stauffer, *Plato's Introduction to the Question of Justice*, 74.

28. Stauffer, *Plato's Introduction to the Question of Justice*, 75.

29. Stauffer, *Plato's Introduction to the Question of Justice*, 76–78.

30. I say "unselfconscious" rather than "unconscious" because the opinions in question are ones which people do, at least in some situations, think and state. In Plato's presentation, most of us have opinions and feelings which we haven't fully recognized or accepted and integrated into our view of ourselves and the world, and which contradict other opinions we hold. We are often loath to admit to ourselves much of what we think and feel; but it is all capable of coming to the surface, at least under the skillful questioning of a Socrates. By contrast, the term "unconscious" suggests thoughts and feelings which people do not consciously experience and which they are therefore incapable of stating or expressing directly (cf. Sigmund Freud, *The Interpretation of Dreams*, translated by James Strachey [New York: Basic Books, 2010], 607–9). Later in the *Republic*, Socrates indicates that lawless desires are often suppressed or repressed by "shame and prudence" (571c). Nonetheless, I believe Plato would doubt that there are wholly unconscious thoughts or feelings. For Plato, what you see is what you get—at least if "you" are Socrates.

31. One might identify two different ways in which art is unselfish. First, the artisan gives his attention to something outside himself. Second, artisans must exchange what they produce with others in order to satisfy their needs. Thus a builder must pay attention both to houses, and to what other people desire in houses. In Aristotle's terms, however, these two are one: The art's end is the good it seeks to provide. Thus a builder seeks to build houses people want.

32. Thrasymachus insults Socrates several times, often after Socrates exposes a genuine problem in what Thrasymachus is saying. The insults suggest that Thrasymachus is irritated by this, but still thinks he can get the better of Socrates. (They also indicate that he is somewhat crude.) The insults stop when Thrasymachus blushes at 350d.

33. I agree with P.P. Nicholson that "the idea that justice is the advantage of another, rather than the idea that it is the advantage of the stronger, i.e. ruler(s)," is central to Thrasymachus' thought ("Unravelling Thrasymachus' Arguments in the *Republic*," *Phronesis* 19 [1974], 216). However, Nicholson seems not to realize that Thrasymachus is *mocking* justice when he initially defines it as "the advantage of the stronger."

34. Stauffer, *Plato's Introduction to the Question of Justice*, 110–11.

35. Thrasymachus switches between singular and plural in this passage. He describes the (single) tyrant's activity, then says "they are called happy and blessed" by people who learn that *he* has done the whole injustice. I am not sure what this means except that Thrasymachus wishes to generalize the statement at its key point, that tyrants are called happy and blessed.

36. Some commentators suggest that Thrasymachus' speech is in his interest insofar as he wishes to attract students who hope to become tyrants. I see two problems with this suggestion. One is that rather than stay to see if he might actually win over any new pupils, Thrasymachus starts to leave immediately after finishing this speech (344d). The second is that his immoralism here is so blunt that it is likely to make his listeners wonder if he is really the man from whom they can learn politically effective rhetoric. Gorgias and Protagoras offer interesting contrasts in this respect as well.

37. The myth of Er, with which the *Republic* concludes, suggests that Socrates largely agrees with Thrasymachus regarding the hypocrisy of people's condemnation of injustice. In the myth, when a man who lived "partaking of virtue by habit, without philosophy" is allowed to choose his next life, he immediately chooses the greatest tyranny, which he regrets only upon discovering that eating his own children and other evils are to be part of his fate (619b–c). The myth suggests that without philosophy, people don't truly embrace justice. They practice it (to some extent) out of necessity, or in hope of reward, not for its own sake. This is consistent with Thrasymachus' insistence that people blame injustice because they fear suffering it, not doing it (344c), though of course Thrasymachus makes no exception for philosophers.

38. Cf. Leibowitz, "Thrasymachus's Blush," 120.

39. Stauffer makes a related point. He argues that Thrasymachus initially seeks to "expose the fraud of justice *as a fraud* . . . his argument has the character of an accusation or a complaint." Paradoxically, he "is directing a moral accusation against justice itself," and even "arguing that justice is unjust" (Stauffer, "Thrasymachus' Attachment to Justice?" 4). This is a valuable analysis, though perhaps Stauffer overstates the extent of Thrasymachus' indignation. Thrasymachus' initial coyness about offering his definition of justice, and his eagerness for praise once he offers it, suggest that he is somewhat less concerned to expose justice than Stauffer indicates. Nonetheless, Thrasymachus does feel some indignation, particularly at fraudulence and hypocrisy. Stauffer reaches a conclusion similar to mine, that Thrasymachus "is more attached to justice than he knows" (10), but on a somewhat different basis. He says little about Thrasymachus' admiration of art, which, as I have argued, is the heart of the strongest part of his attachment to justice. Early in his conversation with Socrates, Thrasymachus turns from the fraudulence of justice to the craftsman who does not err (340c). This turn reveals what most excites him.

40. On the other hand, the Greek gods were less sternly hostile to injustice, and more well-disposed toward success, than the Biblical God. However, I think it would be carrying this point too far to say that many of a rapacious tyrant's subjects would believe him to be blessed. Perhaps some might wonder if the gods were favoring one who seemed to them so successful and fortunate; but given the uncertainty of the matter, they probably would not call blessed someone they had so much reason to hate.

41. Alternatively, it may be that he doesn't really think others think this, but is simply led by enthusiasm to express his own thought or feeling.

42. A finer soul, even a finer immoralist, might emphasize fame or power rather than money. On the other hand, money is more universally pursued than fame or power, and its possession is less susceptible of interpretation or dispute. Therefore amassing tremendous wealth arguably demonstrates more conclusively superiority to others. Thrasymachus himself seems to desire praise more than money (cf. 338b), but it is not clear that he notices this about himself.

43. Beliefs about justice are often deepened, rather than undermined, when confronted. However, it is hard to see how this could happen to somebody who initially prides himself on repudiating justice. Greater self-awareness would compel such a person either to embrace a more consistent, complete selfishness, or (following a period of uncertainty) to embrace justice in a more straightforward manner.

44. Cf. Xenophon, *Hiero or Tyrannicus,* in Leo Strauss, *On Tyranny* (Ithaca: Cornell University Press, 1975).

45. Seth Benardete, *Socrates' Second Sailing: On Plato's Republic* (Chicago: The University of Chicago Press, 1999), 22. At 360c1–2 Glaucon is actually talking about the ring of Gyges, not about tyranny, but the point still seems apt.

46. It is anachronistic but not, I think, irrelevant to mention the history presented in Tacitus' *Annals.* Three of the five rulers of the family of Augustus (Tiberius, Caligula, and Nero) steeped their hands deeply in blood. The latter two were also infamous for sexual depravity.

47. We tend to feel that what we admire should flourish. There may be cases where a person admires without feeling this, but more commonly, the feeling that something is admirable or noble or beautiful is accompanied by a feeling that it is worthy as well.

Chapter Three

Socrates Refutes Thrasymachus

ABIDING BY THRASYMACHUS' DEFINITION OF ART

Thrasymachus has stated in his long speech that injustice is "stronger and freer and more masterful" than justice, and that most human beings think so even if they don't admit it (344c). He has thereby given a clear answer to the questions raised in the Introduction. As we shall see, however, he has difficulty maintaining this answer in the face of Socrates' questions.

Upon finishing his speech, Thrasymachus starts to leave. The others present compel him to remain and defend what he has said (344d). We might be reminded of the beginning of Book I, where Socrates is compelled to come to Polemarchus' house (327c–328b).[1] In both cases the compulsion is playful but nonetheless revealing. Socrates and Thrasymachus are in a different position than the others present. Once Cephalus leaves, they are probably the oldest men there, and more importantly the others view the two of them as teachers who are eager to appeal to them and win them over. The other men resemble the city in their dealings with Socrates and Thrasymachus, who are not exactly members of any city in the ordinary way. Different though they are, Socrates and Thrasymachus both pursue what one might call the life of the mind, which sets them apart. (Thrasymachus of course pursues money and renown, but through teachings and speeches of a cosmopolitan character.)

In his long speech Thrasymachus has shifted his focus from art back to justice and injustice. He introduced art as a model or template for understanding the true ruler's flawless pursuit of his own advantage; however, that introduced complications which he has not been able to address, because of the tension between his admiration of art and his admiration of selfishness, or, to put it another way, because he unselfconsciously holds conflicting opinions about whether art is a means or an end. Socrates will keep the conversation focused on art, however, because Thrasymachus' view of art is the key to the tension in his view of justice.

Socrates demands that Thrasymachus "abide by" (ἔμμενε) the things he said earlier, or else make it clear if he is changing his position. After defining the true doctor, Thrasymachus "no longer thought it necessary to guard precisely the true shepherd." For the shepherd's art, "surely nothing other than that over which it has been set, is a care" (345b–d). As I noted in the previous chapter, Socrates attributes to Thrasymachus the definition of the shepherd as one who takes care of sheep (hence Thrasymachus must "abide by" what he has said). This definition follows from the answer Thrasymachus gave earlier that art considers the advantage of that of which it is the art. At that point Thrasymachus even conceded (reluctantly) that horsemanship considers the advantage of horses, which clearly contradicts what he now says about shepherds (342b–c).

Socrates defends Thrasymachus' earlier definition of art against Thrasymachus' ridicule of it as applied to shepherds. Regarding craftsmen other than rulers, Socrates asks, "Don't you realize that nobody wants to rule voluntarily, but they demand wages as if the benefit from ruling were not for themselves but for those who are ruled?" (345e) Socrates is now explicitly stating that, in effect, human beings are not simply craftsmen: Human beings demand wages. Thrasymachus does not speak at this point, and Socrates goes on to distinguish wage-earning as an art from other arts. "And we say that the benefit for the craftsmen receiving a wage comes to be for them from the use in addition of the wage-earning art." Thrasymachus assents reluctantly (346c). He sees that agreeing to this means agreeing that art as such (at least apart from wage-earning) is unselfish; however, he does not try either to distinguish ruling from the arts, or to focus upon the artisan's demand for wages. Bloom comments about this passage: "The tension between the public good and private good of the individual . . . is admitted with this introduction of the wage earner's art. Thrasymachus, however, is not quick enough to notice this and take advantage of it."[2] This is true, but incomplete. Thrasymachus does not *want* to concede that artisans as such are unselfish, even if it allows him to underline Socrates' concession of a tension between private and public good. Since he despises selflessness (or thinks he does) but admires artisans, he does not want to concede their selflessness *qua* artisans.[3]

One might wonder why Socrates speaks of wage-earning as an art, rather than a different kind of activity. Apparently he wishes to clarify (and for Thrasymachus to agree) that it is distinct from other arts, not part of them. The "private" or "peculiar" (ἰδίαν) benefit of medicine is health, that of the pilot's art is safety in sailing, and that of wage-earning is money (346a–b). Thus the first two, like justice according to Thrasymachus' revised definition, aim at "someone else's good" (though as we have seen, this is not entirely true of piloting). However, if wage-earning is an art, then art does *not* necessarily aim at "someone else's good."[4] As Stauffer notes, "It is not clear why ruling could not be understood on the model of wage-earning rather than the other arts—as the wage-seizing art."[5] Thrasymachus does not mention this possibility, apparently because he is concentrating on resisting the argument for the selflessness of other arts.

In his interchange with Glaucon, Socrates continues to dispute the definition of justice as the advantage of the stronger (347e1), but he does not dispute that it is someone else's good. He does not simply embrace justice in this sense. As he says to Glaucon, the true ruler looks "not for his own advantage, but for that of the one being ruled; so that everyone who knows would choose being benefited by another rather than to have troubles benefiting another" (347d). It is better to be benefited than to benefit.[6]

Having shown that Thrasymachus has not abided by his definition of art in his long speech, Socrates challenges Thrasymachus' claim that the life of the unjust is stronger than the life of the just. As he indicates, he thereby sets aside the question of what justice is (347e). Socrates asks if Thrasymachus asserts that complete or perfect (τελέαν) injustice is more profitable than complete justice (348b). Thrasymachus says it is. Socrates asks if he asserts that justice is virtue and injustice vice. Thrasymachus responds mockingly, "That is likely indeed, most pleasant man, when I also say that injustice is profitable, and justice not." Socrates asks how he identifies them. Thrasymachus replies, the opposite, apparently meaning injustice is virtue and justice vice. However, when Socrates asks if he calls justice vice (κακίαν), Thrasymachus says no, and instead calls it "very high-minded innocence." So Socrates asks if he calls injustice bad disposition, to which Thrasymachus says no, good counsel (348c–d).

In his long speech, Thrasymachus said that those who blame injustice do so because they fear suffering it, not doing it (344c). He thereby suggested that weakness drives people to a hypocritical embrace of justice. Here, however, he suggests that some people (high-minded innocents) are sincerely attached to justice. This shift reflects the fact that Socrates is asking about "complete" (τέλεος) justice and injustice. The hypocritical embrace of justice which he discussed earlier would not seem to qualify. However, he also said in his long speech that injustice rules "the truly simple (εὐηθικῶν) and the just" (343c6–7). Thrasymachus is inclined to think both that nobody is really duped by talk of justice, and that there are high-minded innocents who genuinely embrace justice.

It seems inconsistent that Thrasymachus resists identifying "complete" justice as vice or badness (κακίαν). If justice is someone else's good, and he is right about the absence of a common good, then someone who is perfectly just, who thinks only of the good of others, is incapable of pursuing his own good. Thrasymachus' reluctance to call justice vice apparently reflects a certain underlying restraint, as well as a lack of clarity.[7] He doesn't wholly believe the principles he espouses. To put it another way, for Thrasymachus the choice between injustice and justice is not like choosing between health and sickness, or intelligence and mental disability; it is somehow a choice, if not exactly a difficult one. Of course he thinks "complete" justice is foolish; yet his reluctance to call it a vice suggests that he doesn't quite feel sure he sees to the end of it, or sees everything that might be involved with it.

Socrates says he would know how to respond if Thrasymachus called injustice profitable but vicious or disgraceful, as some others do. He thereby suggests it is relatively easy to show that those who hold this position (such as Polus in the *Gorgias*) contradict themselves. However, Socrates says, it is clear that Thrasymachus will assign to injustice all the good qualities generally assigned to justice. "You prophesy most truly," Thrasymachus replies. Socrates says that he must nonetheless continue to consider the argument, as long as Thrasymachus is saying what he thinks. "For you seem to me now, Thrasymachus, really (ἀτεχνῶς) not to joke, but to say what appears to you concerning the truth" (349a). Thrasymachus has given his opinion about what he seriously considers to be justice and injustice. Socrates' choice of the word ἀτεχνῶς (literally, artlessly) artfully suggests that art isn't necessarily useful for Thrasymachus when he wishes to speak truthfully. Art takes one only so far; sometimes what is needed is simple honesty.

THRASYMACHUS' BLUSH

If Socrates needed a moment to consider how to respond, he quickly recovers. He asks if the just man would want to have more (πλέον ἔχειν) than another just man. Thrasymachus answers that he would not. Socrates asks if the just man would want to have more than the just action, and Thrasymachus says that he would not (349b). It is not obvious what it means to "have more than" an action. It might mean gaining or benefiting from the action, or it might mean gaining more than one has reason to expect. However, this distinction does not matter here, for Thrasymachus thinks one has no reason to expect any benefit from a just action (at least insofar as it is a just action), since justice as such consists in "someone else's good," not one's own. A just person chooses to be just without hope of benefit. Thrasymachus would apparently deny, e.g., that a man helping a friend is performing a just action if he expects to benefit from doing so, even if the benefit consists simply of supporting the friendship. The purity of Thrasymachus' definition of justice is striking, though perhaps not uncommon.[8]

Socrates then asks if the just man would suppose that "he is worthy to get the better of (πλεονεκτεῖν) the unjust man" and that this is just.[9] Thrasymachus responds that he would suppose he is worthy, but would not be able to.

Socrates says he is not asking that, but whether the just man wants and deems himself worthy to have more (πλέον ἔχειν) than the unjust man but not the just man. In restating his question after Thrasymachus initially doesn't fully answer it (and when he therefore may be less certain of how Thrasymachus will respond), Socrates uses "have more than" in place of "get the better of." Thrasymachus answers that the just man thinks thus (349b–c).

Socrates asks whether the unjust man deems himself worthy to get the better of (πλεονεκτεῖν) the just man and the just action. Thrasymachus answers that he "deems [himself] worthy to have more than everyone" (349c). (Thrasymachus doesn't seem to notice any distinction between πλεονεκτεῖν and πλέον ἔχειν. This is the only time in the section from 349b to the blush at 350e when he uses either phrase.) At 343e Thrasymachus implied that the unjust man is willing to help kinsmen and acquaintances against what is just. The way he speaks of the unjust man here makes it sound like he is not interested in helping anybody. Thrasymachus may think the unjust man seeks to "have more than everyone" but is willing to help friends or kinsmen if he thinks doing so will ultimately benefit him. However, as in his description of the tyrant, he tends to speak of the unjust man as purely unjust or selfish.

Thrasymachus speaks in strikingly moral language here: He says the unjust man "deems [himself] worthy (ἀξιοῖ)" to have more than others.[10] He would of course deny that the unjust man expects an *external* reward apart from what he gains as a result of his injustice. And he may be partly joking (mocking the term "deem worthy," which Socrates introduced here). However, he is not simply joking; he later responds that it is "necessary" that the musical man deem himself worthy to have more than the unmusical man, and he doesn't distance himself from the musical man's opinion (349e16). (Thrasymachus also asked at the beginning of the exchange, before giving his definition of justice, what Socrates would "deem [himself] worthy to suffer [ἀξιοῖς παθεῖν]" if shown a better definition of justice [337d2].) To say someone is worthy to have more means he *deserves* more or *should* have more. The term is prescriptive rather than descriptive: It implies a view of justice. In some way Thrasymachus feels that it is just for the better (stronger, wiser, more skilled) to rule and have more than the worse (weaker, less wise, less skilled). To put it another way, he believes more deeply than he realizes something akin to the mocking definition of justice he initially offered. The "advantage of the stronger" is equivalent to the advantage of the better if one understands the stronger as the better, which Thrasymachus does to some extent in defining the stronger as those who do not err.

Socrates concludes that the just man does not get the better of like, but of unlike, while the unjust man gets the better of both like and unlike. Thrasymachus agrees. Socrates asks if the unjust man is prudent (φρόνιμός) and good (ἀγαθὸς). Thrasymachus answers affirmatively. Socrates asks if the unjust man is "like the prudent and the good," and the just man unlike them.

Thrasymachus answers, "How could a man being such not be like such men, and the other, not like them?" Socrates then asks if "each of them is such as those whom he is like (τοιοῦτος ἄρα ἐστὶν ἑκάτερος αὐτῶν οἷσπερ ἔοικεν)." Thrasymachus impatiently answers affirmatively (349c–d). However, the last two questions are different. Thrasymachus first says that one is *like* that which one *is*, which seems incontestable; he then agrees that one *is* that which one is *like*, which is doubtful as a general principle. If Jane is a chess player, then she is *like* a chess player; but if Jane is like a chess player, it does not follow that she *is* a chess player.

Thrasymachus, who is not a genius (though he may be like one), may have lost his bearings and agreed to something he does not really think. However, Socrates did not clearly offer a general principle here. He asked about "each of them (ἑκάτερος αὐτῶν)," the unjust man and the just man, and his relation to those whom he is like, meaning the prudent and good and (by implication) the imprudent and bad. Thrasymachus *does* think the unjust man is like prudent and good men and the same as prudent and good men, and the just man like those lacking prudence and goodness and the same as those lacking prudence and goodness,[11] so he thinks that "each of them" *is* that which he is like. I see no reason to conclude that he doesn't realize what he has agreed to here, though this agreement is a key part of the refutation Socrates offers (at 350c7).[12]

Nonetheless, there might be some significance to Thrasymachus' agreeing to a point which would seem peculiar if generalized. Thrasymachus understands injustice to be the unrestrained pursuit of one's own good, and he thinks the prudent and good man is unjust. He apparently tends to conclude from this that the unjust man is not only *like* the prudent and good man (in being unjust), but *is* the prudent and good man, or that the presence of injustice indicates a prudent and good man. Thus he praises successful thieves as prudent (348d), without much enthusiasm.

Thrasymachus is of two minds. He doesn't simply admire common thieves, yet in some way he feels that injustice as such is a high virtue. In this respect he is like more (or more obviously) moral men: He wants to praise the virtue he admires; he does not want to start noting caveats and limitations.

Socrates next ascertains that Thrasymachus associates being musical with being prudent and good and being unmusical with the opposite qualities. Socrates asks if a musical man tuning his lyre wishes, in the tightening and loosening of the strings, to get the better of (πλεονεκτεῖν) another musical man, or deems himself worthy of having more. Thrasymachus answers no (349e). The distinction (noted above) between πλεονεκτεῖν and the somewhat gentler phrase πλέον ἔχειν may be of some significance here. If the question had instead been whether the musical man seeks to have more than another musical man, Thrasymachus might possibly have hesitated before saying no. Socrates is drawing out a real tension in Thrasymachus' views—but a slight rhetorical or verbal trick helps ensure that the tension comes to light.

Socrates asks if the musical man wishes to get the better of an unmusical man. Thrasymachus answers yes, and once again fails to see that he has taken a decisive step toward being refuted. Having agreed with this example that prudent and good men do not seek to get the better of what is like but rather of what is unlike, he has conceded that the prudent and good behave like the just (349e).

However, Thrasymachus' answer is questionable. Are musical men or doctors (regarding whom Thrasymachus makes the same assertion or agreement at 350a) unwilling to get the better of or have more than other musical men or doctors? If there is one job opening in a symphony or a hospital, they might well clamor to do so. One could say that such competition emerges for them as human beings seeking wages or honor, not strictly as craftsmen. As craftsmen strictly speaking, however, it is not obvious that they try to get the better of anybody.

On the other hand, one could say that a craftsman seeks to get the better of everybody, in the sense of being the best at his craft. Indeed, this seems like the most obvious way to answer Socrates' initial question here: A musical man seeks to surpass or get the better of all other men, most importantly other musicians, in the quality of the music he makes. (By asking about tuning rather than playing [349e10–11], Socrates makes less obvious the ambition to be the best, thereby inviting Thrasymachus to answer as he does. This is another small rhetorical trick which helps expose a genuine tension in Thrasymachus' views.) This ambition doesn't arise for the musical man precisely as a craftsman practicing his craft, but rather as a human being seeking primacy in his craft.

Some scholars do not detect any particular significance in Thrasymachus' holding the view that an artisan does not seek to get the better of his fellow artisans. Stauffer observes that "it would be artless or foolish" for an artisan to "overshoot" the standard at which all practitioners of a certain art aim, "for example, harmony or health."[13] However, there are more and less complex harmonies and variably challenging medical cases, to say nothing of the vast differences among musical composers or medical researchers. If each art aimed merely at one commonly achieved standard, there would be few meaningful differences among competent artisans; but the actual practitioners of the arts are very interested in the manifold differences among them, and in the order of rank they imply. Such differences also provide much of the source of progress in the arts. (Socrates himself later argues for the superiority of Asclepius to Herodicus on the ground that the former's medical art was more philosophic or political than the latter's [407c–e], more in harmony with the proper ends of medicine.)

Catherine Zuckert acknowledges that the differences among actual craftsmen go beyond how competently they pursue a shared standard, but she argues that Thrasymachus and Socrates "both refer to complete knowledge to which it is impossible to add." There is nothing for artisans in this sense "to 'compete' about; all true practitioners of the same art know the same things as all others." Zuckert grants that we may "think it is impossible for a human being to obtain such complete knowledge," but insists this is not relevant to the discussion between Socrates and Thrasymachus.[14] However, a more obvious reading is that Socrates is asking about actual artisans, not hypothetical ones whose knowledge is perfect and as such cannot be bested. He first speaks of musical men in this context simply by asking if someone is musical and another not musical (349d–e), and then mentions details about tuning the lyre (349e). Thrasymachus indeed thinks that craftsmen are truly craftsmen only insofar as they do not err, but he is not self-consciously imagining craftsmen who are radically different than craftsmen as we know them; he means simply that so-called craftsmen fall short of being true craftsmen insofar as they err (340d–e). He does not say that art cannot exist without the "complete knowledge" that Zuckert discusses. One might argue that this is implied in what he does say (though one might also argue that there is a difference between "erring" and simply not knowing everything that might be relevant to one's craft); but it is not clear that Thrasymachus himself draws this implication, while it is clear that he is interested in actual artisans. Despite his interest in actual artisans, however, he fails to notice (at least in this generalizing context) the existence of competition among them.

Thrasymachus is right that a craftsman does not claim superiority to other craftsmen insofar as they too know the craft. Craftsmen pride themselves on their mutual superiority to those who don't know their craft; in this sense they seek to get the better of non-craftsmen but not of each other. Thrasymachus is drawn to this aspect of the relation among craftsmen. He downplays or disregard both the various types of competition that arise among the practitioners of a craft, and the harmony of interest between them and those who do not know their craft and whom they serve. He thinks (at least to some extent) that craftsmen get the better of those who do not know their craft but not of each other. (He does not seem very interested in how the unwise or unskilled behave among themselves, as indicated by his use of Ἴσως at 350b2.) Despite his earlier celebration of injustice and denial of the existence of a meaningful common good, he has an unrealistic or exaggerated view of the common good that exists among craftsmen. He apparently envisages a single degree of craftsmanship, the achievers of which (in any given craft) neither compete with each other nor serve others. This seems incoherent, but like many illusions people cherish, it has some basis in reality, or it reflects an aspect of reality. One might characterize it as a distortion rather than an illusion. Like many such distortions, moreover, it apparently constitutes part of a belief in justice. The common good among craftsmen that Thrasymachus envisages or imagines is something he half-consciously feels they deserve due to their virtue as craftsmen.

His belief that musical men and doctors "get the better of" those who do not know their craft is the reverse side of the same coin. There is also some truth to this belief: Craftsmen pride themselves on their superiority to those who don't know their craft. However, Thrasymachus downplays or disregards the manifest harmony of interest between craftsmen and those whom they serve, which seems (at least to me) much greater than the harmony of interest among the practitioners of any particular craft. His assertion that doctors seek to get the better of non-doctors (350a5) is particularly striking—that's not exactly the Hippocratic Oath. (Here Socrates exploits Thrasymachus' tendency to deny that artisans serve non-artisans rather than refuting it.) Thrasymachus' view that craftsmen get the better of those who don't know their craft also reflects what he half-consciously feels craftsmen and non-craftsmen deserve. Craftsmen, who are prudent and good men (349e7), share a natural harmony or common good; non-craftsmen do not, and thereby face a harsher world. In this context, where he is not thinking about tyrants or injustice as such, Thrasymachus believes that good men tend to be just, at least to a certain group of other good men (practitioners of the same craft).

Enthusiasm for justice, and for those who love justice, invites the belief that a god or godlike moral order supports it. Thrasymachus would of course scoff at such a belief; nonetheless, he apparently feels that artisans have access to a good apart from their skill itself and the real but limited rewards it provides (such as wages and reputation). Like more conventional lovers of justice, Thrasymachus apparently feels that men engaged in a particular selfless activity should prosper.

Given that Thrasymachus unselfconsciously believes in a "should" or in deserving—given that he is more attached to justice than he realizes—one might still ask why his belief doesn't simply take the form of believing that selfish or self-serving virtues deserve to be rewarded. Such a belief would be less glaringly at odds with other beliefs he holds (notably his belief in the rationality of selfishness), while still addressing the common human longing to transcend his limits and his frailty, a longing which apparently makes genuine repudiation of justice impossible for him. To put it another way, one might wonder if self-sacrifice is *necessarily* part of our sense of justice. I think the answer is yes, for to believe in justice (at least in a way that addresses that common human longing) is to believe that something should be *given* to those who are good or deserving. But if this is the fundamental principle at work in the world, then the virtue by which people become deserving must itself partake of that quality of giving. If one's deepest and fondest hope is that those who are worthy will be given something transcendent, one isn't likely to find it plausible that their worthiness itself has nothing to do with giving. If we view ourselves simply as selfish, then we have little ground for hoping that anyone or anything greater than we are will be interested in giving us anything.

Socrates generalizes the questions he has asked regarding musical men and doctors. "See if, regarding every knowledge and lack of knowledge, someone seems to you knowledgeable (ἐπιστήμων) who would want to take (αἱρεῖσθαι) more than another knowledgeable one, or do or say more, and not the same thing as another similar to himself in the same action." Thrasymachus answers, "But perhaps (ἴσως) it is necessary that this be so" (350a). (The Greek word ἴσως ranges in meaning from "perhaps" to "presumably."[15]) Socrates' question broadens the focus from art and prudence to knowledge generally; Thrasymachus' earlier denial that an artisan who errs is truly an artisan invites this broadening.

Socrates does not ask in general terms if the knowledgeable person wishes to get the better of, or take or do or say more than, those who lack knowledge. He next asks if the unknowledgeable one wishes to get the better equally of the knowledgeable and the unknowledgeable one. Thrasymachus merely answers, "Perhaps (Ἴσως)" (350a11–b2). Socrates then asks if the knowledgeable one is wise, and if the wise one is good. Thrasymachus answers both questions affirmatively. Socrates asks if the good and the wise will not want to get the better of the one who is like, but only of the unlike and opposite. Sensing the contradiction in his views, Thrasymachus says, "It seems so" (350b). Socrates asks if the bad and unlearned want to get the better of both the like and the opposite. Thrasymachus says, "It appears so." Socrates reminds Thrasymachus of his earlier statement that the unjust man gets the better of both unlike and like, and the just man only of the unlike. He then continues: "Then the just man is like the wise and good, and the unjust man [like] the bad and unlearned." Thrasymachus replies, "It may be so (Κινδυνεύει)" (350c6). Socrates then reminds Thrasymachus of the earlier agreement that each is such as the one he is like, and concludes that the just man appears to be both good and wise, and the unjust man both unlearned and bad.

Then Thrasymachus blushes. He blushes because he has realized there is a genuine contradiction between his admiration of artisanship and his admiration of injustice: He has realized that he thinks of good men both that they have no cause for conflict with their peers (fellow practitioners of their art), and that they try to get the better of everyone, including each other. Having realized this, which would itself give him pause, he thinks that he has failed in his own art, which is narrowly the art of rhetoric, and broadly that of thinking and speaking well. He views the artisan's skill as the chief form of human excellence, at least for those who are not tyrants; and by his own definition, one who errs is no artisan. His world is one of the proficient and the incompetent; and now he has come to light—in front of others—as one of the incompetent, one who perhaps deserves to suffer and be exploited. He does not really believe he is incompetent, as shown by his refusal in the sequel to renounce his views or even admit uncertainty; but he sees that he has blundered—that he holds contradictory opinions on a question of some significance—which carries a lot of weight for him.

Thrasymachus did not blush earlier in the conversation because he did not see that the earlier refutations indicated any real weakness in his position. To him, Socrates' assertions about the selflessness of artisanship seemed naive and ridiculous, though he was unable to refute them. Even as he blushes, he still does not seem to grasp or digest that the artisan's practice of his craft is inherently self-forgetting, or that there is a tension between pursuit of one's own good and artisanship.[16]

THRASYMACHUS TAMED

After Thrasymachus reluctantly concedes that the just man is good and wise and the unjust man the opposite, Socrates turns to his earlier assertion that injustice is strong. Thrasymachus objects that "what you are now saying is not sufficient," and indicates that he wishes to speak at length without interruption. "So either permit me to speak as much as I want, or, if you want to question, question; and as for me, just as with the old women telling stories, I will say 'All right' and I will nod assent and I will shake my head" (350d–e). Socrates says, "In no way against your opinion," to which Thrasymachus replies that if Socrates will not let him speak at length, that is what he will do. Socrates says he will continue asking questions, which suggests that the heart of his confrontation with Thrasymachus is over. While earlier he indicated that he wished to confront Thrasymachus' real views (349a), now he is prepared to accept insincere responses.

Nonetheless, he continues trying to draw Thrasymachus out. He says it will not be difficult to show that justice is stronger than injustice on the basis of what they have agreed. So rather than building upon those agreements, he approaches the question in a different manner. He asks if Thrasymachus would say that there is an unjust city and that it attempts to enslave other cities unjustly. Thrasymachus heartily agrees and adds, "This indeed the best city will most of all do" (351b).

Socrates then seeks to narrow the question, asking whether a city is powerful with or without justice. Thrasymachus answers: "If it holds as you were saying just now, that justice is wisdom, then with justice; and if as I was saying, then with injustice." Socrates notes that Thrasymachus is not only nodding and shaking his head, but answering "very finely" (351c). Thrasymachus is not adhering to his statement that he will no longer say what he really thinks; his candor gets the better of him. (By contrast, after expressing dissatisfaction with Socrates' mode of conversation at 497b in the *Gorgias*, Callicles becomes terse in his replies.)

Socrates asks if a city or an army or pirates or thieves or any other "tribe" (ἔθνος) with an unjust aim would be able to accomplish anything if they behaved unjustly toward each other. Thrasymachus answers no. Socrates continues, "For injustice produces factions and hatreds and battles with others, and justice produces concord and friendship." Thrasymachus answers, "Let it be, in order that I might not differ with you" (351d). This is the sixth answer (beginning at 351b2) that Thrasymachus gives after stating that he will no longer say what he really thinks, and it is the first one in which he abides by that statement; but he does so in order to evade an obvious difficulty with his position. As Strauss comments, all "human beings (including tyrants and gangsters) who need the help of other men in their enterprises however unjust" must practice justice among their associates.[17]

A proponent of injustice might concede that prudence sometimes requires being just instrumentally, while insisting that it means being unjust or selfish ultimately. However, Thrasymachus doesn't want to concede that men seeking to accomplish something must be just among themselves; he doesn't want to concede any necessity for justice, other than weakness (341a, 344c). He is attracted to a notion of injustice as a pure principle, unsullied by contact with its low opposite. In an odd way, Thrasymachus resembles those lovers of justice who seem more concerned with how the world should be than with how it is. Like them, he tends to define the virtue or excellence he prizes in unrealistically pure or unalloyed terms. Like them, he is at times as concerned about the possession of that virtue as about its actual effect, though, like many of them, he does not see himself this way. Also like many of them, he sees the characteristic opposed to the virtue he prizes in unrealistically pure terms as well, as we saw at 349b.

While Thrasymachus agrees that injustice breeds conflict among people, he is uncomfortable with the unavoidable conclusion that it weakens people. He wants injustice to be a source of strength for its practitioners. Thus he said little earlier about the harm unjust men do to each other, but described with enthusiasm the harm they do to just men. At that point he was arguing that unjust men are less easily harmed than just men because behaving justly makes one vulnerable to being exploited (343d). (Socrates himself later makes a related point, at 409a–b.) However, if unjust men can't harm each other as easily as they can harm just men (at least the relatively innocent ones), they also don't benefit each other the way just men do, especially if they behave the way Thrasymachus suggests here, spurning even instrumentally just behavior among themselves. Thrasymachus is drawn to a strikingly pure vision of injustice, but he resists seeing the obvious difficulties it entails.

Socrates asks if injustice implants hatred and faction among men. Thrasymachus answers, "Very much so." Socrates asks if this also happens between two men, and Thrasymachus answers affirmatively. Then Socrates asks if injustice will retain this power when it comes into being within one man. "Let it remain undiminished," Thrasymachus replies, implying that he doesn't necessarily agree, but doesn't wish to argue about it (351e).

One might wonder what it means to talk about injustice within one man. Nothing in the dialogue before this point has clearly contradicted the common view of justice as the virtue that regulates one's relations with *other* people. The meaning of justice within one man will of course be a major theme later in the dialogue, but its appearance here is a bit surprising.

Socrates clarifies to some extent what he means in the sequel. Injustice within a man "will make him unable to act, he being at faction and not agreeing with himself, therefore hostile both to himself and to just men" (352a). The notion of injustice within one person implies that there are parts of one's soul, and a proper or just relation among those parts. The different parts of the soul have different, potentially conflicting appetites which must be ordered and harmonized for the good of the whole soul. Thus one can compare the soul to a city, as much of the *Republic* famously does.

While this is comprehensible, however, we usually think of moderation and prudence as the virtues that regulate relations among different parts of one's soul, while justice has to do with how one relates to other people. Socrates here not only foreshadows the definition of justice that he will later discuss most extensively (441d–444e); he also tacitly indicates one reason why he will emphasize that definition. Whatever criticism Thrasymachus has offered of justice understood as "someone else's good," he offers no criticism of properly regulating the different parts of one's soul. The chief criticism of justice offered by Thrasymachus, that it is irrational to put others before oneself, is therefore defanged without being fully confronted.

Socrates turns to whether the just are happier than the unjust. He notes that on the basis of what has been agreed, it looks like they are, but says the question should nonetheless be considered (352d). However, it isn't clear that he really considers the question in the sequel, which makes an interesting contrast with the section from 351b1 to 352d2, where Socrates led Thrasymachus to agree that justice is stronger than injustice. There he raised an incontestable difficulty with injustice, and did not invoke previous agreements which Thrasymachus had made reluctantly. In this section, by contrast, Socrates first pursues the somewhat abstract question of what the work of a thing is, and then turns to an earlier agreement extracted from a reluctant Thrasymachus (that justice is virtue of soul) to complete the argument. The section from 352d8 to 353d8 (the discussion of the work of a thing and its relation to the virtue of a thing) does not explicitly say anything about justice, and is not necessary for Socrates' argument. (Thrasymachus has already reluctantly agreed that justice is virtue [350d4], and at 353d10 he readily agrees that the work of a soul is living. On the basis of these two points, Socrates concludes that the just soul and just man will have a good life, and the unjust man a bad one.) For that very reason, however, we should be attuned to what this section might reveal about Thrasymachus.

Socrates asks if it seems to Thrasymachus that there is "some work of a horse" (352d). Thrasymachus says it does. Socrates asks if the work of a thing is "that which someone does either only with it" or best with it. Thrasymachus says he doesn't understand. Socrates asks if there is anything with which one can see other than eyes, or hear other than ears, and Thrasymachus says no. "Would we justly say that these labors are of these things?" Socrates asks, and Thrasymachus replies, "Very much so." Socrates then asks if one can cut a vine with a dagger or a leather-cutter, but less finely than with a cutting knife made for the purpose, and Thrasymachus agrees. Socrates then asks again (this time with wording that focuses on the thing more than the person using it) whether the work of a thing is that which either it alone completes, or completes more finely than other things. This time Thrasymachus says he understands and agrees (352e–353a).

If one is speaking of a body part or a tool, it makes sense to treat its work as that task useful to the person it serves which it does better than anything else, since this is the task at which it is most useful. It is less clear that this is a helpful way to understand Socrates' initial example of a horse, about which one might hesitate before saying that its work is simply serving the needs of a human being. (This is quite a shift from Thrasymachus' earlier reluctant agreement that horsemanship considers the advantage of horses [342c].) One might think the natural work of a horse is simply to satisfy its own needs and live its life.

One must hesitate much more before applying this definition of work to a soul or human being. It doesn't seem correct to say that the work of a person is whatever task he alone does or does better than others, however unsatisfying it might be.[18] Near the end of this line of questioning, Socrates asks if living is the work of a soul (353d9). Thrasymachus heartily agrees. The natural work of a soul or person is living well (or as well as possible), which may involve doing something at which he is less capable than someone else, or something which is not useful for others. The discussion here of the "work of a thing" blurs the difference between tools (which are used by others) and soul (which uses or works for itself). The work of a soul is best understood not as that which one does solely with it or best with it, but rather as that which satisfies its needs.

Socrates asks if there is a virtue for each thing to which a task is assigned. The meaning of virtue here seems to be the quality that enables a thing to perform a particular task. To clarify his question, Socrates suggests they "go to the same things again," and then asks about eyes and ears (353b). He does *not* repeat the examples of the horse or the dagger or leather-cutter cutting a vine, both of which would introduce complications. With the horse, as I noted, it's not so obvious that its natural task is what people want it to do; and Socrates himself noted that a dagger or leather-cutter might be used for cutting vines, which is to say for more than one task. If a tool performs two or more tasks, then the virtue enabling it to perform one task might to some extent detract from its ability to perform the other task. In such cases it would make sense to speak of virtue in terms of the task in addition to the thing doing the task.

Socrates asks if eyes could ever do their work if they did not have their proper virtue, but instead of the virtue, a vice. Thrasymachus says, "How could they? For you probably mean blindness instead of sight." Socrates replies, "Whatever their virtue, for I'm not yet asking this" (353c). Although it is true that eyes are introduced as an example, not as the subject under discussion, it is surprising that Socrates does not agree to Thrasymachus' point. Perhaps he is thinking that eyes can have other tasks as well, albeit much less important ones. For example, people care about how their eyes look, how they contribute to the task of appearing attractive to others. Socrates may be suggesting that there are problems with assuming there is one task for each thing, an assumption which accompanies and reflects Thrasymachus' admiration of art and artisanship.

Socrates then turns to the soul. "Is there some task of a soul that you could not accomplish with any other thing?" He mentions as examples managing, ruling, and deliberating. After Thrasymachus agrees, Socrates adds: "And what about living? Shall we not say that it is the task of a soul?" Thrasymachus replies, "Most of all." Socrates then asks if a soul will ever accomplish its task if it is deprived of its virtue, and Thrasymachus says this is impossible (353d–e).

It seems odd to speak of the soul's virtue (implying there is only one) immediately after identifying some very different tasks the soul performs. If the task of a soul is ruling (the central item in the group of three tasks Socrates mentions at 353d5), then justice (supplemented by or including wisdom) would seem to be the soul's virtue. However, if the task of a soul is living well, then its virtue would be whatever enables that soul to live well. Socrates has indicated that he does not think ruling and living well are the same thing (347c–d). Moreover, in order to live well, a person needs to perform many different tasks, and the qualities that enable him to do one are often quite different than those that enable him to do another. The emphasis here on one virtue reminds us that Thrasymachus is eager to identify one virtue of the soul: injustice (although in some contexts he also or instead stresses the virtue of skill or knowledge). In this, as in other respects, he resembles more conventionally moral people, many of whom feel that there is one virtue or quality (such as justice, or courage, or intelligence) that provides a total answer to their needs. People tend to resist seeing the complexity of their lives, for that complexity leaves us confronting many needs and vulnerabilities. A single virtue, by contrast, might seem to take us out of the realm of neediness, either by satisfying all our needs, or by providing a larger end to which we dedicate ourselves, or both.[19]

Socrates does not raise again the question of what virtue of soul is; instead he reminds Thrasymachus of their earlier agreement that justice is virtue of soul, and injustice vice (353e). Thrasymachus was reluctantly driven to that agreement by his belief that artisans are virtuous and that they behave in a just manner toward each other (350c).

Socrates asks if the just man and the just soul will have a good life, and the unjust man a bad life. Thrasymachus says it appears so "according to your speech (κατὰ τὸν σὸν λόγον)" (353e). After Socrates draws the obvious consequences, Thrasymachus offers his final word in this exchange: "Let these things, Socrates, be your feast at the festival of Bendis" (354a). He implies that the beliefs Socrates holds about justice are fitting for a pious man and a worshipper of the goddess. He does not grasp that the conversation has exposed his beliefs, not those of Socrates.

What does it mean that Thrasymachus agrees that the work of each thing is "that which someone does either only with it or best with it" (352e–353a)? The examples Socrates initially gives are a horse, eyes and ears, and cutting tools; however, Thrasymachus doesn't object or demand a new definition when the discussion turns to the soul. He allows Socrates to blur the difference between tools (which are used by others, and whose work is serving others) and soul (which uses itself, or works for itself). One might think he is simply no longer very involved in the conversation. However, that doesn't seem true; and even if it were, one must consider why Socrates concentrates on the question of a thing's work. As I noted above, this somewhat lengthy discussion of the work of each thing does not seem necessary to secure Thrasymachus' agreement that the work of a soul is living.

Thrasymachus apparently tends to blur the distinction between tools and soul. This is connected to his admiration of artisans. An artisan is somebody who does one thing skillfully, a thing given to him from outside himself, outside his own needs. Of course others pay him to do so, and this may be the best way for him to satisfy his own needs; but his activity as an artisan—the activity Thrasymachus admires and champions—is akin to being a tool of others. Living a good life requires doing many things competently, largely for oneself, not merely one thing skillfully, largely for others. Thrasymachus in some way considers the soul's work to be work for others—which provides a certain justification for Socrates' reliance upon his earlier reluctant agreement that the soul's virtue is justice.

Of course Thrasymachus thinks, or also thinks, that the soul's virtue is not justice but injustice. However, this view is not the correction of the other, but rather a kind of complement or flip side of it. As we have seen, Thrasymachus believes the tyrant's life is the good life, but he doesn't really examine how tyrants live. He understands the tyrant primarily in terms of what he does to others (expropriate their property and enslave them), so in some sense his tyrant, like his artisan, lives in terms of others. Thrasymachus does not carefully consider the good of either the tyrant or the artisan, and in different ways, both his artisan and his tyrant put something before their own good. (His tyrant puts the exploitation of others before his own good.) Thrasymachus is more excited by perfection at a craft, and by getting the better of others, than by examining one's own good—which is a more limited or defined pursuit, and might therefore remind one more of one's own limits.

THRASYMACHUS' CHARACTER AND WAY OF LIFE

Thrasymachus' blush represents a small step toward self-knowledge. However, it seems doubtful that he will get much further. His forceful candor, even when being refuted, indicates that he takes what he says seriously, and is more concerned to be right than to be seen as right, despite his love of praise. He confronts the question of whether to live for oneself or for others vigorously, if not adequately. However, he makes the view that it is sensible to be self-interested, along with admiration of skillful artisanship and tyranny, the center of his thought; I doubt that a very thoughtful man could be satisfied with so little. I also doubt that such a man could fail to notice the tension between self-interest and artisanship in the way that Thrasymachus does during his conversation with Socrates.

Moreover, it suggests a degree of frivolity that Thrasymachus is content at first to argue that justice is the advantage of the stronger, rather than arguing more forthrightly for injustice as a way of life. He is willing to do what his art dictates (by offering clever speeches), as opposed to considering and concentrating on what he really thinks (which might instead lead to dialectic). He pays more attention to his art, or what people today might call his career, than to nature or his life as a whole.

As we have seen, it is hard to imagine that Thrasymachus could concentrate on art the way he does if he did not somehow feel that one's position in life is constituted by what one does for others. While he wants to see art as selfish, he recognizes when considering individual arts that they serve others (341c). He defines ruling as an art that does something "to" others instead of "for" them, and he might understand rhetoric in a similar way. As a teacher of rhetoric, however, he himself does something *for* his students, in exchange for wages; they might in turn use the art to do something *to* their cities. His concentration on art, in deed as well as speech, and indeed his very resistance to understanding art as selfless, suggest that he exaggerates the value for oneself of fulfilling a function for others. He apparently seeks to fulfill such a function, and he clearly prides himself upon mastery of his art; but he also wants to understand himself as selfish. He fails to distinguish between the ends of art and those of the artisan.

On the other hand, Thrasymachus' concern for his art also reflects a kind of seriousness. He believes there is such a thing as excellence, and that achieving it involves work. However, this advantage is outweighed by a significant and related defect. In part because of the confidence he derives from knowledge of his art, he feels sure he knows the answers to all important questions. Notwithstanding his position as a rhetorician who offers shocking arguments, he seems closed in some way, more like Adeimantus than Glaucon or Polemarchus. This also may help explain how he has failed to notice difficulties in his views such as the tension between self-interest and artisanship.

The advantages of tyranny Thrasymachus mentions are expropriating property, exercising power, and being called "happy and blessed" by men (344a–c). By contrast, Glaucon's possessor of the ring of Gyges kills and has sexual relations with whomever he wants. To a large extent he lives outside the city or political life, "equal to a god among human beings" (360c3).[20] Thrasymachus' immoralism is somewhat conventional or tame by comparison. His admiration of tyranny (notably his use of the word "blessed") reflects an unselfconscious longing to transcend mere life; but he thinks less about transcendence than Glaucon does. He is neither truly sober, nor possessed by intense longing for the transcendent or divine.

In judging Thrasymachus, we must also consider his crudity, as revealed especially in his insults of Socrates; and his slow comprehension when confronting unfamiliar arguments. He does not seem as intelligent as Glaucon or Adeimantus, or even his pupil Cleitophon, which limits how far he is likely to go.[21] He is interested in Socrates, as he shows by remaining for the rest of the dialogue. However, he doesn't demonstrate the kind of flexibility or open-mindedness shown by Polemarchus, for example. It seems likely that, after the end of the discussion portrayed in the *Republic*, Thrasymachus will consider his position for a few weeks or months, and eventually alter it so as to remove (to his satisfaction) the contradiction that made him blush, without making any fundamental change in his thought or his life. Indeed, the blush itself suggests that, while he feels he made a blunder, he does not feel that Socrates has anything of vital importance to offer him. He is embarrassed, not excited, or deeply perplexed. He still thinks he knows how to live.

However, a careful reading enables us to learn more from Socrates' refutation of Thrasymachus than Thrasymachus himself does. (We of course have the advantage of being able to consider and re-read.) Perhaps the most striking thing we see is that an outspoken immoralist like Thrasymachus is deeply attached to justice. This is somewhat concealed (including from himself) by his ridiculing justice as commonly understood. However, his half-conscious belief that the skillful and unjust should get the better of the artless and weak is obviously a belief that the world *should* operate some particular way. Moreover, without noticing it, Thrasymachus believes in the selflessness of good men (notably *qua* artisans, and also to some extent in their dealings with each other). He even feels a kind of devotion to injustice, as shown by his incautious praise of it. Like more self-consciously moral men, he feels that devotion to something noble (artistic skill, or injustice itself) makes one a good man, worthy of good things. This feeling colors or distorts his view of how the world works. He exaggerates the importance of the common good among craftsmen (in any given craft); he thinks they get the better of those who lack their skill but not of each other. He exaggerates the happiness of tyrants, and even seems to feel they are favored by gods or godlike forces. By uniting virtue and happiness, as he thinks, the tyrant confirms and completes his moral code.

Jane Austen speaks of "that sanguine expectation of happiness which is happiness itself."[22] I think this is part of the explanation of why Thrasymachus seems to be a relatively cheerful man. Like many men who are not immoralists, he believes himself to be a good man, he believes (at least to some extent) that good men flourish, he therefore expects to flourish, and this prospect cheers him.

NOTES

1. Rosen, *Plato's Republic: A Study,* 51.
2. Bloom, *The Republic of Plato,* 333. Strauss provides an elegant summary of the implications of the introduction of the wage-earning art for the argument, but he does not explore the implications for Thrasymachus' own view of art (*The City and Man,* 81).
3. Leibowitz says "[i]t is revealing" that Thrasymachus does not take advantage of Socrates' introduction of the wage-earning art, and he compares this to Thrasymachus' earlier forgetting that "according to his own definition, the tyrant should not be called unjust" ("Thrasymachus's Blush," 121–22). Leibowitz does not suggest that this failure reveals Thrasymachus' unwillingness to concede that artisanship as such is unselfish.
4. This doesn't exactly mean that wage-earning is selfish. It is actually as well as theoretically possible for people to pursue money in a more or less self-forgetting manner.
5. Stauffer, *Plato's Introduction to the Question of Justice,* 91.
6. Cf. Plato, *Gorgias,* 458a2–7.
7. On this point I agree with Annas, *An Introduction to Plato's Republic,* 48–49.
8. One person who agrees with Thrasymachus on this point is Immanuel Kant. Cf. Kant, *Groundwork of the Metaphysics of Morals,* translated and edited by Mary Gregor (Cambridge, UK: Cambridge University Press, 1999), 11–12.
9. I translate πλεονεκτεῖν as "get the better of." The term can also mean "have more than," but Socrates apparently means by it something different than πλέον ἔχειν, which he also uses in this section, and which I translate as "have more than."
10. Cf. Stauffer, *Plato's Introduction to the Question of Justice,* 101, and Leibowitz, "Thrasymachus's Blush," 123.

11. I speak here of "those lacking prudence and goodness" rather than the imprudent and bad because, as we have seen, Thrasymachus resists identifying justice as vice (348d1). He might also balk at calling the just man a bad man.

12. Strauss's discussion of the confrontation between Socrates and Thrasymachus puts a lot of weight on "the premise that if something is similar to X, it is X" (*The City and Man*, 83). Strauss is right that this premise is explicitly denied later in the *Republic* at 476c6–7. However, as we have seen, neither Thrasymachus nor Socrates clearly offers this premise as a general principle. It is accurate as a statement of what Thrasymachus believes about just and unjust men and their relation to prudent and good men.

13. Stauffer, *Plato's Introduction to the Question of Justice*, 106. Pangle and Burns go further and state that Socrates "forces Thrasymachus to admit" that an artisan does not seek to get the better of fellow artisans; they apparently see this is as a manifest fact which Thrasymachus initially resists accepting (*The Key Texts of Political Philosophy: An Introduction*, 64). I see no indication of such resistance in the text. Socrates does say at 350d1 that Thrasymachus resisted agreeing to "all these things," but this resistance seems to begin at 350b9. During the discussion of artisans getting the better of each other (349e10–350a10), Thrasymachus states his views freely and for the most part firmly.

14. Catherine Zuckert, "Why Socrates and Thrasymachus Become Friends," *Philosophy and Rhetoric* 43 (2010), 179.

15. Cf. Jacques A. Bailly, *Plato's Euthyphro & Clitophon* (Newburyport, MA: Focus Publishing, 2003), 36.

16. Other commentators explain the famous blush differently. Stauffer says that Thrasymachus has come to see that Socrates is "much more prudent than he is" because he gives "at least rhetorical support to conventional opinion" (*Plato's Introduction to the Question of Justice*, 102). However, Thrasymachus remains outspoken in presenting unconventional opinions after the blush (351b–c). His frankness is a trait upon which he prides himself. He initially accused Socrates of being a sycophant who was insincere when discussing justice (see 336c and 341a–b), and I see no sign that he has come to admire the insincerity he initially despised. It is more likely that he blushes because this is the first time he thinks he has been genuinely refuted. Bloom's analysis here is somewhat closer to mine, as he notes that Thrasymachus is "discredited before an audience in his claim to wisdom," but he fails to account for the difference between this refutation and the earlier ones which did not cause Thrasymachus to blush. While Stauffer makes Thrasymachus implausibly prudent, Bloom makes him implausibly petty, a "lover of applause more than of truth" (*The Republic of Plato*, 336). Leibowitz states that because the argument preceding the blush is complicated, he will "provide an overview" instead of "going through it in detail" ("Thrasymachus's Blush," 122). In his overview he does not mention artisanship, which (as we have seen) is the last subject discussed in detail before the blush. I don't see any indication in the text that Thrasymachus recognizes the contradiction in his position whose recognition Leibowitz identifies as the cause of the blush (123), as against the less fundamental contradiction that I have summarized and that the dialogue makes clear. I agree that Thrasymachus contradicts himself in approximately the way Leibowitz indicates: Thrasymachus believes he is wise (or at least not "most simple" [343d]) because he does not believe in justice or deserving; and he unselfconsciously believes he deserves to prosper because of this wisdom. However, he also believes that many or most people share this wisdom (344c), and it seems to be less important as a ground of self-respect than his belief that he excels at his art. Leibowitz's "tentative suggestion" about the root of Thrasymachus' attachment to justice (123) seems to me well stated; however, I think Leibowitz fails fully to grasp the ambiguous significance of *devotion* for Thrasymachus, perhaps because he does not sufficiently focus on Thrasymachus' admiration of artisanship.

17. Strauss, *The City and Man*, 82. Strauss notes that this defense of justice amounts to a "rehabilitation of Polemarchus' view" that justice is helping friends and harming enemies "on the Thrasymachean ground: the common good is derived from the private good via calculation."

18. I myself found during an employment stint in my youth that I was particularly capable at stocking the paper goods aisles of supermarket shelves. I did not conclude that this was my calling.

19. Socrates himself suggests elsewhere that virtue is prudence or knowledge, which might seem a similar simplification (Plato, *Meno,* 88b–89c, in Plato, *Protagoras and Meno,* translated by Robert C. Bartlett [Ithaca: Cornell University Press, 2004]). However, he indicates in various dialogues that the different virtues are different qualities of the soul, even if each is also in some way tantamount to a sort of prudence or knowledge. (Consider Plato, *Meno,* 88b, *Laches,* 194a, and *Republic,* 442c–d. *Laches* is in Thomas L. Pangle, editor, *The Roots of Political Philosophy: Ten Forgotten Socratic Dialogues* [Ithaca: Cornell University Press, 1987].) Later in the *Republic* Socrates describes how the various qualities that form the best natures are rarely found together (503c–d).

20. Benardete, *Socrates' Second Sailing: On Plato's Republic,* 22–23.

21. Cf. Plato, *Republic,* 486c.

22. Jane Austen, *Sense and Sensibility* in *The Complete Novels of Jane Austen* (New York: Random House), 4.

Chapter Four

Callicles' Attack on Justice

SOCRATES PROVOKES CALLICLES

We have seen that Thrasymachus is unselfconsciously attached to justice despite his attack on it, and even precisely as revealed by his attack on it. Plato presents another outspoken critic of justice in the character of Callicles in his *Gorgias*. Socrates' conversation with Callicles is much longer than the one with Thrasymachus, and it penetrates deeper. Plato wishes to show Callicles to us in some detail.

Callicles is the first person to speak in the *Gorgias*. "In war and in battle, they say, Socrates, it is necessary to participate thus," he says, referring in an ironic yet urbane manner to Socrates' arriving at Gorgias' demonstration after it is finished (447a1–2). (The first word of the dialogue is war.) Socrates asks if he has arrived after the feast is over. He thereby suggests that listening to Gorgias resembles eating rather than fighting. Callicles, not averse to this suggestion, responds that it was a very refined (ἀστείας) feast indeed, for Gorgias made a display of "many and beautiful things" (447a).

Callicles is surprised that Socrates apparently wants to listen to Gorgias (447b). Is this because he has some familiarity with Socrates' interests and tastes, or simply because Socrates has arrived too late for the display? Presumably the former, since Socrates and Chaerephon have both attributed their tardiness to Chaerephon. Callicles says that Socrates and Chaerephon are welcome to come to his place whenever they wish, for Gorgias (who is not an Athenian) is staying with him. When Socrates asks if Gorgias would be willing to answer some questions now, Callicles invites him to "ask the man himself" (447c).

The next time Callicles speaks is after Gorgias has been conversing with Socrates for some time, and has suggested that it might be time to end their

59

conversation (485b–c). Chaerephon notes the uproar from the others present that follows this suggestion, and adds that he hopes he will never have too little leisure to hear such arguments. Callicles chimes in, "By the gods, yes, Chaerephon, and indeed I myself also before this have been present at many speeches, [but] I don't know if ever yet I took such delight as now" (458c–d).

Callicles becomes Socrates' chief interlocutor later in the dialogue, after Socrates' exchange with Polus. Socrates concludes that exchange with a series of outlandish statements (481a–b). He asserts that one must seek to prevent one's enemy from paying the penalty if he does injustice. If one's enemy goes to court, one must help him escape. If he is sentenced to death, one must strive to ensure that he escapes being executed, and further one must hope that he may "never die but shall be deathless in being wicked, and if not this, that he shall live for as long a time as possible in being such" (481a–b). One must, in effect, strive to see that one's enemy get everything one might hope for oneself—except being just. Socrates thereby goes beyond the unworldly and anti-worldly Christian injunction that one respond to an aggressor by turning the other cheek; but unlike Jesus, Socrates does not (until the end of the dialogue) promise a reward in another life for the behavior he extols in this one.[1]

Callicles enters the conversation at this point by asking Chaerephon if Socrates is serious about what he has been saying, or if he is joking (481b). (Not surprisingly, he doesn't consider that Socrates may be drawing out something that Polus himself in some way believes.) Unlike Callicles, Chaerephon is not struck by the outlandishness of what Socrates has said; he replies that Socrates seems to be "extraordinarily serious," but invites Callicles to ask Socrates himself. Callicles replies, "By the gods, I certainly desire to do so!" (481b) This is the second time Callicles has sworn "by the gods" (the first was at 458d1).

Callicles says to Socrates that if he is serious and the things he is saying are true, "wouldn't the life of us human beings have been turned upside down and don't we do, as it would appear, all the opposite things to what we ought?" (481c) Callicles thus begins his exchange with Socrates by pointing out the radicalism of what Socrates is saying. Though he himself will soon offer radical statements, he initially reacts to Socrates' challenge to ordinary life as "we" live it. Socrates has found no use for rhetoric apart from accusing oneself and one's friends if they have done unjust deeds, and helping one's enemies avoid punishment if they have done so. He seems to imply (though he does not actually say) that we must not seek our own advantage, except insofar as justice itself is an advantage.[2] Socrates does not even mention that the city's punishment is perhaps not in every case the just one or the one that will truly improve a person's soul. His approach is more suggestive of saints—a type of person even more foreign to pagan Athens than to contemporary America—than of ordinary decent people, to say nothing of the bold criminals whom Callicles will soon champion. Moreover, one might consider what the consequences would be if law-abiding citizens actually used rhetoric to ensure that lawbreakers (who as such are their enemies) escape punishment. Socrates' position would be politically disastrous if it were morally or psychologically possible.

Nonetheless, Callicles is interested in considering what it means if what Socrates says "happens to be true" (481c). This doesn't mean he thinks it is true or even might be true; but he is interested in what Socrates is saying, and in its implications for how one should live. He seems more open, and more concerned with what is truly good, than the earlier interlocutors, whose primary concern was defending the art of rhetoric. (The comparison is imperfect because Gorgias and Polus were responding to arguments explicitly directed against rhetoric; but there still seems to be some difference. It seems unlikely that Callicles would have stayed with the question of rhetoric the way Polus does at 466a.) He also seems more concerned with what is truly good than Thrasymachus, who enters a somewhat similar conversation in the *Republic* eager to denounce Socrates and tell everybody what he himself thinks (*Republic* 336b–c). Of course Callicles is not a teacher of rhetoric like these other three men; but for that very reason he may in some ways be a fuller human being.

Socrates gives a lengthy, humorous, apparently irrelevant, and somewhat disparaging response (481c–482c). Not surprisingly, this provokes Callicles to set aside his politeness and state his opposition to Socrates with candor and force; Callicles' possible openness to Socrates' paradoxical claims is submerged in the heat of argument. This seems to have been Socrates' purpose: He wants to draw Callicles out, and in particular to draw out the part of Callicles most at odds with what he himself has been saying.

Socrates begins by noting that "if some feeling (πάθος) was not common for human beings . . . it probably would not be easy to point out one's own experience (πάθημα) to the other" (481c–d). This surprising remark (which has no obvious connection to the question of whether Socrates has been joking) introduces the still more surprising observation that Socrates and Callicles "happen to have suffered something that is the same" in that they are both lovers (ἐρῶντε), and both in love with two things. Socrates says that he himself loves Alcibiades and philosophy (481d). This is the first use of the word philosophy in the dialogue (earlier the genuine art imitated by sophistry was identified as legislation, not philosophy [465c]), and its appearance, along with that of *eros*, suggests that the exchange with Callicles is going to be more serious or fundamental than what has preceded.

Socrates says that Callicles loves the Athenian *demos* and the son of Pyrilampes, a young man whose name happens to be Demos (481d). (Apparently Socrates himself does not love either Demos or the *demos*.) This serendipitous fact about Callicles (assuming it is a fact, which Callicles never denies) gives Socrates an opportunity to inject a bit of humor into a serious suggestion. While the two beloveds of Callicles have the same name, they pull him in different directions. Socrates says to Callicles, "you turn yourself around up and down" because "you are not able to oppose either the proposals or the speeches of your boyfriends." By contrast, Socrates does not say that he himself is compelled to agree with Alcibiades when Alcibiades presents "various speeches at various times," and there is no suggestion that he ever agrees with Alcibiades rather than philosophy. We might suspect that his love of Alcibiades is not merely subordinate to but a result or part of his love of philosophy or of wisdom (481d–482a).[3]

Socrates makes a striking statement regarding Callicles' need to refute the argument he himself has presented. "So then either refute that [speech], as I was saying just a while ago, by showing that doing injustice and not paying the just penalty when one does injustice is not the utmost of all evils; or else, if you leave this unrefuted—by the dog, the god of the Egyptians—Callicles will not agree with you, Callicles, but will be dissonant in his whole life" (482b). This statement lays the foundation for the rest of the exchange between Socrates and Callicles. Callicles, apparently in contrast to Socrates himself, will not be in harmony with himself unless he can refute the argument Socrates has been making. Socrates clearly doesn't expect him to refute it, and indeed he doesn't. It seems that Callicles is divided within himself even apart from his concern to appeal to his two beloveds.

Socrates presumes that Callicles' inability to refute the view that doing injustice with impunity is the utmost of evils means that Callicles himself *holds* this view, at least in some important way. This makes sense, at least to some extent: If one genuinely disagrees with something, one has a basis for arguing against it. On the other hand, one might think Callicles could fail to withstand Socrates' dialectical abilities even while genuinely disagreeing with him. At the end of their exchange, this is clearly what Callicles thinks has happened. Socrates suggests, however, that on the particular question of whether doing injustice with impunity is the utmost of evils, this isn't really a possibility. If one truly does not hold this view, one is able to refute it; otherwise one does hold this view, perhaps in spite of oneself. Since Socrates tells us that nobody in his experience has been able to refute this view, it must be one that *everybody* holds, except possibly a few who are unlike those with whom Socrates has discussed it.

Socrates does not mention as a possibility that Callicles will come, even upon examination or later in life, to *agree* with this view. His alternatives are to refute it, or to be at odds with himself. Socrates suggests that even though Callicles holds this view, whatever in him resists it will never be overcome.

Why is Socrates so sure of this? Callicles is a fairly young man (cf. 515a, where Socrates says Callicles is "just now beginning" to engage in politics). His views might someday change. However, people never wholly believe things that are clearly untrue. Regarding the view that doing injustice with impunity is the utmost of evils, Socrates never refutes the case that Polus makes at 473c, where he cites the likely penalty for someone who is caught plotting to establish a tyranny. Instead Socrates dismisses it, and moves on to another, more abstract argument. How could he refute it? The evils Polus cites are clearly worse (in themselves, leaving aside the possibility of divine retribution after death) than the evil of successfully perpetrating injustice—which isn't to deny that it too is an evil. (Stalin was likely harmed by his way of life, but he was alive, and not in evident agony.) Socrates later says that he doesn't "know how these things are, but of those people I fall in with, as now, no one who says something different is able not to be ridiculous" (509a). That surely reveals something; but its inadequacy as an argument for the view that doing injustice with impunity is the utmost of evils is suggested by Socrates' own criticism of Polus for relying on ridicule rather than refutation (473e).[4] Moreover, Socrates himself leaves open the possibility that this view *can be refuted* (482b).[5] Perhaps he is consistent with himself because, unlike Callicles, he does *not* believe that doing injustice with impunity is the utmost of evils.

I also note Socrates' oath here (482b5). He occasionally swears "by the dog," but this is the only time in the Platonic corpus that he spells out that the dog is the god of the Egyptians.[6] Socrates' dog is presumably Anubis or Anpu, the jackal-headed god who, Egyptians believed, was a guardian of the dead. In some Egyptian texts, Anubis protected the dead in their journey to the afterlife; in others Anubis judged the souls of the dead, deciding whether they would be sent to a heavenly afterlife or devoured by a monstrous deity named Ammit.[7] Socrates seems to be suggesting that the inability to refute the claim that doing injustice with impunity is the utmost of evils will leave Callicles at odds with himself in a way that has something to do with an afterlife, or perhaps with Callicles' hope of attaining an afterlife.

NATURE AND CONVENTION

Callicles is stung by Socrates' description of him as enslaved to the whims of the *demos*, as Socrates surely expected him to be. He responds by calling Socrates a "popular speaker" (δημηγόρος) (482c). Notwithstanding his interest in rhetoric, Callicles clearly considers this a term of opprobrium; in some way he despises the one art he seems to consider worth studying. He declares that rather than seek the truth as he claims to do, Socrates has used "the custom of human beings" or popular speech in order to refute Gorgias and Polus. Polus was refuted because "he conceded to you that doing injustice is more shameful than suffering injustice," a concession which caused him to get his "feet entangled and his mouth gagged by you in the speeches."

Callicles thinks that, like Gorgias before him, Polus contradicted himself because he was "ashamed" to avow his real opinions. Now this does not actually seem true of either Polus or Gorgias. Gorgias avoids making shocking statements out of caution rather than shame, while Polus really thinks that doing injustice is more shameful than suffering it. We may surmise that Callicles himself overcomes a feeling of shame when saying what he thinks about such matters.[8] If this is true, however, he does not dwell upon this hint of restraint in himself. Moreover, he seems to assume that intelligent people, including Socrates, think as he does about these matters. Thus he thinks that Socrates speaks as he does because compelling others to contradict themselves "is the very thing you are fond of," not because he really believes the arguments he makes (482d).

Callicles explains that Socrates leads the discussion into things suited to a popular speaker, things that "are fine not by nature, but by convention," in order to shame and silence his interlocutors. He adds that nature and convention are "in most cases opposed to each other" (482e). This distinction is of course familiar to philosophy, and is close to the heart of philosophy; nonetheless, Callicles exaggerates the opposition. Surely in many areas nature and convention agree. Both generally consider health better than sickness, friendship better than enmity, small children and senile people incapable of taking care of themselves, etc. While Callicles would no doubt grant such points if asked, we see in him a certain inclination to exaggerate the opposition of nature and convention, or to exaggerate the extent to which one must oppose common or conventional opinion if one is to lead a genuinely good life.

At the same time, however, Callicles' distinction between nature and convention is inadequate, even feeble. He continues: "If, therefore, someone feels ashamed and doesn't dare say what he thinks, he is compelled to say contradictory things. And now, having thoroughly understood this piece of wisdom, you work evil in the arguments: if someone speaks of things according to convention, you slip in questions about things according to nature, and if he speaks of the things of nature, you ask about the things of convention" (482e–483a). Callicles thinks that people who speak according to convention are merely ashamed to say what they think. (This supports the suggestion made above that he himself feels shame while saying what he thinks—a feeling he overcomes, to be sure.) Callicles does not view convention as opinion in contradistinction to reality; he views it as what people claim to believe in contradistinction to what they really believe, which he does not distinguish from nature or truth.

Callicles appears to have spent time listening to philosophers or (more likely) to people who have been influenced by philosophy, perhaps including Gorgias himself; but he has not digested the fundamental distinction they make. He has not really grasped or accepted philosophy's radical critique of opinion, for he doesn't really grasp or accept that sincerely held opinions are mere opinions.[9]

This is not to deny that what he says has some validity. Insincerity indeed helps constitute convention, both because people defer to the statements of those who are powerful, and more deeply because people don't wholly believe the untrue opinions they hold or claim to hold or try to hold. How could they? In holding untrue opinions about important matters, people somehow avert their glance from truly looking at those matters, or at the limits of their knowledge; and they can't wholly avoid being aware that they are doing so. Nonetheless, in equating convention with shame or hypocrisy, Callicles shows that he does not really grasp what it is and what it means for people; for the heart of convention is not hypocrisy but beliefs which are held sincerely and passionately (if also only partially), beliefs which people cherish and which constitute the core of their lives. These are above all beliefs about justice.

Callicles overestimates the extent to which people are insincere, and underestimates the extent to which they are sincere. (These are of course two sides of a coin.) Like Thrasymachus, he detects a certain hypocrisy in what people say about justice (do they *really* believe that successful injustice is unenviable?), but he exaggerates its extent, and underestimates the extent to which people do in fact believe what they say, or feel that they should believe it (which means they do believe it in some way). He doesn't see that people have a genuine stake in the truth of what they say, not merely a stake in proclaiming its truth. His failure to see the importance such beliefs have to people, coupled with his opinion that he does understand the root of these beliefs, suggests that he himself has kindred beliefs which he doesn't recognize as satisfying a kindred need in himself.

Spelling out the opposition between nature and convention, Callicles continues: "For by nature, everything more shameful is also that which is worse, such as suffering injustice, whereas by convention doing injustice is more shameful" (483a).[10] Socrates suggested when talking with Polus that he himself considers the shameful to be bad (474c8–9), so he and Callicles agree there. The disagreement is over whether suffering or doing injustice is genuinely more shameful and worse. Callicles continues: "Nor does this misfortune, suffering injustice, belong to a man (ἀνδρὸς), but to some slave (ἀνδραπόδου) for whom it is superior (κρεῖττόν) to die than to live, who, suffering injustice and being trampled in the mud, is unable to help himself or anyone else he might care for" (483b).

This vehement statement is among the most revealing Callicles makes, in large part because it doesn't really make sense. Surely most of us occasionally suffer injustice (as commonly understood) in minor matters. Does this make us slaves who are unable to help ourselves or anybody we care for, and who would be better off dead? Callicles uses a particularly contemptuous term for slave, τὸ ἀνδραπόδον, a composite word which one might translate literally as the thing at a man's foot, instead of the more common ὁ δοῦλος. This accentuates the contrast with man or real man (ἀνδρὸς) in the previous phrase.

Suffering occasional injustice in minor matters is part of ordinary human life, which isn't to deny there is something slavish about it. Callicles may be thinking primarily of suffering injustice in more serious matters; however, no degree of power or virtue can fully remove this possibility. His belief in a position of freedom from any possibility of suffering injustice is fantastic.

Callicles seems to consider his own life worth living, which implies that he thinks he himself is able to avoid suffering injustice. He suggests later that men who are active in law courts and political affairs are better equipped than others to avoid suffering injustice (486b1–d2).[11] But is this true? Politically active men are indeed stronger than private men; but they are also likely to encounter stronger foes. One might think they are less likely to face injustice in minor matters (since others fear incurring their wrath for small gain), but more likely to face injustice in important matters (since they have powerful rivals). Moreover, circumstances vary—a fact with which lovers of virtue, however they understand it, tend to be uncomfortable. During times of political turmoil, as competing parties try to destroy each other, private life might be a better strategy for avoiding injustice than public life, and meekness better than boldness.

Callicles knows at least much of this, at least with part of his mind. He is aware of the difficulties encountered by prominent Athenian political men of the past, and in the case of Pericles he indicates that he thinks Pericles suffered unjustly (516a). Now if Pericles was not powerful enough to be free from suffering injustice, then no political man is, except possibly a king or tyrant. This latter alternative is obviously part of what inspires Callicles' praise of tyranny. Even tyrants, however, face the danger of conspiracy and assassination, though one might maintain that a tyrant as such cannot suffer injustice because whatever harm anyone does him is just.

Whether or not the political man is truly safer than the private man, for Callicles he is what a man should be. Thus one becomes "unmanly" (ἀνάνδρῳ) through "fleeing the central area of the city and the agoras" (485d). While Callicles thinks with half his mind that a real man can't be pushed around, he thinks with his whole mind that a real man can't *easily* be pushed around. The private man isn't a real man because he can easily be pushed around, which is disgraceful and somehow means he doesn't deserve to live. The political man, the one who counts in the city, is a real man and deserves to prosper, even if his way of life entails dangers. This is the key to Callicles' vehement overstatement: It's a statement about what should be purporting to be a statement about what is (which is by no means to deny that Callicles believes what he says about what is, at least at the moment he says it). The real man *should* prosper, and the merely private man *should* be trampled upon, or should die. So this statement is very much an appeal to justice as he sees it.

Callicles exaggerates both the vulnerability of the private man and the security of the political man because he is eager for those he considers virtuous, and only those he considers virtuous, to overcome the possibility of suffering injustice, and to flourish more broadly. While he does not seem to have thought it out clearly, he also feels that those he admires attain a kind of invulnerability to any misfortune or harm. His vehement exaggeration of the difference between the ways of life he describes suggests that what is at stake is not only freedom from suffering injustice, but a radical difference of desert and fate.

Callicles knows that doing injustice is generally blamed much more strongly than suffering injustice, so he feels he must support his contention that in truth it is less shameful, or not shameful at all. He offers a somewhat theoretical explanation.

> But, I think, those who set down the laws are the weak human beings and the many. It is therefore in reference to themselves and their own advantage that they set down laws and praise their praises and blame their blames: frightening away the more forceful human beings and those with power to have more, so that they won't have more than themselves, they say that taking more is shameful and unjust, and that doing injustice is this—seeking to have more than the others. For they are quite contented, I think, if they themselves have an equal share, since they are lowlier. (483b–c)

Callicles' explanation reflects his view of convention as what people say rather than what they believe. He doesn't quite state that "the many" self-consciously view justice as a mere word to use in pursuing what benefits them, but clearly their genuine concern is not with justice but with their interest. (When he suggested earlier that people speak in accordance with convention out of shame [483a1], he might not have been thinking of the many, who seem to speak out of interest rather than shame; either way, however, convention is not what people really believe.) This gives his explanation an element of caricature—which is not to deny that there is also some truth to it. However, Callicles is less vehement and certain here than earlier, as shown by his twice saying "I think" (οἶμαι). He does not feel altogether confident that he knows why the many speak of justice the way they do, unlike Thrasymachus, who offers a similar explanation without any such reservation (cf. *Republic* 344c). Each man offers an incomplete or partial account of why the many disagree with him, but Callicles is less confident of his account. This may be because he is a more delicate man than Thrasymachus, or because he has less of a stake in claiming to understand the many, or both.

Callicles' explanation has a paradoxical element: The "weak" (ἀσθενεῖς) human beings "frighten" (ἐκφοβοῦντες) the "more forceful" (ἐρρωμενεστέρους) ones. This is possible, he suggests, because the weak are many and united, while the more forceful are few and apparently not united.[12] Nonetheless, it seems odd to identify men who are frightened as more forceful, at least without qualification.

Callicles' speech then takes an interesting turn. "But nature herself, I think, reveals that this very thing is just, for the better to have more than the worse and the more powerful than the less powerful" (483c–d). He does not assert, as one might have expected (and as Thrasymachus does in the *Republic*), that justice is merely a word people use to disguise their advantage. Instead he says it is *just* for the better and more powerful to have more than the worse and less powerful.

Of course it is not unusual to distinguish natural justice from conventional justice; anybody who believes there are unjust laws does so at least implicitly. Moreover, the way Callicles distinguishes natural and conventional justice is in part comprehensible from a decent point of view. As Aristotle says, justice means that "if [people] are not equal, they will not have equal things."[13] However, this is not all that Callicles has in mind, as shown by his speaking of the more and less powerful (τὸν δυνατώτερον and τοῦ ἀδυνατωτέρου) as well as the better and worse (τὸν ἀμείνω and τοῦ χείρονος). While it is not unusual to assert that it is just for the better to have more, it *is* unusual to assert that it is just for the more powerful to have more. The more powerful do of course have more, but it seems to nullify the meaning of justice to identify that as justice, since it offers no standard apart from what is by which to judge what is. Nonetheless, Callicles is not mocking the term justice, as Thrasymachus does.

One could resolve this peculiarity by translating δυνατώτερον as more able or capable rather than more powerful, and thereby interpret Callicles simply to be specifying what he means by "the better" who should have more than "the worse." However, this does not capture the whole of what he means. As indicated by his examples of Xerxes and Darius (483d), and by his later reference to sons of kings (492b), he is thinking in part of men who lack any apparent superiority other than power itself. Power is of course a kind of superiority; but most of us understand political power as extrinsic or conventional superiority, and virtue as intrinsic or natural superiority. For Callicles, political power seems (at least some of the time) to constitute or give rise to a form of intrinsic superiority. His claim that it is just for the more powerful to have more points to a feeling that they are somehow more deserving. He will later relinquish this view when Socrates challenges it, but that does not mean he genuinely ceases to hold it in part of his mind. His bias in favor of the powerful is rooted in an eagerness to believe that power and virtue coincide, or that genuine (not conventional) justice prevails in the world.

In earlier chapters I distinguished two meanings or aspects of justice as commonly understood. Justice is both a virtue and a principle. It is putting something before oneself, and it is the principle that a just person puts before himself. Callicles believes in deserving or distributive justice as a principle, but does not seem to believe (self-consciously) in self-sacrifice or justice as a virtue. We might wonder how he can believe that some men or qualities are deserving without believing that others should subordinate themselves to those men or qualities.

According to Callicles, contrary to what convention claims, "nature herself" reveals justice to be as he describes. "And it is clear in many places that these things are so, both among the other animals and among the cities and the races of human beings taken as wholes, that the just has been decided thus, for the stronger (τὸν κρείττω) to rule and to have more than the weaker (τοῦ ἥττονος)" (483d). I have noted that the word κρείττων can have the connotation of better; likewise ἥττων can have the connotation of worse. However, the context makes it clear that Callicles primarily means stronger and weaker rather than better and worse, or that the stronger and the weaker *are* the better and the worse. Thus it is just, not merely a brute fact, that the strong rule and have more. "Indeed, making use of what kind of justice did Xerxes lead his army against Greece, or his father against the Scythians?" (483d).

Callicles continues: "I think these men do these things according to the nature of the just, and yes, by Zeus, according to the law of nature (νόμον γε τὸν τῆς φύσεως), though perhaps not according to this one that we set down" (483e). The phrase "law of nature" probably sounds paradoxical to the other men present. Law or convention (νόμος) was seen by Greeks who thought about such matters as the restriction of nature (φύσις), or even the opposite of nature, a view which remains comprehensible to us if we set aside so-called natural laws and think of law in the usual sense.[14] Indeed Callicles himself has just said that νόμος and φύσις are in most cases opposed to each other (482e). As Nichols remarks, Callicles' oath to Zeus reveals that he himself is "somehow aware" of the paradoxical character of the phrase.[15] (The particle γε also suggests that.) He's aware of the paradox but, by Zeus, that's the way it looks to him.

Nature is of course a positive standard for Callicles. Xerxes and Darius were behaving as powerful men should. Those with the power to exploit others, should do so; to do otherwise is unnatural. When mentioning relations among cities and races, Callicles is likely mindful of the Athenian empire, which was built upon exploitation of less powerful Greek cities.[16] However, he probably cites Xerxes and Darius, rather than imperial Athens herself, because he feels that natural justice is demonstrated more clearly by the behavior of a powerful king than by that of a powerful city (especially a democracy), where men must cooperate and treat each other in accord with conventional justice in order to be able to exploit others. He probably also wishes to show that such behavior is universal, as he emphasizes in the next sentence: "Or one could tell of myriad other such cases" (483e).

However, Xerxes' attack upon Greece and Darius' attack upon the Scythians both ended in defeat, which makes them odd examples. Callicles doesn't really seem to consider that these ventures were unsuccessful. His attention is on the example they provide of how powerful men behave, rather than on whether that behavior benefited them. To be sure, he thinks powerful men benefit by exploiting others. He thinks such men owe it to themselves to exploit others, and would be foolish not to; however, his lack of concern for the success of the ventures he mentions is striking. Without having thought it out clearly, Callicles seems to feel that powerful men need not, and perhaps even should not, consider very carefully the possibility of failure, or more broadly whether it's truly good for them to seek to exploit others. That sort of consideration, if carried so far that it produces inaction or peaceful behavior, would likely strike him as timorous, spiritless, possibly even somehow overly self-absorbed or selfish. One might say he feels that powerful men should behave as he describes *whether it's good for them or not*. In some half-conscious way he considers his lawless "law of nature" to be a law in the usual sense—a way people are obliged to behave.

However, there is a striking proviso to this law. Callicles says "these men" (οὗτοι) behave according to the law of nature, whereas "we" (ἡμεῖς) set down unnatural laws. The law of nature dictates the behavior of men who are powerful enough to exploit others openly, which is to say very few people, of whom Callicles does not consider himself one. Of course such a law implies that people generally would exploit others if they could. The behavior of the most powerful reveals what all of us would do if we were equally powerful. Nonetheless, it is striking the degree to which the most powerful men are not merely a kind of thought experiment or touchstone for Callicles, but the focus of his concern. It is important to him that some men be free to dominate and exploit others boldly and openly, even though he himself isn't, so that they can uphold the "law of nature" against the hypocrisy and injustice of convention. He is selflessly interested in their injustice—and, as we saw above, he expects them to be as well.

Conventional law of course opposes the law of nature. "By molding the best and most forceful of us, catching them young, like lions, subduing them by charms and bewitching them, we reduce them to slavery, saying that it is necessary to have an equal share and that this is the noble and the just" (483e–484a). Thus the weak overcome natural justice, to some extent. "But, I think, if a man having a sufficient nature comes to be, he shakes off and breaks through all these things and gets away, trampling underfoot our writings and deceptions and enchantments and the laws which are all against nature, and rising up the slave is revealed as our master; and there the justice of nature shines forth (ἐξέλαμψεν)" (484a–b). Callicles' enthusiasm here vindicates Socrates' description of him as an erotic man. For Callicles the shining forth of natural justice has some of the character of a genuine revelation, as distinguished from the "charms" and "enchantments" of the many. I commented in Chapter Two that the tyrant is a kind of hero for Thrasymachus. Callicles experiences the tyrant as something even higher, almost godlike in power and righteousness. One might say that for Thrasymachus the tyrant is a hero in the current American sense of the term, while for Callicles he is a hero in something like the ancient Greek sense; thus he compares him to Heracles (484b).

Callicles speaks of the many "subduing by charms" (κατεπᾴδοντές) and "bewitching" (γοητεύοντες) and using "deceptions" (μαγγανεύματα) and "enchantments" (ἐπῳδὰς). He uses these terms to disparage devices which the many employ to tame the few. These devices seem to include religious beliefs and practices. He does not use similar language when speaking of the "law of nature" or of the behavior of men like Xerxes and Darius. The weak must deceive in order to overcome those who are otherwise stronger; the strong, if liberated from or immune to deceptive devices, apparently do not need them, but can frankly rule in their own interest. But is this true? Can an individual ruler be so strong that he does not need the ruled to believe that he serves the common good or that gods support his rule? Surely Xerxes and Darius rely upon such beliefs no less than the Athenian *demos* does. Unvarnished tyrannies sometimes arise, but usually do not last long. More generally, in what sense can one man be "stronger" than many? Socrates will pursue this question in the sequel.

I noted earlier that, paradoxically, the weak frighten the strong in Callicles' account. He suggests here that they also deceive the strong, inspiring them with belief in conventional justice or fear of the city's gods or both. The strong may even be more genuinely concerned about justice than the weak, though the weak set down the laws and define (conventional) justice in their own interest. This too seems paradoxical. Callicles may think that the weak, in their weakness, are compelled to be realistic about their interests and needs, while the strong, in their strength, have more freedom for and therefore susceptibility to illusions or being deceived.

Callicles evidently dislikes the hypocrisy of the weak, though he uses the first person plural when speaking of it. This hypocrisy seems justifiable on the basis of the apparently selfish law of nature that vindicates Xerxes and Darius; however, this is not Callicles' view, or his whole view. He is thrilled by the behavior of men like Xerxes and Darius, even though he might be harmed by it. The freedom from limits that such men seem to him to experience represents the possibility of human happiness. He apparently feels the rest of us should respect this condition and its deeds. This is at least partly a duty to ourselves: Only through recognizing and admiring the greatness of such men can we at least vicariously transcend our comparatively paltry lives. Likewise, as discussed above, Callicles feels that these men have a duty to behave with bold injustice (as conventionally defined), even though it might turn out badly for them (to say nothing of us). They must vindicate for all the freedom and greatness of unencumbered human beings—one could almost say they have a kind of *noblesse oblige*. Both strong and weak, in different ways, have a kind of duty to bold, unencumbered selfishness which transcends their narrow self-interest. They must honor this happy condition in order to be in any way worthy of it. Now this is a bit strange, and Callicles would not come out and say there are such duties; but it is part of what he feels and thinks.

Callicles tries to take the world as it is without making claims about how it should be.[17] He thinks it is futile to expect the world to be gentler or more "just" than it is. On the contrary, there is no genuine justice except the justice of "nature herself." Those who have what it takes to flourish deserve to do so, and those who do not deserve to suffer. Thus he defines natural justice as the rule of the stronger (483d5), and he identifies the better with the stronger (483d1–2). However, there are limits to how far he wants to go in this direction. He is disturbed that the "law we set down" enables people he despises to triumph over people he respects. His soul is both too strong and too weak to believe fully that whatever is, must be.

Callicles believes it is just for the strong to exploit the weak, and he finds it unjust that the weak often prove clever enough to turn the tables and exploit the strong. (He actually identifies three different groups: those with great power, like Xerxes or the tyrant he imagines; those with some strength who are tricked and enslaved by the many; and the many themselves.) Like any avid believer in justice, Callicles looks forward to the righting of this wrong, which will occur when the justice of nature "shines forth" in tyranny. Like Thrasymachus but more explicitly and even eagerly, Callicles identifies himself as one of the weak, one of those whom the godlike tyrant will trample upon. His immoralism entails enthusiasm for an imagined ruler who is likely to harm him personally; in other words, it resembles devotion to a moral principle.[18]

Callicles then offers a quote from Pindar, which has the effect of making him seem mildly ridiculous, since as he admits he remembers only part of the quote, and it isn't necessary for his argument. So why does he offer it? As he finishes speaking of the "man having a sufficient nature" who "rising up . . . is revealed as our master" and thereby enables the "justice of nature" to "shine forth," Callicles is enthused, caught up in his vision of justice. At this moment he feels himself to be the mouthpiece of something bigger than he is. It seems fitting to cite a source larger than himself, a famous poet who writes eloquently of "mortals and immortals" and the great Heracles. It isn't that Callicles feels his argument needs logical support (the quote would probably provide little logical support even if it were complete), but rather that he feels what he is saying has a dignity that merits a poetic conclusion, even a kind of divine testimony. Needless to say, one might wonder how this feeling jibes with the principles Callicles proclaims. The paradox posed by Callicles, and by other outspoken immoralists, is an enthusiastic, self-forgetting adherence to selfishness.

Regrettably we possess only the following fragment of the poem from which Callicles quotes.

> Law is king of all
> Both of mortals and immortals;
> It leads, deeming just the greatest violence,
> With a most high hand. I judge by
> The deeds of Heracles, when the cattle of Geryon
> Into the Cyclopean courtyard of Eurystheus
> Were driven by him, unasked and unpurchased.[19]

Insofar as we can judge from this fragment, Callicles' use of the poem to support his argument is perhaps tendentious, but not baseless. While Callicles argues that "the worse and weaker men's cows and all other possessions belong to the better and stronger man" (484c), Pindar simply says that when such violence occurs, law decrees that it is just. Callicles embraces what Pindar merely describes.

CRITICIZING PHILOSOPHY

Callicles then turns from justice to philosophy. As befits a criticism of philosophy, the remainder of his speech is less radical, and less hostile to conventional morality. "The truth, therefore, is thus, and you will know it if you proceed to greater things, once you have let philosophy drop" (484c). Callicles indicates there are greater things than philosophy, things which philosophy tends to conceal from its devotees. "Philosophy, to be sure, Socrates, is a graceful thing, if someone engages in it in due measure at the proper age; but if he fritters his time away in it further than is needed, it is the corruption of human beings." While Callicles is not hostile to philosophy in the way that, e.g., Anytus shows himself to be in Plato's *Meno*, there is nonetheless some similarity, as shown by Callicles' use of the word "corruption" (διαφθορὰ). "For even if he is of an altogether good nature and philosophizes far along in age, he must of necessity become inexperienced in all those things that one who is to be a noble and good man, and well reputed, must have experience of. And indeed they become inexperienced in the laws of the city, in the speeches one must use to associate with human beings in dealings both privately and publicly, in human pleasures and desires, and in sum they become all in all inexperienced in customs and characters" (484c–d).

For Callicles, as for Anytus and other practical men, the "noble and good man" (καλὸν κἀγαθὸν) has reputation and influence in the city. However, unlike Anytus, Callicles does not believe in a common good. Callicles understands political activity as fundamentally selfish, not public-spirited, and therefore as a duty to oneself, not others. As we shall see later in the dialogue, he also holds a more public-spirited view of what makes an admirable political man (to say nothing of the self-sacrificing element in his immoralism). Nonetheless, Callicles thinks (at least much of the time) that he views political activity as selfish, so one might expect him to view someone who prefers another activity as ridiculous or pitiable rather than evil. Indeed he claims to find a grown man who philosophizes ridiculous; but he also speaks of wanting to give him a beating (485c). On the whole his reaction seems more hostile than amused.

Political activity is what counts for Callicles. It is what makes someone a man, and one who shirks it is not quite what a man should be. Political activity is therefore a kind of duty. Callicles might accept this statement of his view, and add that the duty is to oneself. However, his hostility to philosophy suggests that he feels the duty is not simply to oneself. It is not precisely to other people either, but to a world in which those who can take care of themselves deservedly prosper, and those who can't are deservedly "trampled in the mud." In other words, the world presents itself as a kind of moral order or force to Callicles; it rewards and punishes according to men's deserts. Of course he does not think he believes in a moral order of this kind; nonetheless, he feels that men who engage in philosophy are self-indulgent, perhaps even impious, and that they deserve punishment. Like more conventional moralists who feel that those who behave badly should be punished, he wants to see a confirmation of the moral order which he believes in and respects.

We might distinguish two targets of this punishment: disobedience of the moral law, and disbelief in it. These two overlap to a great extent, but not completely, and we might ask which inspires greater hostility. Do moralists feel more hostile to believers who sin, or to skeptics who do not (apart from their disbelief itself)? The answer of course is generally the latter. (We might consider the Biblical emphasis upon belief, the New Testament's readiness to forgive the sinner, and even the story of the Fall itself, as well as Socrates' own fate in Athens.) And that makes sense, for the believing sinner does not call the moral order into question the way the disbeliever does. For Callicles, philosophers are both sinners and doubters, but his hostility seems stronger to the latter activity.

To be sure, Callicles also feels a certain respect for philosophy. He mentions that political men make themselves ridiculous when they try to philosophize, just as philosophers do when they try to engage in politics. (As Stauffer notes, Callicles may have seen Socrates in conversation with political men.[20]) He invokes Euripides in support of his view that people praise the activity at which they excel, in the belief that they thereby praise themselves, and he asserts, "I think the most correct thing is to partake of both" politics and philosophy (484e–485a). He also feels friendly toward Socrates, or at least "fairly" friendly (compare 485e3 and 486a3). He is hostile only insofar as philosophy poses a threat to his views.

However, he believes that philosophy truly educates only those who are young. "It is fine to partake of philosophy to the extent that it is for the sake of education, and it is not shameful to philosophize when one is a lad" (485a). To continue philosophizing after this initial exposure is to engage in mere subtleties without real learning.

> Whenever I see a small child, to whom it is still proper to talk in this manner, mumbling and playing around, I rejoice and it appears graceful to me, befitting a free man, and suitable to the small child's age; whereas when I hear a little boy talking distinctly, the thing seems to me rather disagreeable, vexes my ears, and seems to me to be something slavish. But whenever one hears a man mumbling or sees him playing around childishly, it appears ridiculous, unmanly, and deserving of a beating. (485b–c)

In Callicles' view a child who speaks distinctly is slavish, overly eager to appeal to others, while a man who mumbles is unmanly and deserving of a beating. Callicles presumably thinks that a man must speak clearly in order to participate in adult life, the most important part of which he considers to be political life. However, Callicles also thinks that the chief reason one needs to participate in political life is to protect oneself. One might infer that the critical difference between a boy and a man is that the latter must appeal to others in order to protect himself, or, to put it more bluntly, he must *accept* his slavery. To be sure, Callicles also thinks of political life as an end, as the activity that completes a man, but regarding ordinary political activity (as distinguished from being a tyrant) he emphasizes this less than the need to protect oneself.

Something similar is at the root of Callicles' disapproval of grown men who philosophize.

> So then, I feel this same thing towards those who philosophize, too. For seeing philosophy in a young lad, I admire it, and it seems to me fitting, and I consider this human being to be a free man, whereas the one who does not philosophize I consider illiberal, someone who will never deem himself worthy of any fine or noble affair. But whenever I see an older man still philosophizing and not released from it, this man, Socrates, surely seems to me to need a beating. . . .It falls to this man, even if he is of an altogether good nature, to become unmanly through fleeing the central area of the city and the assemblies, in which the poet says men become highly distinguished, and through sinking down into living the rest of his life whispering with three or

four lads in a corner, never to give voice to anything free and great and sufficient. (485c–e)

The poet Callicles mentions is of course Homer. In the *Iliad* Phoinix reminds Achilles of how Peleus sent him to accompany Achilles when Achilles did not yet know of battle or of assemblies "where men become highly distinguished."[21] Callicles' quote downplays the significance of battle in this passage and throughout the *Iliad*. This is not surprising given his selfish principles, but it makes us wonder why he chose to quote the *Iliad*. When we come later to the political men he admires, we shall see that Callicles is actually impressed by the willingness to risk one's life for one's city. His selectively quoting the *Iliad* seems to reflect the ambivalence he feels toward the courage and devotion of the warrior.

Callicles thinks that a young man who throws himself directly into politics, without any attention to philosophy, reveals a nature that is illiberal, incapable of anything fine. One might wonder why this criticism doesn't apply to older men who engage in politics. As with speaking clearly instead of mumbling, part of the answer seems to be that older men *need* to engage in politics. One is vulnerable, and therefore unmanly, if one gains no power in the city. (Callicles does not consider that it might be manly to accept vulnerability for the sake of a higher pursuit; he does not believe there is a higher pursuit.)

That's not the whole story, however. For Callicles politics offers the only arena in which one can accomplish anything "free and great and sufficient." His use of the word "free" (ἐλεύθερον) is particularly interesting. One might think the political man is especially unfree, and more closely resembles the child who talks distinctly than the private man does: Being involved in politics intensifies one's need to appeal to others. However, Callicles' coupling of free with "great" (μέγα) suggests that what he means is not so much free of obligations as free of limits (insofar as these meanings of freedom are distinct). The rulers of a powerful city or empire can propose and lead great projects like the invasions he mentioned earlier, or the Athenian attempt to conquer Sicily, which are, in his view, unbounded by the mundane necessities that constrain private life. Such men rise above their own private lives; they alone among mortals reach for the limitless or infinite. One might point out that reaching does not equal attaining, and that bold political projects often turn out badly; but as we have seen Callicles tends to disregard actual results. What excites him is men's ability and willingness to make the attempt, without being constrained by morality, necessity, or moderation. In some way he feels that making the attempt itself propels one into the realm of the infinite, that one becomes limitless in pursuing the limitless, and that the actual result is secondary.

This invites the question of the difference between a Xerxes and a madman who fancies that he is pursuing a great project. The difference for Callicles seems to be that other people are forced to follow and react to Xerxes. One might wonder if this difference makes all the difference.

For Callicles politics is the realm that counts. His chief criticism of the young man who does not initially engage in philosophy seems to be that his vision of politics itself will never reach great heights. One might assume Callicles considers it more substantial to be doing than talking, but that isn't what he says here. He speaks of the opportunity to "give voice to" (φθέγξασθαι) something free and great, not simply to *do* such a thing. Of course he is right to suggest that politics is largely a matter of talk, especially in a direct democracy like Athens. However, insofar as talking is what counts, philosophy would seem to have the advantage over politics, since it means talking about whatever is ultimately most important, not merely about what is politically important. Obviously Callicles doesn't see it this way. For him the talk in politics is about what is "free and great and sufficient," apparently because this talk involves doing as well as talking. Numbers also seem to matter—the greatness of Xerxes and Darius is established not by the goodness of what they accomplished or hoped to accomplish, but by the number of people they set in motion. A multitude of people acting together can do something "free and great and sufficient," which seems to mean above all an act of force or conquest. The most desirable position for Callicles is where one's "talking" leads to many people's "doing."

The youth who does not philosophize is "someone who will never deem himself worthy of any fine or noble affair." Since it seems unlikely that Callicles would describe himself this way, we may infer that he was attracted to philosophy in his youth. He is still willing to talk dialectically with Socrates about their respective ways of life; initially he even seems to enjoy it. In this respect he is of course very different from Anytus. Callicles' feeling toward philosophy is not wholly unlike what a person feels toward an activity he has outgrown. He wants to articulate the ground of his rejection, above all to himself, as a way of confirming that he has left it behind. However, this does not account for the degree of hostility he shows. He also experiences philosophy as a challenge or threat to his current beliefs. He cannot ignore philosophy, for he thinks it liberated him. However, the way of life it offers seems unsatisfying to him, amounting merely to "whispering with three or four lads in a corner."

The distinction between nature and convention seems to be among the things Callicles thinks one learns in one's initial exposure to philosophy.[22] Making this distinction, even as imperfectly as he does, is tantamount to raising (or raising more deeply) the question of how to live, which he considers a necessary question, though of course unlike Socrates he does not think philosophy is the answer.[23] In particular, distinguishing between nature and convention entails asking whether justice (as commonly understood) is genuinely good, or merely said or thought to be good. Whatever the limits of his understanding of the distinction between nature and convention, Callicles has thought about whether justice is good, and decided that it is not, that it makes more sense to live for oneself than for others. As we have begun to see, however, this considered decision reflects only part of Callicles' feeling and thought about justice.

Callicles thinks both that someone who is never attracted to philosophy is limited by nature, and that philosophy expands the vision of the youths who engage in it. Thus the initial impulse toward philosophy is healthy and liberal, and it yields genuine benefits. However, continuing with philosophy is unhealthy and unmanly, and it is sterile. In this respect the world is favorable to human beings: Their healthy and admirable impulses lead to good ends. By contrast, Socrates suggests in the *Republic* that unhealthy or peculiar qualities make possible the greatest benefit, philosophy. (He specifically mentions Theages's sickliness and his own *daimonion* [*Republic* 496b–c].) In this respect Socrates' vision of the world is more unsettling than that of Callicles. It is not clear that Callicles has considered the possibility that the most impressive qualities might fail to produce the best ends. Yet if there are no gods, and the world is not organized for the flourishing of human beings, this is a genuine possibility. (One might for example consider Samuel Butler's suggestion that success comes to those whose capacity is "a little above the average . . . not too much so. It is on this rock that so many clever people split. The successful man will see just so much more than his neighbors as they will be able to see too when it is shown them, but not enough to puzzle them."[24]) In this as in other respects, Callicles is less tough than he thinks he is.

Callicles asserts that he is "fairly friendly" (ἐπιεικῶς φιλικῶς) toward Socrates, and says, "I have now probably felt what Euripides' Zethus felt toward Amphion" (485e). This is a reference to a play called *Antiope*, which presents two brothers who argue for different ways of life. Much of the play is lost, but based on existing fragments, scholars think that Zethus, a shepherd, argues for an active way of life, while Amphion, a musician, argues for an artistic or contemplative one.[25] Callicles knows this play better than he knew the Pindar he earlier quoted. After quoting some lines spoken by Zethus, he asks, "does it not seem to you to be a shameful thing to be in such a condition as I think you and the others are, who are forever pushing further on in philosophy?" (486a). He makes at least one change to the text of Euripides, saying that Socrates makes himself conspicuous "in a shape belonging to a youth (μειρακιώδει)" instead of "in a shape belonging to a woman (γυναικομίμῳ)" (485e–486a).[26] He considers philosophy youthful rather than womanish.

He continues in words that have since become famous: "For now, if someone seized you . . . and carried you off to prison, claiming that you were doing injustice when you were not at all doing injustice, you know that you would not have anything of use to do for yourself, but you would be dizzy and gaping, without anything to say; and when you stood up in the law court, happening to face a very lowly and vicious accuser, you would die, if he wished to demand the death penalty for you" (486a–b). Although somewhat prophetic, this vivid statement is also exaggerated. It is hard for any reader of Plato to imagine Socrates "without anything to say." Callicles himself has just heard Socrates refute Gorgias and Polus, and has characterized him as a "popular speaker" (482c). He clearly exaggerates philosophy's (or at least Socrates') impotence in public speech—which is not to deny that Socrates would be much more vulnerable in such a situation than a prominent political man. Callicles probably draws his opinion of philosophy's impotence partly from common opinion in Athens at the time. Aristophanes' *Clouds* famously presents a Socrates who seems destined to have difficulties in law courts.[27] However, the Socrates of the *Gorgias*, the one Callicles actually sees, behaves very differently than the one in the *Clouds*. Callicles' eagerness to find fault with philosophy prevents him from seeing it as it actually presents itself. Moreover, his emphatic and exaggerated description of the danger Socrates faces suggests a certain desire to see Socrates experience what he describes, a desire arising not so much out of ill will toward Socrates as out of an unselfconscious desire to see his own way of life and beliefs vindicated. The fate Callicles describes is what he feels, or hopes, Socrates deserves.

One might contrast Callicles in this respect with the young Alcibiades of *Alcibiades I*, who, despite his attraction to political life, does not disparage philosophy. Of course in that dialogue Socrates presents philosophy as a necessary aid to political life, rather than a hostile alternative; and Alcibiades has not (yet) had Callicles' experience of moving away from philosophy after an initial attraction to it. However, even allowing for these differences, Alcibiades seems to want what he wants, without being much bothered if others want something different. The older Alcibiades of the *Symposium* has more complicated feelings toward Socrates, but does not seem hostile to philosophy. Callicles is clearly bothered by philosophy. In itself this is no vice, since of course people choose different ways of life at least partly due to different views of what is good, and it is reasonable to wonder if the choices others make cast light on one's own. However, Callicles does not, and probably cannot, maintain the openness or honesty with himself that his concern that others live differently seems to demand; so rather than liberating him, that concern makes him uneasy and angry, and leads him to exaggerate the goodness or necessity of his way of life, and to distort the alternative he confronts.

Callicles' statement about philosophy's vulnerability also suggests a contradiction in his own views. He speaks of doing injustice in the usual, conventional sense. (The key phrase in this regard is "claiming that you were doing injustice when you were not at all doing injustice [φάσκων ἀδικεῖν μηδὲν ἀδικοῦντα]" [486a]. The infinitive ἀδικεῖν refers to what the imaginary accuser says, but ἀδικοῦντα is in Callicles' own voice.) Shortly afterwards he speaks of "paying the just penalty (διδόναι δίκην)" (486c3) for striking a harmless man on the side of the head, though he himself has defined (natural) justice in such a way that this act is not unjust. One could argue that Callicles intentionally speaks in these cases of merely conventional justice; however, that doesn't seem like the most natural reading. He doesn't distance himself from the way he speaks of justice in these statements, and his "not at all" (μηδέν) in the former statement emphasizes it. Callicles does not consistently adhere to the view of "natural justice" he has articulated.

I note also a difference in emphasis between Callicles' quote from *Antiope* and what he himself says. Zethus speaks of Amphion's likely irrelevance, and suggests that merely private life lacks maturity and dignity. While Callicles seems to share those views, what he emphasizes is the possibility of being harmed if one lacks political influence and the ability to speak in law courts. "Yet 'how can this be a wise thing,' Socrates, 'an art that took a man with a good nature and made him worse,' unable to help himself or to save either himself or anyone else from the greatest dangers.[28] . . . To say something rather rude, it is possible to strike such a man on the side of the head without paying the just penalty" (486b–c). Callicles' imagination runs quickly to the possibility of being harmed by others—which may not be entirely unreasonable, but is nonetheless striking, especially in a young man.

While the challenge Socrates poses to his own beliefs provokes hostility and a certain eagerness to see Socrates suffer the fate he deserves according to those beliefs, Callicles nonetheless feels some concern and friendliness toward him. In the middle of his warning he addresses Socrates as his friend (ὦ φίλε Σώκρατες) (486a3). He suggests that Socrates has a good nature (486b5), and he addresses him as good (486c4). However, he never calls him noble (καλός), or a real man (ἀνήρ). As we have seen, Callicles thinks a real man cannot be struck with impunity, while a man who can be is ignoble, akin to a slave (483a–b). We have seen that Callicles considers the noble to be good (483a). Socrates is good in some way, but not in every way; the fully or truly good man is able to take care of himself. However, this defect may be reparable, if Socrates will follow Callicles' advice.

Callicles later asks Socrates whether it is not "infuriating" (ἀγανακτητόν) when a base man kills a noble and good one (511b). He can't accept that this might be the fate of a noble and good man, so he understands the noble and good man as the man to whom this can't happen (or the man to whom he thinks it can't happen).[29] However, this description could be understood in two different ways. Callicles might view the noble and good man as one who can protect himself primarily because this seems to him good, a strength, and the opposite situation seems to him bad, a weakness; or primarily because he finds it intolerable to contemplate that a noble and good man can be struck with impunity. In other words, is he drawn to understanding the noble and good man as (conventionally) just, only to recoil at the prospect that such a man is vulnerable? Or do strength and ability to protect oneself seem to him a critical part of virtue from the outset, as it were, not primarily in response to the vulnerability of those who lack this ability? Does Callicles become an immoralist because he believes in justice and grows frustrated at its weakness, or simply because he feels a noble and good man must be able to take care of himself? I shall return to this question when we come to the "infuriating" comment.

REPUTATION

Callicles concludes with an appeal to the advantages of the way of life he favors. "Good man, be persuaded by me, stop refuting, 'practice the good music' of affairs, and practice there whence 'you will seem to be prudent, giving up to others these refined subtleties'—whether one must say they are silliness or drivel—'from which you will dwell in an empty house,' envying not the men who make refutations over these small matters, but those who have livelihood, reputation (δόξα), and many other good things" (486c–d).[30] Callicles' concern for reputation reminds us of the incompleteness of his earlier attack on convention. Concern for reputation means concern for the opinions of others, and not as a possible source of knowledge. Callicles resists conventional justice, but not opinion or convention as such. Indeed, one might say he attacks the higher part of convention (concern for justice) while lauding the lower part (concern for what others think of one).

Callicles' concern for reputation is obviously related to his lack of confidence in a common good or an effective moral order in the world; since one cannot count on any such thing, one depends upon the goodwill of others. One could say something similar of his interest in rhetoric. However, his attachment to reputation extends further than a purely negative desire to be well regarded in order to avoid persecution. He presents reputation as a good, not merely a means of avoiding harm, or a means to other goods. He apparently takes pleasure in reputation itself, which suggests, whether or not he fully recognizes it, that in some way he feels that if others think one is good, then one is good.

Perhaps this contention requires defense. Reputation helps one attain security, prosperity, and friendly social intercourse. It is also a promise of those goods, an indication that one is likely to enjoy them, and as such it is pleasant. However, particular goods external to reputation itself are probably not what cause Callicles to mention it so prominently—it is one of only two goods he mentions in this context, the other being "livelihood" (βίος) (486d1). Reputation itself, apart from other goods it helps one enjoy or gives one hope of enjoying, is pleasant because it makes one feel one is good. Thus one would not take pleasure (or not much) in thinking others *incorrectly* thought one was good (unless one prided oneself on deceiving them and took that as the mark of one's goodness, which is not Callicles' approach). It is true that feeling one is good is pleasant largely or chiefly because it makes one feel one is likely to enjoy good things, but not so much particular good things one has concrete reason to expect as something more vague, the good things of which one feels one is worthy, culminating in happiness. Callicles' enjoyment of reputation suggests an unselfconscious belief that those who gain the good opinion of others are good people who are worthy of good things. In other words, it suggests a belief in justice or deserving.

To be sure, reputation or praise can foster a belief in one's goodness which is not necessarily attached to a belief in justice. A practitioner of an art, e.g., may be gratified by the praise of other practitioners of his art because such praise confirms his skill and understanding, and thereby causes him to expect to fare well. By contrast, if a knowledgeable person sharply criticizes something one has done, one is pained because one doubts that one knows what one is doing. However, the pleasure and pain produced by praise and criticism are relatively specific and limited if they do not (as they usually do) spill over into a more general feeling that one is or is not a good and worthy person. Praise and reputation can be gratifying for reasons which have nothing to do with a belief in justice, but they are not *deeply* gratifying unless they contribute to the feeling that one is a good person who deserves good things. The emphasis Callicles puts upon reputation suggests that he experiences it as pleasant in this deeper way. The concrete but limited hopes to which reputation gives rise are accompanied by a less concrete, less limited hope. Of course it is common to attach this sort of meaning to reputation; but it less common to do so while purporting to disdain convention.

Callicles says in his speech that the man who suffers injustice is unable to take care of "anyone else he might care for" (483b4). Tentative though it is, this is the strongest indication he gives in the dialogue of attachment to others. He also quotes Euripides regarding speaking politically "on behalf of another," but as part of a long quote, without focusing on this point (486a). He later indicates that a ruler would be foolish not to distribute more to his friends than to enemies (492c), a statement which is similar to one Thrasymachus makes in the *Republic* (343e). However, Thrasymachus speaks of all unjust men, not only rulers, and it is clearer in what he says that men expect to benefit from their relatives and acquaintances. Both men deny that a genuine common good exists politically, but Thrasymachus seems more confident that there can be a common good (at least in the sense of shared interests) in subpolitical groups. Callicles' world does not seem to be one of very warm or dependable connections to other people.

It is worth considering the less radical tone of what Callicles says after he turns to criticizing philosophy (beginning at 484c). One might think his speech as a whole reveals yet another division in him. The radical Callicles champions immoral principles and offers a paean to tyranny; the milder Callicles praises the life of respectable citizens. The radical Callicles presents a philosophic doctrine, albeit in a distorted form; the milder one criticizes the philosopher as a ridiculous and vulnerable figure. The radical Callicles insists that nature and convention are usually in opposition; the milder one holds out reputation as a great good.

On the other hand, Callicles does not offer any explicitly moral or (conventionally) just argument in the second part of the speech. One might distinguish the two parts in terms of discussing what is possible for the rare unfettered individual, who as such casts light on what we all want or on human nature, versus what is possible for the rest of us, including Socrates and Callicles. This seems to be how Callicles himself views his speech. Even in his citizen frame of mind, he is attracted to freedom from moral and other restraints. As individuals, ordinary people can't shake off the bonds of convention; but united as a group, perhaps they can.

However, this doesn't wholly account for the difference in character between the two parts of the speech. The first part reflects what he thinks when he self-consciously confronts fundamental questions, but he slips into a more ordinary, more friendly frame of mind much or most of the time. As he implies by grouping himself with the many rather than with the powerful men he discusses (real and imagined), he does not live by his self-conscious views on fundamental questions. This is not simply because he lacks power; lack of power need not prevent him from taking his bearings by these views, and living by them in principle if not in deed. To some extent he does this; thus he does not view himself as devoted to justice or to his city—at least not most of the time. His usual frame of mind is shaped to some extent by his radical views; but to a greater extent it partakes of ordinary friendliness and restraint. Whether or not he discusses it with himself, he seems to feel that living by his radical views would be uncomfortably harsh and demanding. The way of life he envisages as the culmination and confirmation of these views is not wholly attractive to him. It is not a hope, and not really a touchstone by which he guides his life, but a fantasy which has some elements that thrill him and capture his imagination.

Callicles' actual life is not so exciting to him. We do not see in his practical moments the kind of enthusiasm he shows when discussing natural justice or the slave who rises up to be revealed as our master; thus the second part of his speech is somewhat tepid compared to the first. Natural justice somehow promises transcendence for Callicles—as justice generally does for people. He is in a way devoted to it, which gives flight to the hopes connected with it. By contrast, when he praises a way of life that secures livelihood and reputation, Callicles still feels some hope of transcendence, but it seems weaker. His greatest excitement in the second part of his speech comes when he describes not his way of life but the dangers to which philosophy is exposed.

In his theoretical moments, Callicles thinks that because there is no common good, one must live *against* others. Even if one accepts the premise, however, the conclusion does not follow. One might distinguish one's good from that of others, one might even be wary of them, while still forming alliances with them, and perhaps enjoying their company. Callicles himself is aware of this in his more ordinary frame of mind, so we might ask what draws him to a more radical position in his theoretical and enthusiastic moments. We have seen that he does not trust people, that his instinct is to feel that others can harm one and one must take care of oneself. If others are generally threatening, if they are potential enemies, then it is indeed better to dominate and exploit than to be dominated and exploited. It is better to be above than below. However, being securely above isn't possible, at least not for anybody who is neither godlike nor born a king. Callicles has not digested this. He believes, at least in part of his mind, that the danger others pose can be overcome. He thinks that being a real man enables one to take care of oneself, to be secure. To be sure, that is true to some extent; however, Callicles is not interested in examining the extent to which it is true. He feels that if one is wholeheartedly a real man, if one gives oneself to this noble thing, then one will fare well—or at least deserve to.

I have suggested that the politically active man is not necessarily safer than the private one. However, discretion, which Callicles does not practice, is usually safer than outspokenness. His outspokenness in attacking conventional justice and hailing the tyrant who will trample upon it reveals that he is not really as concerned about security as he sometimes sounds, notably when faulting Socrates for living insecurely. Although an awareness of insecurity somehow inspires Callicles' thought, he does not soberly consider how to maximize his security. That sort of consideration is not really attractive to him; it does not answer his longing for a complete solution to the problem of insecurity, and of vulnerability more generally.

It is in part this longing for a complete solution that leads Callicles to feel that the best life is lived against others. A man who could successfully live against others would overcome the danger they pose. Callicles knows he does not have this sort of invulnerability, which makes him feel he must not be worthy of it. Instead of accepting that invulnerability is simply unattainable, he (unselfconsciously) raises the bar of what constitutes worthiness to a fantastic extent. Somewhere, he feels, there is a man who can live against and dominate all others; that heroic man is somehow the touchstone of what is possible. Although he does not think he himself is such a man, the imagination of that man enables him to believe that the limits of human life can be transcended. (More precisely, the imagination of that man both results from and crystallizes his belief that those limits can be transcended.)

Callicles' imaginary hero exemplifies the virtues he admires, intelligence and courage (491c). He does not consider justice a virtue, nor moderation, as we shall see. Despite (or because of) his admiration of virtue, however, Callicles is not deeply attracted to a virtue which is good in itself rather than for benefits it might bring. Insofar as he conceives of such a thing, he is not deeply attracted to a virtue which is good as an end or for the sake of an activity in which it is exercised, which is to say philosophy is not deeply attractive to him. He wants virtue to be secure, to flourish, to dominate—he feels it is worthy of these things—not simply to be practiced for its own sake.

Callicles fails to grasp that ultimately one cannot do all that much to ensure one's survival, to say nothing of invulnerability. (Of course there are many things one can do, but only to limited effect.) We might ask, is this failure fundamentally due to his admiration of virtue, or to an inability to accept his mortality? The answer seems to be both. He is reluctant to accept the limits of human power. He averts his glance to some extent—unselfconsciously of course. This is shown above all by his hostility to philosophy. He resists seeing clearly how little people can do for themselves—not with any precise sense of what he is resisting, but with a sense that this is not what he wishes to think about, not the direction in which he wishes to go. He wishes instead to think of the real man, the one who (he believes) can hold his own among men, and even, in the extreme case, so dominate them as to transcend the vulnerability to which the rest of us are subject. This is not a belief he wants to question; he does not want to lose what it seems to promise. This is the deepest reason why he is hostile to, not merely contemptuous of, philosophy. He senses that philosophy is unimpressed by the sort of virtue he admires, and skeptical that it will attain the reward he expects. Perhaps he senses also that philosophy questions the very possibility of deserving to transcend one's vulnerability or mortality.

However, this does not mean awareness of vulnerability is the cause, or sole cause, of Callicles' admiration of virtue. On the contrary, his admiration makes it possible for him to believe that virtue is capable, or worthy, of reaching beyond the normal fate of human beings. To some extent he even admires virtue apart from any clear sense of what it is. (Thus in the sequel he is slow to specify what characteristics he considers superior [489e–491c].) He feels that there must be impressive, demanding, deserving qualities prior to or apart from focusing on any particular qualities. For Callicles, the belief or feeling that virtue is worthy arises apart from awareness of vulnerability, but awareness of vulnerability intensifies and broadens that belief. An unwillingness or inability to accept his limits as a mortal being works in tandem with admiration of virtue (as he understands it) to shape his peculiar attachment to justice—which is not simply peculiar.

NOTES

1. Note, however, "godlessly (ἀθέως)" at 481a5. Of course what Socrates says does not reflect the spirit of Jesus' injunction, since he assumes that one wishes one's enemy to be harmed. This assumption also contradicts the argument he develops with Polemarchus in the *Republic*, according to which "it is not the work of the just man to harm . . . either a friend or any other, but of his opposite, the unjust man" (335d). If it is unjust to harm anyone, and just punishment improves men, as Socrates and Polus have agreed, then it is unjust to prevent an enemy from being justly punished.
2. Socrates says at 480e that one must beware of suffering injustice, but the bulk of what he says points in another direction.
3. As E. R. Dodds notes, the claim that he loves Alcibiades erotically is a kind of joke on Socrates' part (*Plato: Gorgias*, 261). A truer glimpse at the relation between them is offered by Alcibiades himself in Plato's *Symposium*.
4. Nichols, "The Rhetoric of Justice in Plato's *Gorgias*," interpretive essay in Plato, *Gorgias*, 145.
5. Stauffer, *The Unity of Plato's Gorgias*, 140.
6. The shorter form of the oath occurs in *Charmides*, *Lysis*, *Phaedo*, and twice in the *Republic*.
7. Robert A. Armour, *Gods and Myths of Ancient Egypt* (New York: The American University in Cairo Press, 2001), 141.
8. Cf. Leo Strauss, unpublished transcript of class taught on Gorgias (1957), 132. A transcript of this class is available online through the Leo Strauss Center.
9. Cf. Leo Strauss, *Natural Right and History* (Chicago: The University of Chicago Press, 1953), 91–92.
10. Stauffer says that Callicles argues "that nobility has no genuine meaning beyond what is advantageous" (*The Unity of Plato's Gorgias*, 117). It seems to me this is not quite correct. Callicles says that everything more shameful is also worse, which implies that everything more noble is also better; but he does not say that the noble is nothing more than the good, or that it has no independent meaning. As we shall soon see, Callicles is strongly and consciously attached to nobility. He seems to feel that whatever is noble is as such good, or that the (genuinely) noble as such has a goodness which is not reducible to other goods. (Thus at 499b he cheerfully abandons hedonism for the sake of virtue.) He does not spell out this view, and might resist doing so, for it seems to conflict with other views he expresses; but neither does he reduce the noble to the advantageous. Stauffer seems to assume that Callicles is somewhat more consistent or has greater clarity in these matters than is in fact the case. He also seems to assume (and this may in part cause the first assumption) that an attachment to justice must accompany an attachment to nobility. (Thus immediately following the statement I quoted above, Stauffer writes: "and that it is simply a manifest fact that should not be lamented that the strong dominate the weak." This is indeed an opinion that Callicles holds, but he does not derive it from the opinion that "nobility has no genuine meaning beyond what is advantageous.") While it may ultimately be true that attachment to justice must accompany attachment to nobility, Callicles does not think it is true.
11. Callicles does not clearly distinguish between being active in politics and in law courts. Of course there was much less boundary between them in ancient Athens than there is in America.
12. Cf. Plato, *Republic* 492a–b, where Socrates identifies the many as the "biggest sophists."
13. Aristotle, *Nicomachean Ethics*, 1131a23.
14. As Dodds notes, the fact that most laws were not written meant that law and convention were less distinct for the Greeks than they are for us (*Plato: Gorgias,* 266).
15. Nichols, footnote 75 in Plato, *Gorgias*.

16. We see later that he admires Pericles, who revealed the exploitative character of the Athenian empire with striking frankness. See Thucydides, *The Peloponnesian War*, II.63.

17. One might compare this to what Nietzsche calls *amor fati*. See Friedrich Nietzsche, *The Gay Science*, translated by Walter Kaufmann (New York: Random House, 1974), aphorism 276.

18. To be sure, if a tyrant subdued Athens, Callicles might seek to attach himself to him, and his enthusiasm for tyranny might help him do so. However, calculations of this kind are obviously not the basis of that enthusiasm.

19. Dodds, *Plato: Gorgias,* 270. The translation is mine. Callicles gives the quote correctly, as far as we know, for the first four and a half lines.

20. Stauffer, *The Unity of Plato's Gorgias*, 90.

21. Homer, *The Iliad* (Cambridge, MA: Harvard University Press, Loeb edition, 1999), IX.441.

22. We have seen that Callicles understands convention as something people claim to believe rather than as something they actually believe. That might make us surprised at the significance he attributes to philosophy for helping him break free of convention. However, it is not necessarily easy to dismiss a commonly expressed opinion even if one has doubts about it. Moreover, before he encountered philosophy, Callicles might not have concluded that few people really believe the conventional statements they make. Whether or not philosophy gave him this insight (the truth of which he exaggerates), it might have liberated him to develop it on his own.

23. Strauss, 1957 class, 83.

24. Samuel Butler, *The Way of All Flesh* (New York: Rinehart & Co., 1948), 18.

25. Dodds, *Plato: Gorgias*, 275–76. One recent scholar suggests a somewhat different interpretation of the disagreement between Zethus and Amphion. See John Gibert, "*Apragmosyne* in Euripides' *Antiope*" (paper presented at annual meeting of American Philological Association, 2001). However, the way Callicles (and Plato) make use of the play tends to support the traditional interpretation.

26. Dodds, *Plato: Gorgias*, 277. Dodds also considers other possible changes Callicles and Plato may have introduced (276–77).

27. For that matter, so do Plato's dialogues. However, Plato's Socrates does a better job defending himself in the *Apology* than one would expect of the Socrates in the *Clouds*.

28. Dodds and Nichols think this question contains another quote from *Antiope* because of the poetic word φώς (φῶτ' in accusative) for man. See Dodds, *Plato: Gorgias*, 278, and Nichols, footnote 81 in Plato, *Gorgias*. I am following Nichols' translation in this section in distinguishing where Callicles is quoting Euripides.

29. To be sure, this view makes sense to some extent. It is surely a disadvantage to be someone who can be struck with impunity, to say nothing of being killed. However, the question remains whether what it takes to avoid such a position is worth the time and effort involved, given the brevity of human life, and the uncertainty that one will in fact fare better if one is more highly respected. Callicles doesn't pay attention to these considerations. He is inclined to believe that the way of life he favors can overcome, or at least greatly minimize, evils endemic to life.

30. According to Dodds, an ancient quotation of *Antiope* indicates that Callicles replaces "wars" (πολέμων) with "affairs" (πραγμάτων) at 486c5, but he also notes there are reasons to doubt this quotation (*Plato: Gorgias*, 278).

Chapter Five

Socrates Questions Callicles

STRONGER AND BETTER

We have seen from his speech criticizing (conventional) justice and philosophy that Callicles has ambivalent and complicated feelings and opinions about justice. These feelings and opinions come into sharper focus under Socrates' questioning.

When Callicles finishes speaking, Socrates asks a peculiar question. "If I happened to have a golden soul, Callicles, would you not think I'd be pleased to find one of those stones with which they test gold . . . ?" When Callicles asks what he means, Socrates explains that "if you agree with me on the things that my soul holds opinions about, these at last are the true things themselves" (486d–e). This is very high praise of Callicles—higher, I think, than can be wholly sincere. Callicles is an energetic and engaging man, but not a careful thinker, so it is hard to see how his agreement could establish the truth of Socrates' opinions.

Socrates offers three criteria for whether someone can serve as a "sufficient test of a soul's living correctly": knowledge, goodwill, and outspokenness (487a). The evidence Socrates offers that Callicles meets the first criterion, "you have been sufficiently educated, as many of the Athenians would say," is more humorous than compelling (487b). (Socrates doesn't even claim *most* Athenians would say so.) Callicles does seem to meet the third criterion; as Socrates says, Callicles' speech supports his claim to be outspoken or shameless (487d).

Regarding the middle criterion, goodwill, Socrates mentions having heard Callicles speak with three close friends about how far one must practice wisdom. "You urged each other not to be too eager to philosophize to the point of precision, but to be cautious lest, by becoming wiser beyond what is needful, you should be corrupted unawares" (487c–d). This is presumably a humorous restatement of what Socrates heard Callicles and his friends saying.[1] Probably they discussed not the danger of becoming wise but the danger of spending time philosophizing which could be better spent some other way. Possibly they also discussed philosophy as a form of corruption apart from the time it consumes; if so, they would have spoken of it not as genuine wisdom, but as a kind of folly which might appear to be wisdom. "Since, therefore, I hear you giving the same counsel to me as to your own closest comrades, it is sufficient evidence for me that you are truly of goodwill towards me." This is inadequate as a proof that Callicles feels goodwill toward Socrates—his candor seems to reflect anger as much as goodwill—but it does confirm that he is being candid.

Socrates concludes that "when you agree with me on something in the speeches . . . there will be no further need to carry it back to another touchstone . . . . Your and my agreement, therefore, will really at last attain the goal of truth" (487e). This conclusion seems at least largely ironic, but Callicles may nonetheless be a touchstone of some significance to Socrates, enabling him to confirm that he understands the opinions and moral attachments of people who think they are free of moral attachments.

Given what Socrates has said, one might expect him to share his opinions with Callicles and see how Callicles reacts. Instead he turns to what Callicles has been saying, and asks him to take it up again "from the beginning (ἐξ ἀρχῆς)" (488b).[2] Callicles acts as a touchstone for Socrates (insofar as he genuinely does) not by judging what Socrates says, or even by telling Socrates what he himself thinks, but rather through Socrates' *probing* him, presumably to find out what he *really* thinks. Socrates must examine Callicles to find out what Callicles truly thinks and whether they agree.

Socrates asks Callicles if he is saying that the just according to nature is that the stronger carry off the things of the weaker, the better rule the worse, and the superior have more than the inferior. After Callicles agrees, Socrates focuses on the most obvious question this raises: "And do you call the same man better (βελτίω) and stronger (κρείττω)?" (488b) He asks if Callicles calls the mightier men stronger, and if it is necessary for the weaker to obey the mightier. "Or is it possible for one to be better but weaker and feebler, and to be stronger but more vicious? . . . Are the stronger and the better and the mightier (τὸ κρεῖττον καὶ τὸ βέλτιον καὶ τὸ ἰσχυρότερον) the same or different?" Callicles replies, "But I say to you distinctly that they are the same" (488c–d). One might detect in Callicles' use of "I say to you" (ἐγώ σοι . . . λέγω) an incipient awareness that there may be a difficulty in what he is saying.

Socrates asks if the many are stronger than the one by nature. "How could they not be?" Callicles replies (488d). Therefore the lawful usages (τὰ νόμιμα) of the many are those of the stronger, and therefore of the better,

Socrates says, and Callicles agrees. Socrates asks if such usages are fine by nature, since they are those of the stronger. Callicles answers, "I say so." Socrates assumes that since the lawful usages of the many are fine, what the many say about justice must be true. Callicles does not contest this assumption, and (after some hesitation) he concedes that he has misspoken (488d–489b). However, the assumption that everything fine is true or truthful is questionable. (To be sure, truthfulness as such seems finer than its opposite; yet under some circumstances untruthfulness is the finer course. We do not consider someone a fine husband if he tells criminals where his wife is hiding.) Callicles does not seem to notice this assumption, but he would if he instinctively doubted it. We may infer that despite his immoral principles, he more or less assumes that everything fine is true or truthful. Indeed, his own outspokenness, and his criticism of Polus and Gorgias for not being outspoken, suggest that he admires frankness. Moreover, he presents his self-made tyrant as frankly dominating others, without need for spells or charms (484a–b). Callicles believes in a condition of such power that no falsehood is necessary; this fantasy provides his touchstone for what constitutes the fine or noble.

Still more questionable is the conclusion that the lawful usages of the many are fine because the many are stronger, a conclusion with which Callicles explicitly agrees. As his view of natural justice implies, Callicles somehow believes that everything the stronger do is fine. He tends to forget the complexity of life, its unavoidable drawbacks and compromises, when he considers "the stronger" as such. At a similar point in his conversation with Thrasymachus in the *Republic*, Socrates asks whether the stronger sometimes make mistakes in ordering what is to their advantage (339c). Socrates' procedure here reflects Callicles' greater concern for the fine or noble, in contrast to Thrasymachus' greater concern for knowledge or technical ability; however, Callicles would likely agree with Thrasymachus that the stronger as such do not err. Both men admire strength or power, and tend to think it is wholly without blemish. Indeed, this seems to be a general characteristic of immoralists. A man who embraces injustice turns from what should be to what is, but doesn't quite make it all the way. (If he did, he would be more conscious of the pitfalls of injustice.) His preference for what is turns out to be a (more or less unselfconscious) opinion that what *is* is what should be, or that strength or power constitutes or reflects true righteousness and is truly deserving.

However, this is not an opinion any person can wholly embrace—certainly not Callicles, who despises the many despite their undeniable strength, and who denounces (conventional) justice because it denies that true virtue is deserving. Socrates refutes Callicles where it matters to him by showing that his admiration of strength points to accepting conventional justice. Since the many are stronger and what is said by the stronger is fine, it is by nature, not only by convention, that doing injustice is more shameful than suffering it and that having an equal share is just. Callicles responds by redefining the stronger, and by criticizing Socrates. "This man here will not stop driveling!" he exclaims. He accuses Socrates of hunting after small errors in speech, and asks, "Do you suppose I say that being stronger men (τὸ κρείττους) is anything other than being better men (τὸ βελτίους)?" (489b–c). As I have noted, the word κρείττων can have the connotation of better as well as stronger; nonetheless, Callicles' question highlights his tendency to believe in the coincidence of power and virtue. He uses the word κρείττων in two different senses, as stronger and as better, and thereby implicitly claims that the stronger are better and vice versa.

Callicles continues: "Or do you think I am saying that, if a rabble of slaves and human beings of all sorts, worthy of nothing except perhaps to exert strength of body, was collected together, and if these people asserted some things, these things are lawful (νόμιμα)?" (489c). A critic of democracy might object to it precisely on the grounds that when a "rabble of slaves and human beings of all sorts" gathers, its decrees become law. I think it is not putting too much weight on his use of the word "lawful" to suggest that Callicles is interested in the dignity or nobility of law. We saw above that his distinction between nature and convention was sharp but incomplete. We see here that he seems interested not only in transcending convention or law, but also in purifying it. We might even take this as an aspect of his enthusiasm for the tyrant who will trample upon the low and hypocritical devices of men.

Callicles' behavior toward Socrates, though not as rude as Thrasymachus' at a similar point in his conversation with Socrates, is neither gracious nor philosophic. On the other hand, as I noted above, Socrates was somewhat insulting at the beginning of their exchange (481c–482c), so I think we should not criticize Callicles sharply for this. Unlike Thrasymachus, Callicles admits he has made a mistake; but he faults Socrates for having uncovered it, and insists that it was clear what he really meant (489c). In fact his restatement is quite a shift. Before he was saying that it is just for the stronger to have more than the weaker, so that the way things are is the way they should be; now he is saying that the true meaning of stronger is better, and that he does not consider the many to be stronger in this sense or deserving of rule simply by virtue of bodily might. This is not to deny, as Socrates says (489d1), that it was fairly clear earlier that Callicles meant some such thing by "the stronger."[3] Nonetheless, once he abandons the claim that whatever is, is just, it is unclear that what Callicles describes should be called "natural justice," though he continues to use the phrase (490a7, 491e7).

Socrates asks Callicles to clarify who he says are the better (βελτίους) men. Callicles replies that he means the superior (ἀμείνους) men (489e).[4] Socrates declares that this clarifies nothing; but that isn't entirely true. Callicles has backed away from identifying the better with the stronger; saying that they are the superior, while far from adequate, does give some suggestion about what he now means. Nonetheless, it is striking how slow Callicles is to speak more precisely. Socrates asks if he means the more intelligent (φρονιμωτέρους), to which Callicles emphatically agrees (489e). Later he says that the better are also courageous, and specifies that they are intelligent regarding the affairs of the city (491b). It seems that he has not defined in his own mind exactly who the better are. To be sure, he has a vague idea; but he has not considered it explicitly.[5] I noted earlier that he seems to admire excellence apart from any particular idea of what it is, but this does not explain why he has not more carefully considered what it is. He is to some extent a man of action rather than words; but only to some extent, as we have seen. (We might consider how much more developed his thoughts are on the related subject of nature and convention.) His lack of clarity about the better men results at least partly from his eagerness to believe that power and virtue coincide. He avoids thinking about who the better men are because he vaguely senses that if he does, he might see that they are not the same as the stronger, and that men he considers better are sometimes weaker than men he considers worse. He is eager to take the world as it is without making futile claims about how it "should" be, but he can do so comfortably only insofar as he thinks "natural justice" is truly just.

Socrates says: "Many times, therefore, one man who thinks intelligently is stronger according to your argument than ten thousand who do not, and it is necessary that this man rule, and that those be ruled, and that the ruler have more than (πλέον ἔχειν) the ruled." Callicles confirms that this is what he means. "For I think that the just by nature is this, for one who is better and more intelligent both to rule and to have more than the lowlier ones" (490a).

Socrates seeks to clarify what Callicles means by the phrase "have more than" (πλέον ἔχειν), which Callicles used in his long speech, and which Socrates has reintroduced here. He asks if a doctor, being more intelligent about matters of food and drink, is therefore better and stronger about them, to which Callicles agrees (490b). Socrates asks if the doctor should have more food than others, because he is better; Socrates suggests the doctor will "pay a fine" if he eats too much. In a situation where food is scarce, however, a doctor might well wish to take what he needs rather than suffer deprivation along with everybody else. However that may be, Callicles replies that he is not talking about "food and drink and doctors and drivel." They repeat the exchange regarding cloaks, shoes, and farm supplies, at which Callicles exclaims, "How you always say the same things, Socrates!" Socrates agrees and adds, also about the same things. Callicles continues, "By the gods, you simply always talk without stopping about cobblers, clothiers, cooks, and doctors, as if our speech were about these people!" (490b–491a). He is irritated, as Stauffer notes, because Socrates' questions seem to "make a mockery out of something deserving of respect—the question of the true good that is sought and deserved by the men he most admires."⁶ Socrates did not actually mention cooks in this context, but he did speak of farmers, whom Callicles omits. Callicles probably does not despise farmers as much as the other craftsmen mentioned, since of course wealthy farmers are not considered mere craftsmen.

Socrates also treats farmers differently than the other craftsmen. With the others he asks if they should have more of the fruit of their labor. Regarding a man who is "skilled in farming, intelligent about land, and fine and good," Socrates asks if he should have more *seeds,* or more of a raw material of production, which is by no means an unreasonable suggestion (490e). However, Callicles does not notice this shift, which immediately precedes his accusing Socrates of always saying the same things. Socrates and Plato seem to be suggesting that in some contexts, the view that the better and stronger should have more than others is unobjectionable.

Callicles is slow to explain what the better and stronger ought to have more of, just as earlier he was slow to explain who the better and stronger are. He says later, when the focus of the conversation shifts from justice to moderation, that the man of courage and intelligence should satisfy his desires (491e–492a). He does not say that here, where the focus of the conversation is justice, probably because it is not obvious (even to him) that this is a fitting or just reward for superior ability at ruling. (It is not obvious, for example, that ability at ruling should enable a man to gratify himself sexually with whomever he desires.) The view that it is just for the better to have more can be a decent view of justice if one connects having more to being better, and thereby defines and limits the scope of having more. (One might, for example, think that superior ability at ruling entitles a man to political power and the honor that accompanies it.) Callicles does not wish to limit the rewards of virtue in this way; nonetheless, he is slow to claim that the better men should satisfy all their desires, no matter how low or exploitative. He shows a certain hesitation in making the leap from justice to "natural justice." He seems to feel (unselfconsciously) that there is something fitting in justice which is lacking in "natural justice." However, this does not lead him to question the justice of "natural justice," for two reasons: his eagerness to embrace what is without making claims about what should be, and his eagerness to embrace virtue without restraint. There is a tension between these two tendencies, but they work together in leading Callicles to feel that the rewards of virtue are great, even limitless. He believes, and wants to believe, both that the powerful are virtuous, and that the virtuous are powerful.

Thus he understands virtue in terms of ruling. He explains that he is talking about those who are intelligent "regarding the affairs of the city and how they may be well managed" (491b). In this context the phrase "well managed" (εὖ οἰκοῖτο) seems to imply the existence of a common good, or at least a good of the city as a whole, meaning that the virtuous do not rule solely for their own good. (One could interpret "well managed" to mean managed effectively with an eye to the advantage of the ruler, but this does not seem like the most natural reading.) Callicles is suggesting that it is just for the virtuous to rule in part because it is good for all if they do. We see again that he has not thoroughly considered or digested his radically selfish principles. He adds, "And not only intelligent but also courageous, being sufficient to accomplish what they intend and not flinching through softness of soul." Socrates responds by complaining that Callicles never says the same things about the same things, and contrasts this with Callicles' earlier criticism of him for always saying the same things. First Callicles said the better and stronger were the mightier, then the more intelligent, and now the more courageous (491b–c). Callicles responds that he means those who are intelligent regarding the affairs of the city and courageous. "For it is fitting that these men rule the cities; and the just is this, that these, the rulers, have more than the others, the ruled."

RULING ONESELF

Socrates then asks a surprising question: "But what in relation to themselves, comrade?" Since Callicles does not understand, Socrates explains, "I mean that each one rules himself. Or is there no need of this, that he rule himself, but only that he rule others?" (491c–d).

Why does Socrates turn in this direction? Callicles has now stated who he considers the better and stronger men to be. He still has not specified what these men ought to have more of, other than rule itself, but in his long speech he implied that they should have more of whatever they want (483d–484c). Apparently Socrates doubts that it would be particularly fruitful to pursue the question of why such men should have more of goods that are extraneous to political rule itself. Callicles evidently thinks they should because they can. While this fails to provide a standard that meaningfully obliges other people (despite Callicles' partial feeling that it does), it is not so obvious why rulers or potential rulers should refrain from pursuing genuine goods that are within their grasp. So Socrates turns the conversation toward what is good for such men themselves. Why does he do this by asking about the ability of the ruler to rule himself? He seems to suspect that Callicles will have radical and revealing things to say about moderation. As noted above, Callicles has hesitated to say it is just by nature for a ruler to satisfy his desires, no matter how low or exploitative. He is more confident, however, that behaving this way is good for oneself, as he makes clear when the conversation turns from justice to moderation.

When Callicles asks what Socrates means by ruling himself, Socrates replies, "Nothing complicated but just what the many mean: being moderate and in control of oneself, ruling the pleasures and desires that are in oneself." Callicles declares that Socrates is saying the moderate are the foolish, a response whose peculiarity scarcely needs underlining. Socrates claims that there is nobody who would not understand that this is not what he is saying, which suggests that he doubts Callicles' sincerity (491d–e). Callicles may indeed be playfully attributing his own opinion of moderation to Socrates.

Callicles continues, "How would a human being become happy while being a slave to anyone at all? No, this is the noble and just according to nature, which I am now telling you outspokenly: The man who will live correctly must let his own desires be as great as possible and not chasten them, and he must be sufficient to serve them, when they are as great as possible, through courage and intelligence, and to fill them up with the things for which desire arises on each occasion" (491e–492a). Callicles speaks here of the noble and just, not, as we might have expected from what he then says, of the noble and good, or the good and noble. He treats the just and the good as compatible or even equivalent, even though he does not believe in a common good or in a justice which is good for all; as I have noted, he tends to think from the perspective of the few for whom he thinks (natural) justice is good. What is striking here is that "the noble and just according to nature" seems more important to him than the good. Callicles seems to think both that the noble is whatever is good, and that the good is what counts; and that the intelligent and courageous pursuit of what is good shows one is noble or justly deserving of good things, and that this is what counts. Perhaps he would not state the latter thought, but it is revealed by such things as his speaking here of the noble and just but not the good. Indeed, this latter thought seems to be more important to him than the thought that the noble is simply subordinate to the good. It is characteristic of immoralists to pride themselves on their hardheaded rejection of illusory hopes for more than the world offers, and then (unselfconsciously) to raise their very rejection of such hopes into a basis for such hopes.

Callicles characterizes ruling oneself as a form of slavery—which makes sense to a limited extent. To rule oneself is to control and resist at least some of one's desires, which is arguably tantamount to enslaving part of oneself.[7] Someone might believe this is necessary even while thinking that living well ultimately consists of satisfying one's desires or some of one's desires. Callicles treats this rule or enslavement of part of oneself by another part of oneself as essentially similar to being enslaved to another person, which seems excessive. And he does not mention that if part of oneself is ruled or enslaved, then another part of oneself is exercising rule or mastery.

Callicles' positive view of desire is the flip side of his negative view of ruling oneself. He finds in desire the limitless vista for which he longs. When imagining the life of unchecked desire, he doesn't think of the frustrations and pains that would arise if somebody actually tried to live this way. (It is hard to imagine an older man having a similar view of desire.) As we saw when considering what he says about Xerxes and Darius, he feels that pursuing the limitless is in some way tantamount to achieving it. Moreover, while he admires the courage and intelligence required by the life he describes, he does not exactly view them as ends in themselves. He views the satisfaction of desire as the aim of and reward for these virtues, even though his admiration of them is stronger than his eagerness for the satisfaction of any particular desire. He feels that virtue must aim at something different in kind than virtue itself, something free of labor and pain in a way virtue cannot be; and he feels the virtues he admires are worthy of a limitless reward.

The aim of and reward for virtue must also be consistent with his disdain for conventional justice, which the satisfaction of desire obviously is. "For those for whom it is possible from the beginning to be either sons of kings or themselves by nature sufficient to supply for themselves some rule or tyranny or dynasty—what in truth would be more shameful and worse than moderation and justice for these human beings, and that they, who can enjoy the good things (and with no one blocking their path), should impose a master on themselves, the law and speech and blame of the many human beings?" (492b). Callicles is convinced of the folly of behaving unselfishly if one has the power to do otherwise. He considers desire to be selfish; yet he also seems in a way devoted to it, as he reveals when he describes how one must "serve" (ὑπηρετεῖν) one's desires (492a1). Callicles feels to some extent that desire is something large and limitless to which one gives oneself.

Callicles views moderation as a companion or form of (conventional) justice, the "law and speech and blame of the many," rather than a rule one imposes on oneself for one's own good. At 492c1 he treats moderation and justice as one thing, "this fine thing," speaking sarcastically. There is some truth in this view: Those who are immoderate are more drawn to unjust behavior than those whose desires are more limited or restrained. Nonetheless, moderation can of course be defended on purely selfish grounds, without regard to justice. Callicles' hostility to justice makes him suspicious of the claim that one benefits by limiting oneself to desires that can be satisfied justly. He suspects this claim is merely an attempt to justify or lead people to justice (as indeed it may sometimes be). His hostility to moderation is partly a result of his hostility to justice. However, it also, and more deeply, results from the longing for the limitless which I have considered.

Callicles speaks here of sons of kings (492b2). He had backed away from presenting the merely powerful as having a claim according to natural justice; but here they reappear. He is of two minds about the merely powerful, which reflects the fact that two somewhat contradictory opinions are joined in his view of natural justice. On the one hand, he thinks that what is, is right, or that the "justice of nature" is true justice. On the other hand, he thinks it is just by nature for the better to rule and have more. The latter opinion can draw him away from championing the merely powerful, but the former brings him back. The two opinions are more attractive in combination than either of them would be in isolation. The former, though perhaps unappealing in itself, enables Callicles to feel that the latter is not merely a claim about how things should be, but a description of how they are. However, the opinions don't really fit together; Callicles can hold both simultaneously only insofar as he believes that actual rulers are in fact better men. (One might perhaps find comparable pairs of uneasily combined opinions in people who are not immoralists.)

There has been no mention, either in this section or in Callicles' long speech earlier, of a good to which one might think rulers (or good rulers) are preeminently entitled: honor (τιμή).[8] (Callicles mentions being dishonored as an evil at 486c2, but dishonor is not simply the absence of honor, as he makes clear.) To be sure, when Callicles spoke of the "slave" who rises up to be "revealed as our master" (484b1), he implied that it is satisfying for a superior man to compel others to recognize his superiority; but this is not exactly honor. Honor presupposes a friendly relation and a common good between rulers and ruled. It presupposes an attachment to justice. Callicles (at least in his theoretical moments) believes that rulers and ruled are naturally hostile to one another. To love honor is to believe that others are, at least to some extent, competent and fair-minded judges of one's excellence. Callicles feels that others would like to harm one. Honor presupposes too much trust of one's fellow men for it to seem solid and attractive to him. He feels a certain harsh attraction to recognition in his theoretical moments, and a desire for reputation (δόξα) in his more practical moments, but the love of honor is absent. (Reputation seems higher than what we now call popularity, but lower than honor.) He thinks political men pursue lower things than honor, notably unrestrained satisfaction of physical desires for extraordinary men, and security, wealth, and reputation for ordinary politicians like himself.

Yet we might wonder if these things are really the reason for Callicles' interest in politics. Although he doesn't love honor, he admires courage and intelligence, particularly as demonstrated in political activity. He is eager to see men with these virtues flourish, and presumably to demonstrate them himself. A noble ambition is present to some extent; but he doesn't consciously devote himself to virtue. Indeed, he doesn't think it is virtuous to devote oneself to virtue. Perhaps one cannot think this unless one believes in justice as a virtue, in the virtue of selflessness or giving.[9] Callicles' distrust of the world makes him doubt that one will benefit through devoting oneself to anything. While it is natural to wonder if devotion or self-sacrifice is good, Callicles' distrust prevents self-conscious devotion from even arising. Nonetheless, he has some confidence that virtue will protect him from suffering injustice, and he nurtures an impossible dream of invulnerability to be gained through outstanding virtue. His feelings about virtue seem to draw him to politics more strongly than the lower aims he discusses. To be sure, the desire for security is something he discusses and actually feels; yet to a large extent he pursues security through pursuing virtue rather than directly. This suggests, as I have noted, that the security he seeks is not so much the limited security a person might actually gain as the more imaginary security of being protected because one is worthy or because the world smiles upon virtue. (Of course he pursues this sort of security precisely because he does not see it as imaginary.) In other words, he does devote himself to virtue, to some extent, unselfconsciously.

Socrates praises Callicles' outspokenness in attacking moderation. "For you are now saying distinctly what the others think but are unwilling to say" (492d). Who are these others? Are they the many whom Socrates cited in explaining what he meant by ruling oneself (491e1)? The view that ruling one's desires is not merely a regrettable necessity for those who lack great power and wealth, but choiceworthy regardless of power and wealth, may be limited to a few, perhaps only to philosophers. Perhaps only the genuine desire to see one's situation and its limits is capable of taming or ruling other desires, notably the desire to transcend those limits; or perhaps only the self-conscious desire to transcend one's apparent limits is capable of taming or ruling desires which unselfconsciously attempt to do so.

Socrates asks if Callicles is saying that one must not chasten the desires, but rather let them be as great as possible, "if one is to be such as one should" (492d). Callicles agrees. "Then those who need nothing are not correctly said to be happy?" Callicles replies, "No, for in this way stones and corpses would be happiest" (492e). Socrates' last question may refer to the gods, who are said to need nothing yet to be happy.[10] Callicles' reply seems to assume that there are no gods, but he might also deny that gods would be happy if they did exist. Might not a pleasant awareness of one's existence be possible for a god? But would that awareness be pleasant if existence was eternal and necessary?

Be that as it may, it is striking that Socrates (or Plato) initially lets Callicles' radical position on moderation stand without serious challenge. Callicles' point about stones and corpses is reasonable, and it is followed by Socrates' offering myths or images which he clearly does not expect to convince Callicles. Socrates comes to the first myth in a circuitous and complicated manner (he quotes Euripides, then a wise man, then the person who told or invented the myth, and then again the wise man who apparently told the myth to Socrates and interpreted it for him), and he presents it with less than his usual clarity (492e–493c). Moreover, its persuasive force relies upon an assertion about what happens in Hades. Socrates then concludes rather feebly: "Am I persuading you somewhat and do you change to the position that the orderly are happier than the intemperate? Or even if I tell myths of many other such things, will you nonetheless not change anything?" It is hardly surprising that Callicles chooses the latter response (493d). Nonetheless, Socrates then offers another myth or image, which is somewhat clearer and more effective, but which not surprisingly also fails to convince Callicles (493d–494a).

It may be that Socrates has a certain respect for Callicles' view of moderation. Perhaps he lets it stand for a few minutes because it has a partial truth to it, at least regarding what being without needs or desires would mean. Alternatively, or in addition, Socrates (or Plato) may proceed as he does in order to demonstrate (perhaps to Gorgias, as well as the reader) that Callicles cannot be convinced either by appeals to an afterlife as in the first myth, or by prudential arguments about the good as in the second. Callicles' attachment to immoderation is shaken only when the hedonism with which it is linked appears to deny the existence of virtue.

I noted the circuitous route by which Socrates arrives at the first myth. Euripides suggested that perhaps living is being dead, and being dead is living (492e). An unnamed wise man told Socrates that we are now dead and that our body is a tomb (σῆμα), a word which also has an older meaning of sign or defining mark, and that the part or aspect of the soul in which desires exist can be persuaded and can change or move.[11] The myth-telling man, punning with this persuadable (πιθανόν) character, called this part or aspect of the soul a jar (πίθον), and called thoughtless people uninitiated (ἀμυήτους), a word which may also carry a connotation of leaky.[12] "This man surely points out what contradicts you, Callicles: that of those in Hades—meaning the unseen—these, the uninitiated, are most wretched," for they carry water to their perforated jar with a sieve. The wise man interprets the myth for Socrates to mean that the sieve is the soul, and the soul of the thoughtless is akin to a sieve since it is perforated, meaning "that it cannot hold anything on account of disbelief and forgetfulness" (493a–c).

The jar is said to be the desiring part or aspect of the soul (literally, "this [thing] of the soul"). The jars of the thoughtless are perforated, which seems to mean their desires are difficult or impossible to satisfy, apparently because they do not persuade or tame them. The sieve is said to be the soul of the thoughtless, though the jar has been identified as part of the soul. Since it ministers to the desires, the sieve seems to represent the rational part of the soul, as distinguished from the jar, the desiring part of the soul; one might well consider the rational part of the soul to be the soul. A sieve is a fitting image for the rational part of the soul, since even thoughtful people cannot avoid allowing most of what they perceive to slip through their minds; at best we grasp and hold only large or important things. However, the thoughtless are said to carry water to their jar with a sieve, which is impossible, no matter how fine the mesh of the sieve. Perhaps the chief desire of the thoughtless is for something which is simply impossible to acquire, so their sieves are on an impossible quest. Moreover, Socrates says the soul of the thoughtless "cannot hold anything on account of disbelief and forgetfulness," which suggests greater permeability than we would expect from a functioning sieve; the soul of the thoughtless is perhaps perforated or pierced (τετρημένος) apart from or in addition to being like a sieve (i.e., it may contain a large hole or holes in addition to the tiny ones which characterize a sieve). At any rate, the myth suggests that thoughtlessness makes it impossible for people to satisfy their desires in two ways, by making the desiring part of the soul impossibly leaky or needy, and by undermining the soul's ability to gather the means to satisfy one's desires.

Socrates calls the second image a "likeness from the same school" rather than a myth (493d). Apart from this cryptic reference to the "same school," he presents the likeness on his own rather than as something someone has told him. "If each of two men had many jars, and those of the one were healthy and full (one of wine, one of honey, one of milk, and many others of many things), and the sources of each of these things were scarce and difficult and to be supplied for oneself with many difficult toils; the one man, then, having filled his jars, conducts no more supplies to them nor gives any heed . . . ." For the other man, filling the jars is equally difficult, but they are perforated and decayed, "and he is always compelled, night and day, to fill them, or he suffers the utmost pains." In this case, unlike in the first myth, Socrates spells out that the man with the perforated jars is intemperate, while the other is moderate (493d–494a).

The second image does not mention Hades, and generally seems somewhat closer to life as we know it, as Socrates suggests in calling it a likeness rather than a myth. Thus Callicles explains why he is unconvinced by the second image, but does not bother doing so with the first. His response to the second image shows that prudential appeals to the good will not shake his attachment to immoderation.

In the first image, people carry water to their jars; in the second the jars hold a variety of potables. In the first, the jar is the desiring part of the soul, and each person has only one. The second describes the "life" of each person, and each person has many jars. The soul is not mentioned, but it seems the jars represent our various desires or needs, and the man himself represents reason or the rational part of the soul. In the first image, intemperate people have both a leaky jar and a perforated sieve or rational part of the soul; in the second, only the jars of the intemperate man are said to be perforated. Thus the second image presents the moderate and intemperate man as differing in their jars or desires, but not in their thinking or rational faculties. In this respect the first image seems more realistic. Many or most desires are bound up with opinions; the immoderate desires that make people unhappy are generally less similar to hunger (where opinion plays little role) than to vanity (where it plays a considerable role).

Chapter 5

PLEASURE AS THE GOOD

Responding to the second image, Callicles says, "That man who has filled his jars no longer has any pleasure; indeed this, as I was saying just now, is living just like a stone, when one has been filled up, no longer either rejoicing or feeling pain. But living pleasantly consists in this, in keeping as much as possible flowing in" (494a–b). If much is flowing in, Socrates asks, must there not also be much flowing out? Callicles says yes. Socrates says, "You in turn mean some life of a stone-curlew (χαραδριοῦ), though not indeed of a corpse or a stone" (494b). This may refer to a bird that excretes at the same time it eats.[13]

In speaking of "keeping as much as possible flowing in," Callicles is thinking of pleasure and desire generally, not only of bodily pleasure and desire. He is speaking in terms of the image Socrates has introduced. Nonetheless, his use of a physical or bodily metaphor indicates that he thinks pleasure and desire generally can be understood in the same manner as physical pleasure and desire. In the same vein, he said earlier that the man who lives correctly must be able "to fill up [his desires] with the things for which desire arises" (492a). Desire is a void or absence of something we want or need, and pleasure arises through filling the void. This suggests that Callicles does not think of opinion as a critical element of desire. No doubt he would agree that people sometimes take pleasure in opinions, including false ones. (For example, a man might think he is secure when in fact he is in danger.) However, Callicles does not think desire (such as the desire for security) depends upon opinion, and he seems to think pleasures that depend upon false opinion or that falsely seem to satisfy desire are the exception rather than the rule. He does not view the desire for reputation, for example, as bound up with believing that if others think one is good, then one must indeed be good, and deserving of good things. It is not that he thinks this description is false; more likely he hasn't thought much about it.

One might wonder about the adequacy of the image of "keeping as much as possible flowing in" on other grounds as well. Some pleasures, such as eating and drinking, fit this image; others, notably male sexual pleasure, are better described as flowing out. Philosophy arguably resembles eating in this respect; but at least one important pleasure related to political life, the exercise of power, primarily involves something moving out. Love of honor involves both virtuous deeds moving out and admiration flowing in. Of course no image or metaphor is perfect, and this one clearly captures something. (A similar image is used in Plato's *Philebus*, where Socrates says that when we are empty, we love to be filled, and Protarchus agrees; but it is not clear there that they are discussing all forms of pleasure.[14]) Nonetheless, Callicles' readiness to use this imperfect image invites the suspicion that he hasn't really thought much about what pleasure is. He has given more thought to his rejection of justice than to his embrace of pleasure.

Indeed, Callicles seems to some extent to stumble into arguing for hedonism. In attacking moderation, he says that a man who lives correctly must let his desires be "as great as possible and not chasten them," and "through courage and intelligence" he must "fill up [his desires] with the things for which desire arises" (491e–492a). This does not exactly mean that all pleasures are good and all desires worthy of satisfaction, for he has in mind a certain sort of man with certain sorts of desires, as his disgust when Socrates later mentions self-scratchers and catamites makes clear (494d–e). He is eager to deny that justice and moderation should restrain the virtuous man's pursuit of pleasure. Since he has not considered any other basis of restraint, however, this leads him to championing hedonism.[15]

Socrates asks if Callicles means something such as being hungry and, being hungry, eating. Callicles agrees. Socrates asks the same question regarding thirst, and Callicles answers that he means that someone who has all the desires and can fulfill them rejoices and lives happily (494b–c). Socrates asks if someone is living happily who itches and has as much scratching as he desires. Callicles responds only by saying, "How strange you are, Socrates, and simply a popular speaker!" Socrates urges Callicles to answer the question, and Callicles says that such a man would live pleasantly. He does not say that such a man would live happily until Socrates specifically asks (494c–d); it seems unlikely that he really believes it.

Socrates draws out one implication of what Callicles has said. "Is this the case if he should scratch only his head . . . the culmination of such things as these, the life of catamites, is this not terrible and shameful and wretched? Or will you dare to say that these men are happy, if they have an ungrudging amount of what they want?" Callicles asks if Socrates is not ashamed to lead the arguments into such things. Socrates asks if it is he who leads them there, or rather the one who asserts that those who enjoy pleasure are happy, "and who does not distinguish among the pleasures what sort are good and what sort bad" (494e–495a). Socrates could have emphasized that Callicles' indiscriminate praise of pleasure compels him to praise lives that seem empty, instead of ones that seem shameful. However, the emptiness of pleasure as such was implied in the earlier question about scratching, which did not greatly disturb Callicles. If he had reacted more strongly to that question, Socrates might instead have examined the difference between pleasures that are good and those that are empty or insubstantial. He might then have criticized pleasure in terms of the need for self-consciousness in a good life, as he does with Protarchus in the *Philebus*.[16] Callicles reacts more strongly to the mention of catamites, and perhaps to the allusion to onanism. This is what leads Socrates to distinguish between pleasures which are good and those which are bad (495a2), with bad particularly meaning shameful (495b).

The fact that Callicles is disgusted by what Socrates says confirms that his hedonism is less considered than his political views. He feels some things are shameful even if they are pleasant (at least to some people), or that some things are shameful and therefore bad rather than bad and therefore shameful. Notwithstanding his radical principles, he has some notion of decency. Given his emphasis on manliness and the ability to take care of oneself, it is not surprising that he despises a physically passive and submissive activity. But how does this reaction sit alongside his love of the young man Demos? Does he feel no such desire for Demos? Given what Socrates has said—without any objection from Callicles—and what we know of Athenian practices, that seems unlikely. Does he understand himself as wishing to lead Demos into a shameful life? Perhaps he thinks it is not terribly degrading for a youth to engage in such an act a few times, or perhaps he has simply avoided considering the question. We don't know enough to judge.

It is perhaps worth noting that hedonism does not necessarily imply the desirability of a life of scratching, let alone of being a catamite. Obviously it is pleasant to scratch if one has an itch; but that does not mean one would choose to have an itch, which is as such painful. More importantly, the pleasure of scratching an itch, unless one takes "itch" in a very broad sense, is very narrow. Other activities engage our minds and faculties far more fully, which means they can provide much more substantial pleasure. To put it another way, while scratching a painful itch might in itself be intensely pleasant, any human being who for a whole day had no other sensation would grow thoroughly sick of it. Moreover, the deepest human pleasure is the pleasure of hope, since it addresses the deepest pain, our awareness of vulnerability and mortality. No merely bodily pleasure can be comparably satisfying. Callicles is right that hedonism means denying there is such a thing as a bad pleasure (495a5), but he doesn't see that it is nonetheless consistent with distinguishing between more and less engaging and satisfying pleasures.[17] I say this not to endorse hedonism but to cast light on the limits of Callicles' understanding of the position he champions.

Socrates asks if Callicles asserts that the pleasant and the good are the same, or whether some one of the pleasant things is not good. Callicles says, "In order that the speech should not contradict me, if I assert that they are different, I assert that they are the same" (495a). In other words, he doesn't really think they are the same—the reference to catamites has affected him to that extent—but he doesn't want to contradict himself. As Tarnopolsky says, Callicles seems to be "more concerned with how the immediate witnesses to this debate . . . will view his defeat at the hands of Socrates than he is with how he himself views the life of a catamite."[18] However, earlier Callicles admitted a contradiction and restated his position when he disagreed with a conclusion Socrates had drawn from his initial statement (489c), so he is not utterly incapable of admitting he has misspoken. While wanting to avoid this if possible, Callicles also seems to be curious to see where the discussion will go if he insists on hedonism. During the subsequent conversation, he seems engaged and genuinely considers at least some of the points Socrates makes. While he is disgusted at catamites, he seems to feel that this does not necessarily settle the question of hedonism. He knows that hedonism is championed by sophisticated people, perhaps including those who taught him to distinguish between nature and convention, and he may recognize that he himself has not thought carefully about the subject.

Strauss suggests that indifference to contradiction and a certain view of manliness cause Callicles to stick to hedonism. "To contradict oneself is of course not by nature shameful. That he shows by his own action. While to abandon one's view—for example, because these views have been shown to be self-contradictory—this is by nature shameful. Namely, why? . . . A sign of lacking manliness. You budge; you don't stick to your guns . . . he has a military view of intellectual battles."[19] He calls Callicles "the prototype of the man who cannot be persuaded."[20] While this interpretation casts some light, there are difficulties with it. Callicles later renounces hedonism when it is shown to conflict with his admiration of virtue (499b), and he earlier admitted that he had initially misspoken in defining the stronger men (note ἁμάρτῃ at 489c1). So he is capable of changing his position, and even of admitting he has made a mistake. On the other hand, the one time he admits having made a mistake, he blames Socrates for having heeded what he said instead of what he meant (489b–c). When he later renounces hedonism, he claims that in advocating it he was merely joking (499b). He does seem to feel, as Strauss says, that it is unmanly to admit one has erred.

However, it is incorrect to say that Callicles "is not ashamed to contradict himself."[21] Callicles actually says he is trying to avoid contradicting himself (495a5). Elsewhere he responds to being shown that he has contradicted himself by denying that he was truly doing so (489b–c), by angrily resisting the admission that he has done so (497a–b), and by claiming that he was joking (499b). These responses (which are not unusual, of course) surely indicate that he is ashamed of contradicting himself. Strauss seems both to overestimate and to underestimate Callicles. On the one hand, he does not acknowledge Callicles' attempts to conceal or deny that he has contradicted himself; on the other, he does not acknowledge that Callicles does sometimes change his position in response to realizing he has contradicted himself, or that regarding hedonism he is genuinely interested to see where the conversation will go if he sticks to his position. Nonetheless, despite feeling somewhat ashamed about it, Callicles doesn't seem to care deeply about contradicting himself. As he tells Gorgias, Socrates "asks small things, of little worth, and refutes them" (497b). He does not seem to feel that his views are really being put to the test, except on the question of hedonism, which is not of fundamental importance to him. (The mistake he concedes at 489c1 is in what he considers a merely semantic matter.)

Strauss asks "whether this dedication to opinions without any concern about the grounds of these opinions, and the perfect willingness to contradict oneself provided one does not retract these opinions, is not the characteristic of the vulgar mind."[22] I offer two objections to this suggestion. First, a person may be convinced of the truth of his opinions even if he cannot defend those opinions against a clever interlocutor. Callicles seems to feel this way at least to some extent when he says that Socrates "asks small things, of little worth, and refutes them" (497b). Second, those Strauss calls the "vulgar" often genuinely believe not so much that their opinions are correct as that they are the correct opinions to hold, the opinions that good people hold. More broadly, many people tend to view opinions less in terms of truth or understanding than in terms of conduct; but they are concerned that they behave in a manner that is genuinely good. Callicles' feeling that it is manly to stand one's ground, for example, implies a view about virtue, about how a virtuous man behaves. One might say that Strauss examines "the vulgar" (among whom he of course includes Callicles) on his terms rather than their own. This is not to deny that those who resist examining their opinions are less concerned with what is true than those who welcome such examination; but Strauss seems to overstate the difference.

However, Strauss is right that Socrates is unable to convince Callicles, even to the extent to which he convinces Polus or Thrasymachus. One reason for this difference is Callicles' feeling that it is manly to stand one's ground. Another is Callicles' doubt that words and speeches have a necessary or complete correspondence to the things they represent, a doubt he expresses in what he says to Gorgias about Socrates refuting small things of little worth (497b). In both respects Callicles differs from Thrasymachus and Polus, whom we might call intellectuals. Both of them feel comfortable with words and enjoy manipulating them. To some extent both of them experience words as mere play, which is not true of Callicles: He gives words more weight, but for that very reason he is more wary of them. His lack of interest in playing with words is shown by the mildness of his praise of Gorgias' rhetorical display at the beginning of the dialogue, while his taking words seriously is shown by his eagerness to consider the implications for how one should live of what Socrates says to Polus. He is a more serious man than Thrasymachus or Polus, but a less open one: more engaged by serious questions, but less open to considering that his answers to them might be mistaken (which means he is not truly or ultimately serious).

Indeed, to some extent Callicles is less open than Thrasymachus and Polus *because* he is more serious. Perhaps the deepest reason why he is less open is that he is less confident that the world supports justice in any form that might do him good. Thrasymachus and Polus both have confidence in the worth of their art, and a belief that practicing it makes them worthy. They are more open because they are more closed; their belief in the worth of their art enables them to question other beliefs with somewhat more security or complacency than Callicles generally feels. Less confident that the world has a place for him, Callicles holds more rigidly to the beliefs he does have and the limited sense of significance they provide. His beliefs are more exposed and more fiercely defended. This is also the cause, in part, of his greater wariness of words.

Socrates asks if Callicles calls something knowledge, and then if there is also courage, and Callicles agrees. Socrates asks if these two are the same or different, and Callicles answers that they are different. Socrates asks if pleasure and knowledge are the same or different, and Callicles replies, "Different, I suppose, you wisest man" (495c–d). He considers this a ridiculous question. Socrates asks if courage is different than pleasure, and Callicles asks how it could not be. "Let us remember these things," Socrates summarizes, "Callicles the Acharnian asserted that the pleasant and the good are the same, and that knowledge and courage are different both from each other and from the good." As Dodds notes, Socrates speaks in the form of a legal deposition, "in which the name of the deponent's deme had to be stated."[23] Callicles answers, "And does Socrates of Alopece not agree with us on these things, or does he agree?" Socrates answers that he does not, "nor do I think that Callicles will either, when he himself looks on himself correctly" (495d–e).

Socrates asks if those who are doing well have suffered the opposite experience than those who are doing badly. Callicles agrees. Socrates says, "So then if these things are opposed to each other, must one of necessity be in the same condition concerning them that one is in concerning health and sickness? For a human being is not, I suppose, healthy and sick at the same time, nor is he released at the same time from health and sickness" (495e). However, there is one thing which releases us "at the same time from health and sickness," at least if Callicles' apparent disbelief in the gods is warranted, namely death. If one suffers from an illness and then recovers, in some sense of course one becomes healthy; however, it seems more true to say that a mortal being as such is "healthy and sick at the same time." Recovering from an illness means becoming healthy (or more healthy) in a particular and limited respect. Socrates' question invites Callicles to affirm a fantasy of perfect health, something which could be possible only for a perfect and immortal being.

After a pause, Callicles takes the bait. First he asks what Socrates means. Socrates says one may consider any part of the body by itself as an example, and asks if one may be sick in the eyes at the same time that one is healthy in the eyes. Callicles answers, "Not in any way whatsoever (Οὐδ' ὁπωστιοῦν)" (496a). This response shows he does not doubt there is such a thing as perfect health. Socrates asks if somebody released from ophthalmia is at the same time released from health of the eyes. Callicles answers, "Not in the least (Ἥκιστά γε)," thereby showing that death is "not in the least" at the forefront of his mind (496a).[24] To be sure, the answers Callicles gives are not unusual; it is common, at least among the young, to believe in a state of perfect health, and to disregard our directedness toward death.

But have I not suggested that Callicles is, like all human beings, influenced by a sense of his mortality? An awareness of mortality or finitude looms in the background of his consciousness, not fully digested or accepted, yet nonetheless disposing him toward beliefs or hopes that it can be overcome or evaded. This is a common condition, one which is avoided only by those who confront mortality directly and become self-conscious, at least to a significant extent, about the importance it has for them. (Consider the medieval Christian injunction *memento mori*.) However, even those who do this generally fail to do so completely honestly and rationally. Mortality is a very tough pill to swallow; or rather it is impossible to swallow for almost everybody almost all the time. Our immoralists reject any self-conscious belief in a god or moral order which might address the problem. They thereby avoid some of the distortions that such beliefs introduce; but they also avoid the ability that such beliefs bring to confront to some extent a situation which is otherwise intolerable. Immoralists are less self-conscious about the importance mortality has for them than thoughtful believers in a just god or gods. They are less able to see and accept how much mortality matters to them because they do not (consciously) believe there is any escape from it.

Socrates asks if a person "gets and loses each [sickness and health of the eyes] in turn." Callicles agrees. Socrates asks if the same is true regarding strength and weakness, and speed and slowness. Callicles agrees in both cases (496b). As with health and sickness, however, it seems truer to say we are compounded of opposite things. The springs of our strength and speed are themselves in some sense sources of weakness. Each muscle is dependent on what constitutes it and on the nourishment it receives; its very strength entails dependency or weakness. In addition, a muscle's or a body's form both makes possible and limits what it can do. To be strong is in some sense to be weak. By the same token, to be weak is to be strong, but weakness or sickness can destroy all of one's strength, while strength can never destroy all of one's weakness.

This is beyond what we might expect Callicles to consider in the midst of the conversation; but it is striking that he agrees that we gain and lose strength and weakness, and speed and slowness, in turn. Our strength and speed generally grow during our childhood, peak in our young adulthood, and then fade as we age. To the extent that we get and lose these qualities in turn, this occurs in tandem with health and sickness (which we do gain and lose in turn to some extent), as well as fatigue and other passing conditions.

Apparently Callicles agrees here because he has in mind these passing conditions, rather than the fundamental human condition.

Perhaps Callicles would not so readily have accepted this way of thinking about strength and weakness or speed and slowness if Socrates had not first asked about health and sickness; nonetheless, anyone who had thought much about life as a whole would resist viewing strength and speed this way. Callicles does not experience our fundamental situation—as mortal beings who wax and then wane—as fundamental. This seems to be because he believes in a state of unmixed health and strength, a state where death is remote and need not be confronted, except the danger of death at the hand of others. Callicles not only assumes there is such a state, but also feels he experiences it; he would not take its existence for granted the way he does if he felt he did not partake of it. Of course all this is common among young men.[25] By contrast, the view that our health always partakes of sickness (in some sense) and our strength always partakes of weakness, even when we are young and healthy, entails awareness that our lives are fundamentally characterized by limits and directed toward death.

Socrates now asks about happiness. "And as regards good things and happiness and their opposites, bad things and wretchedness—does he get each in turn and lose each in turn?" (496b). Callicles agrees, both because the conversation about health and strength and speed has at the moment led him to think in this rubric, and because in some way this is what he thinks about happiness—as his view of health and strength suggests. (The fantasy of unmixed happiness both encourages and is encouraged by a similar view of these other, related things.) We have already seen that he feels his imaginary tyrant enjoys a state of unmixed happiness (484b). He does not feel he himself enjoys unmixed happiness, however, or that most other people do; he does not take it for granted as he does unmixed health, but fantasizes about it and perhaps longs for it, from a distance. Socrates says, "Then if we find some things that a human being is released from and that he has at the same time, clearly these would not be the good and the bad. Do we agree on these things?" Callicles answers, "I do agree, preternaturally so" (496c).[26]

There is obviously a tension between what Callicles is saying here and his view that pleasure is the good. (Of course the tension is more obvious to us than we could expect it to be to Callicles in the midst of a demanding conversation.) Socrates asks if being hungry is pleasant or painful, and Callicles says painful (496c). He says the same about thirst. Socrates then asks if all need and desire are painful. Callicles says he agrees (496d). Socrates asks if the thirsty man's drinking is pleasant, and Callicles says it is. "So then you are speaking of rejoicing during the drinking?" Socrates asks. "Very much indeed," Callicles replies. "When one is thirsty, that is," Socrates says, and Callicles agrees (496d–e).[27]

Callicles does not seem to have anticipated the conclusion which Socrates draws: "Do you then perceive the consequence, that you are saying that the man feeling pain rejoices at the same time, when you speak of the thirsty man's drinking? Or does this not come into being at the same time in relation to the same place, whether of soul or of body, as you wish? For, I think, it makes no difference. Are these things so, or not?" Callicles agrees (496e). Only the first question Socrates asks here is necessary to show the contradiction in Callicles' position. In fact the second question seems to muddy the waters. Socrates might be suggesting that if one looks closely, one sees pleasure and pain do *not* exist at the same time in relation to precisely the same place in the soul or body. As the thirsty man drinks, the pleasure of satisfied thirst replaces the thirst which preceded it at any given spot in his mouth or throat or appetite; pleasure succeeds pain, rather than being coincident with it.[28] Callicles does not notice this suggestion, probably because, as noted above, he has not examined pleasure very closely.

Even if this suggestion is valid, however, it remains true of course that we feel pleasure and pain at the same time, though perhaps not in relation to precisely the same place in ourselves. More broadly, as Callicles agrees, pleasure is bound up with pain. What he says about the good shows that he does not fully believe his own statement that pleasure is the good. He also believes in a good of a different character.

Nonetheless, if one wished to defend hedonism more effectively than Callicles does, it would be helpful to note that in relation to any particular part of our body or soul, pleasure succeeds pain rather than coinciding with it. Moreover, while it is true that pleasure is generally bound up with pain, different experiences have widely varying pleasure to pain ratios. However, considering pleasure to pain ratios is far from the pure or unmixed good for which Callicles longs; and one might doubt that anybody would really be content putting the search for a favorable pleasure to pain ratio at the center of his life. The desire for a pure or unmixed good, however unrealistic, is some sort of response to our mortality (albeit an attempt to transcend or evade it)—and however we vary, we all have some response to our mortality.[29]

Socrates reminds Callicles of his assertion that it is impossible for the man who is doing well to do badly at the same time. Callicles says he does assert this; he has not backed down in light of the consideration of pleasure. Socrates then reminds him that he has agreed that it is possible for a man suffering pain to rejoice. "So it appears," Callicles says, now seeing the contradiction (496e–497a). Strictly speaking, these two statements do not necessarily add up to a rejection of the view that pleasure is the good, since the second statement does not preclude the possibility that someone might rejoice without feeling pain, and this might be what "doing well" means in the first statement. Of course Callicles has agreed that all need and desire are painful, which suggests that pleasure necessarily involves pain (though he never actually says so); but it is noteworthy that Socrates presents the contradiction in a less compelling manner than one might have expected. I don't have an interpretation of this detail, except to suggest that Callicles might not agree that it is possible for a man who rejoices to suffer pain (as distinguished from agreeing that one who suffers pain can rejoice). He might somehow believe in a pleasure or rejoicing which is wholly free of pain, even though he has discussed pleasure in terms of relief from pain. (This is not an uncommon belief, especially among the young, who are sanguine and for whom pleasure is less bound up with pain than for older people.) Perhaps he has not self-consciously articulated this belief, yet it may nonetheless dwell in his mind; and this complete, unmixed pleasure may be, or be part of, the unmixed good in which he believes.[30]

Socrates concludes that rejoicing is not doing well, nor is suffering pain doing badly, so the pleasant is different than the good (497a). Callicles replies, "I don't know what sophisms you are making." He tries to stop conversing with Socrates, but agrees to continue at Gorgias' request. The exchange that follows concentrates on the view that pleasure ceases at the same time as pain, which Callicles does not dispute or reconsider. Socrates asks about thirst and hunger, where this view is arguably close to being true (497a–d). A more capable proponent of hedonism would likely speak of experiences where pleasure clearly outlasts pain rather than ceasing with it. In particular, we see again that sexual pleasure does not seem to be at the forefront of Callicles' mind, for in this experience (at least for men—I can't speak for women), the pleasure can outlast and dwarf the preceding pain of desire. This is especially true when one loves one's partner and believes oneself loved in return. Callicles may be too distrustful to experience love of another person this way; indeed, those who have this experience don't tend to view pleasure as the highest good. He is erotic in the broad sense, a man of strong desire, but not in the specific sense of being strongly inclined toward love of another person.[31] However, even sexual pleasure in a man who does not think he loves his partner can extend beyond the preceding pain of desire. It seems that even this experience is a relatively minor part of Callicles' life, whether because he is distrustful, or because (notwithstanding his hedonism) mere pleasure cannot satisfy him, or both.

Callicles is unconvinced by this refutation of hedonism. How is it possible for him not to be struck by the disparity between the purity of the good (as he sees it) and pleasure's coinciding with pain? Perhaps he is undisturbed because, as I suggested above, he also somehow believes in a pleasure which *is* a complete, unmixed good, even though he has not articulated this belief to himself. It is not the pleasure of the lover he has in mind, but that of the virtuous and powerful man, the man who in his view *deserves* unmixed happiness. So it is fitting that Socrates now turns to the relation between pleasure and virtue.

PLEASURE AND VIRTUE

Socrates asks if Callicles calls good men good because of the presence of good things, just as he calls those beautiful in whom beauty is present. Callicles says he does (497e). Socrates asks if he calls fools and cowards good men, or rather the courageous and intelligent. Callicles of course says the latter. "Have you ever seen a thoughtless child rejoicing?" Socrates asks, and Callicles says he has. When Socrates asks if Callicles has ever seen a thoughtless man rejoicing, Callicles says he thinks so, "but what of it?" Apparently he suspects that Socrates thinks there is a tension between this and the view that pleasure is the good, but he does not yet grasp it. Socrates asks if he has seen an intelligent man feeling pain and rejoicing, and Callicles says he has. "Which rejoice and feel pain more, the intelligent or the fools?" Socrates asks. Callicles says he thinks there is not much difference. "Well, even this is enough," Socrates says, implying that he himself thinks the fools rejoice and feel pain more than the intelligent. "And have you ever seen a cowardly man in war?" When Callicles says he has, Socrates asks, "When the enemies went away, which seemed to you to rejoice more, the cowardly or the courageous men?" Callicles answers perhaps the former, or if not, about equally. And when the enemies advanced, Socrates asks, do the cowards alone feel pain, or do the courageous too? Callicles answers that they both do, and when Socrates asks if they do so equally, he says the cowards perhaps feel more. "So then," Socrates concludes, "the foolish and the intelligent and the cowardly and the courageous men feel pain and rejoice about equally, as you assert, and the cowardly more than the courageous?" Callicles agrees. Socrates then asks if the good and bad rejoice and feel pain about equally, to which Callicles agrees. Socrates concludes: "So are the good and the bad therefore about equally good and bad? Or are the bad still more good?" (497e–498c).

Callicles exclaims, "But by Zeus, I do not know what you are saying" (498d), but there is clearly some weight to this line of questioning. Shouldn't there be more of the good in good people than in bad ones? To put it another way, shouldn't being good either be equivalent to, or tend to ensure, the experience of whatever is good? However, while the foolish and cowardly might feel more pleasure than the intelligent and courageous in particular situations, the overall ratio of pleasure to pain might be higher in the lives of the intelligent and courageous. Nonetheless, Socrates is pointing to a genuine disjunction between the way Callicles defines good men and the way he defines the good. True virtue must enable us to achieve what is truly good; or else what do we mean by calling it virtue? If pleasure is the good, then good people must be those who tend to experience the most of it.[32] In this light we see clearly that Callicles is not truly a hedonist; his admiration of men he considers virtuous is not based on their ability to achieve pleasure, a subject on which he seems to have thought little. Thus he does not even think to claim here that the men he admires live more pleasantly than others.

Callicles identifies pleasure as the good chiefly because he wants there to be some undeniable good which virtue enables men to attain, and he has no other suitable candidate. However, he does not truly believe that intelligence and courage are good only insofar as they produce pleasure. To a large extent, despite his partial immoralism, he believes in virtue the way most believers in virtue do: as something good in itself, something one should pursue whatever the consequences. Like most believers in virtue, he also believes that its presence makes one worthy of (other) good things; but calculation about gaining such things is not the basis of his belief in virtue. Although he might resist saying so, he believes not that virtue is noble because good, but that it is good because noble. This belief in turn enables him to believe (unselfconsciously) in a complete, unmixed good which truly virtuous men both deserve and attain. As I noted while discussing Thrasymachus, people are built to believe that one must give if one is to get; it is in giving to something beautiful like virtue, for *its* sake not our own, that we feel we may perhaps become worthy of getting something transcendently good. That good may encompass unmixed pleasure, but it bears little relation to pleasure and pain as we know them.[33] Callicles thinks (at least much of the time) that he believes in virtue in a mercenary manner, but the fact that he has not derived his view of virtue from a consideration of how to attain pleasure or any other good indicates that his love of virtue is actually more generous, and more erotic.

Since Callicles does not grasp the contradiction in his position, Socrates leads him over the same ground again, but with a different emphasis. Socrates asks, "Don't you know that you are asserting that the good are good through the presence of good things, and the bad of bad things? And that the good things are pleasures and the bad things pains?" (498d). Callicles agrees. Socrates asks if the good things are present for those who rejoice, to which Callicles replies, "How they could not be?" We might wonder why Socrates bothers to ask this question. It is probably to underline and prepare the conclusion that those who experience pleasure are as such good, which is somewhat counterintuitive. When Callicles first agreed that good men are good because of the presence of what is good (497e), he did not really grasp this implication; Socrates wants to be sure that he does now. "So then with good things present, are those who rejoice good?" Socrates asks, and Callicles agrees (498d). Callicles then agrees that bad things, pains, are present for those who suffer pain, and that "the bad are bad because of the presence of bad things." Socrates asks, "Are they who rejoice therefore good, and they who suffer pain bad?" Callicles replies, "Certainly." Socrates asks, "Those who do so more, more; and less, less; and about equally, about equally?" Callicles agrees. Socrates then again spells out the contradiction between this view and the admiration of virtuous men (498d–499b).

We see here another indication of the character of the moralism underlying Callicles' immoralism. It is not clear that he really thinks those who feel pleasure are as such good and those who feel pain are as such bad. In the sequel he readily gives up this view, and he may answer as he does here because he is still arguing for hedonism. However, he does seem to think that whatever the good truly is, it is present in those who are good; and likewise regarding the bad. As I noted above, this must be true in some way, or else calling men good and bad doesn't make any sense. Nonetheless, the role of chance, and more broadly the great limits to human power, are missing in this exchange. Callicles never says that a good man is capable at procuring pleasure, but can't always succeed. His repeated agreement that "the man who suffers pain is bad" (499a) is especially striking, since of course nobody lives without suffering pain. Callicles may not entirely believe that assertion; but he does seem to believe that something similar is true of whatever is truly bad (if not of pain), or that somebody is bad if he suffers whatever is truly bad. Alongside his immoralism is a belief in the complete coincidence of virtue and enjoyment of the good on the one hand, and vice and suffering what is bad on the other. This belief is not unique to Callicles; I think we are all somewhat disposed to such a belief, which is attractive to beings who are hopeful but aware of our fragility. Callicles' partial immoralism is in tension with this belief, but nonetheless bolsters this belief in him by concealing it and thereby preventing it (at least to some extent) from being tempered by his experience of life.

Once he accepts that hedonism is at odds with his admiration of intelligent and courageous men, Callicles gives it up, and tells Socrates that he was joking in claiming that he did not consider some pleasures better and others worse (499b). The claim that he was joking is obviously a feeble attempt to conceal that he has been refuted, though it is true he felt some reservation about hedonism. One may at least commend the cheerfulness with which he now gives it up, though it would have been better to do so without mocking Socrates. As noted above, Callicles feels it would be unmanly to admit he has made a mistake. To an outside observer, it might seem more manly to admit it than to deny it, especially in so obvious a case; but Callicles is hardly the only man to feel as he does. Moreover, like many people who are not naturally philosophic, he seems to feel he hasn't really made a mistake, or at least not as much of a mistake, if he hasn't admitted to one. Admitting a mistake gives it a palpable and undeniable reality which it doesn't otherwise have for him (though in this context his claim that he was joking may be too feeble to weaken that reality). To recognize that he has made a mistake in a matter of importance would make Callicles uneasy; such a recognition would call into question beliefs upon which cherished hopes rest, starting with his belief in his own virtue. In this too he is similar to many people. Hedonism is too important a subject for him to comfortably admit having made a mistake in embracing it, but (unlike natural justice) not so fundamental that he can't recede from that embrace.

This refutation of hedonism is much more effective than the earlier ones because it concentrates not on the nature of pleasure, which is not really very important for Callicles, but on the goodness of intelligent and courageous men, which is. As we have seen, Socrates' two myths or images had little effect on Callicles. The observation that his position implied that scratching itches or being a catamite would be a good life made some impression, but was not decisive. The argument that pleasure could not be the good because it ceases at the same time as pain made the least impression of all. Callicles initially embraced hedonism not so much because he was attracted to pleasure as because it seemed to complement and complete other beliefs he held more deeply: admiration of virtuous men, immoralism or injustice, and (less significantly) contempt for moderation. Having given up hedonism, he doesn't really have a general opinion about what is good apart from virtue itself, which he does not (self-consciously) see as an end or as good in itself.

We are now in a position to consider why Socrates shifts the conversation from justice to moderation (491d–492d) and then hedonism (492d–499b). We have seen that Callicles' opinions on these subjects are particularly questionable, and hence particularly revealing. Attacking his view of justice directly would not produce so effective or revealing a refutation, for it's not so unreasonable to think that better men should have more. The critical question (as Socrates indicates before turning to moderation, at 490c–491c) is, more of what?[34] Callicles' answer is, more of whatever they desire. The man who lives correctly "must let his own desires be as great as possible . . . and he must be sufficient to serve them, when they are as great as possible, through courage and intelligence" (492a). Unchecked desire is both the proof and the reward of superior virtue. Callicles' view of moderation and hedonism is in some sense the justification of his view of justice, the reward for excellence, the jewel in the crown. If the desires of the best men are limitless, then in pleasure they can find a limitless reward for their virtue; or so Callicles feels. However, he himself is clearly less moved by desire (at least as usually understood) than by admiration.

Callicles is confused about whether virtue is a means or an end. While he justifies virtue in terms of pleasure, his non-mercenary attachment to it goes deeper than this justification.[35] This non-mercenary attachment entails a hope that devotion to virtue will produce a happiness of a different character than mere pleasure.

NOTES

1. Apparently Socrates likes to overhear the conversations of others. As Strauss notes, when it was a question of deciding how to live, Callicles behaved in a manner similar to the one for which he criticizes Socrates: talking quietly with three others in a corner. "Even Callicles had to withdraw when he chose his way of life" (1957 class, 111). Of course Callicles emerged from the corner once he had answered this question to his satisfaction, and undertook what he considers the serious business of life.

2. As Stauffer notes, there are two ways to understand this phrase (*The Unity of Plato's Gorgias*, 96). Socrates turns both to what Callicles discussed first in his speech, and to what seems primary for Callicles, the foundation or starting point of his thought.

3. Socrates calls Callicles "demonic man" (δαιμόνιε) while making this observation. Perhaps he means to suggest that Callicles is in the grip of a belief about justice which seems to promise or uncover supernatural power.

4. There is not a large difference in meaning between βελτίων and ἀμείνων. Both adjectives are comparative forms of ἀγαθός, which means good, but ἀμείνων tends particularly to suggest more able. Above I translated ἀμείνω at 483d1 as better, because there it was juxtaposed with χείρονος, worse.

5. Cf. Stauffer, *The Unity of Plato's Gorgias*, 99, and Nichols, "The Rhetoric of Justice in Plato's *Gorgias*," in Plato, *Gorgias*, 143.

6. Stauffer, *The Unity of Plato's Gorgias*, 100.

7. Of course rule as such is not the same as enslavement, but that is because rulers (or good rulers) aim at a common good, and appeal to the reason of the ruled, and because the ruled might someday take their turn as rulers. Other than the pursuit of a common good, these considerations do not apply to one's reason ruling one's desires.

8. Leo Strauss, unpublished transcript of class taught on Gorgias [1963], IX, 24. A transcript of this class is available online through the Leo Strauss Center.

9. As I indicated in an earlier note, I don't disagree with Stauffer on this point. One might say Callicles embraces virtue, insofar as he denies there is any limit on what the truly virtuous deserve, but he does not self-consciously devote himself to it. One also might doubt it is truly possible to feel the virtuous are deserving without somehow devoting oneself to virtue; but this is the position Callicles tries to maintain.

10. Cf. Plato, *Symposium,* translated by Seth Benardete (Chicago: The University of Chicago Press, 2001), 202c–d.

11. Strauss notes that if we consider the older meaning of tomb (σῆμα), the myth suggests that "individuality is due to the body" (1957 class, 119). The soul which can be separated from the body, therefore, is not the individual's soul, and cannot experience happiness as an individual. Thus the myth seems to suggest, in agreement with Callicles, that the body and desire are part of whatever happiness people can attain.

12. Nichols, footnote 103 in Plato, *Gorgias*.

13. Nichols, footnote 107 in Plato, *Gorgias*.

14. Plato, *Philebus,* translated by Seth Benardete, in *The Tragedy and Comedy of Life: Plato's "Philebus,"* by Seth Benardete (Chicago: The University of Chicago Press, 1993), 35a–e.

15. Stauffer says that Socrates "foists on Callicles an interpretation of his position according to which pleasure should be pursued not only immoderately but also indiscriminately" (*The Unity of Plato's Gorgias*, 109). This seems to me an overstatement of a valid point. It is true that Socrates interprets Callicles' attack on moderation as an argument for the indiscriminate pursuit of pleasure, an interpretation which Callicles accepts (492e2). However, Callicles has already come close to championing the satisfaction of all desires without discrimination, and he apparently sees no reasonable basis for any such discrimination. Although he is not genuinely a hedonist, he is not reluctant to argue for hedonism.

16. Plato, *Philebus*, 21b–d.

17. Hedonism is of course consistent with viewing some pleasant activities as bad because they can be harmful, meaning harmful with an eye to their future effect in terms of pleasure and

pain. However, in such a case one is not exactly saying that the pleasure is bad, but rather that the activity, all things considered, causes more pain than pleasure.

18. Tarnopolsky, *Prudes, Perverts, and Tyrants: Plato's Gorgias and the Politics of Shame*, 81.

19. Strauss, 1963 class, X.14–15.

20. Strauss, 1957 class, 128.

21. Strauss, 1957 class, 132.

22. Strauss, 1957 class, 149.

23. Dodds, *Plato: Gorgias*, 308.

24. Stauffer offers a similar interpretation of this line of questions (*The Unity of Plato's Gorgias*, 113–14).

25. I think young women are less prone to these particular illusions.

26. The "preternaturally so" (ὑπερφυῶς) of Callicles' response is a rare moment in Plato which does not quite ring true to me. I don't quite believe that Callicles would give so vehement an agreement here, because I suspect Socrates' somewhat leading question would alert him to the danger of being refuted, and might inspire a vague sense that there is a tension between what he is now saying and his view that pleasure is the good. However, it goes without saying that my suspicion may well be misplaced. More importantly, it is clear that in some way, and quite strongly, Callicles believes that the good is not mixed or bound up with the bad.

27. Strauss notes that Callicles does not object here, as he had at 490d, to talking of food and drink (1957 class, 143). The difference seems to be that in the earlier context he and Socrates were discussing what superior human beings should have more of according to (natural) justice, a topic in the light of which food and drink seemed to be paltry matters, while here he is defending the view that the good is the pleasant, a topic which apparently does not seem as elevated to him. Of course it would be odd to refuse to discuss food and drink while talking about pleasure—but a true hedonist would not object to discussing food and drink while defining justice. The difference in Callicles' reaction supports our doubt that he really feels mere pleasure is the sole or chief reward due to outstanding virtue.

28. Cf. Plato, *Phaedo*, translated by Eva Brann, Peter Kalkavage, and Eric Salem (Newburyport, MA: Focus Publishing, 1998), 60b–c.

29. Some experiences, such as smelling a flower, are at least arguably pure pleasures, unmixed with pain. (Consider Plato, *Philebus*, 51a–e, and *Republic*, 584b.) However, they do not grip us deeply, for they fail to address our mortality, the awareness of which of course involves pain. Our most intense pleasures arise precisely through the hope or belief that our mortality is in some way transcended. What we seek by nature is not so much pleasure as the good; the greatest pleasure results from feeling that we have secured the ultimate good. On the other hand, especially as we age, many of us come to suspect that we can't really attain the transcendent good for which we long, and instead seek the *feeling* that we have it. In other words, many of us do move in the direction of hedonism as we age; but it is not our preferred or initial position.

30. A belief in unmixed pleasure or rejoicing seems to be attractive not so much because of the sheer pleasure involved as because of the freedom from evils that unmixed pleasure seems to entail; a being feeling unmixed pleasure is a being who is not worried about anything, or who has no worries. What is most seductive, in other words, is the image of anticipating a future free of pain or death.

31. Cf. Plato, *Symposium*, 205d.

32. As David Bolotin puts it, if one believes that one ought to pursue pleasure, then "the good man in the fullest sense will be the one who pursues what he ought to, either the most earnestly or skillfully, or else the most successfully" (Bolotin, "Socrates' Critique of Hedonism: A Reading of the *Philebus*," *Interpretation* 13/1 [January 1985], 3).

33. Stauffer says that Callicles' hedonism is part of an effort to deny, "even to himself, that he is concerned with any kind of virtue and any form of happiness beyond the enjoyment of pleasure" (*The Unity of Plato's Gorgias*, 116). This statement seems to me to understate Callicles' love of virtue, and to overstate how close he is to thoroughgoing hedonism. He never denies that he admires virtue, though it is true he doesn't (self-consciously) view it as good for its own sake. His concern for virtue is by no means wholly buried or unselfconscious, as we see

clearly when Socrates shows him that he must choose between virtue and pleasure (499b). As I suggested earlier, Stauffer seems to interpret Callicles in light of the view that virtue includes justice, but Callicles does not share this view (at least self-consciously).

34. Another relevant question is, better in what? However, pursuing this question directly would probably be less fruitful than the procedure Socrates follows. A person is revealed above all by what he or she deems to be an end, and Callicles thinks he considers virtue to be a means to some other end.

35. Stauffer treats the turn to moderation and then hedonism as caused primarily by Socrates' "education of Gorgias in a nobler form of rhetoric" (*The Unity of Plato's Gorgias*, 122). This seems incomplete at best. Stauffer does not make it clear that by attacking Callicles' view of moderation and hedonism, Socrates *is* attacking his view of justice, and at its most vulnerable point. This is a bit surprising since Stauffer deftly analyzes a comparable turn in the conversation between Socrates and Polus (*The Unity of Plato's Gorgias*, 54–55).

Chapter Six

Callicles Retreats

TWO WAYS OF LIFE?

In the previous chapter we saw that Callicles' enthusiasm for "natural justice" and disdain for "conventional justice" lead him to defend hedonism. Socrates challenges Callicles' hedonism with several lines of questioning, only one of which has much effect. That line of questioning begins with the simple suggestion that whatever is good must be especially present in men who are good. If pleasure is the good, then good men must be those who experience the most pleasure. Since Callicles admires intelligence and courage much more than the successful pursuit of pleasure, he balks at this conclusion, and repudiates hedonism. While he does not repudiate immoralism or "natural justice," the discussion of hedonism confirms that rejection of morality is not truly the basis of Callicles' views. More important is his admiration of virtue as he understands it, and his feeling that virtuous men deserve an unmixed and unlimited good.

While repudiating hedonism, Callicles mockingly claims that he has been joking. Socrates returns his mockery with greater justification, and says, "What you are now saying, as it would appear, is that there are some pleasures that are good, and some that are bad" (499b–c). Callicles agrees. Socrates asks if the beneficial pleasures are good and the harmful ones bad, to which Callicles agrees. Socrates asks if this means, regarding the pleasures of the body, that those which produce health or strength or some other virtue of the body are good, while those which produce the opposites are bad. Callicles again agrees. Mentioning an earlier agreement with Polus, Socrates asks if Callicles also agrees that it is necessary that all other things be done for the sake of good things, and Callicles says he does. Socrates says therefore it is necessary to do pleasant things and other things for the sake of good things, not good ones for the sake of pleasant ones, and Callicles agrees (499d–500a).

The questions Socrates asks here do not express the genuine basis of Callicles' repudiation of hedonism. Having embraced pleasure as the reward of virtuous men, Callicles turns away when he realizes that hedonism entails denying that they are truly virtuous. As we saw also from his disgust at catamites, he rejects hedonism out of concern for what is noble and base rather than what is good and bad. Socrates works with what Callicles explicitly gives him, however, which is Callicles' statement that all men "consider some pleasures better and others worse" (499b). Callicles has given up hedonism, but he has not given up immoralism. Nonetheless, his unselfconscious attraction to a moral standard is revealed in his agreeing to what Socrates says here. He does not suggest that pleasure is *a* good even if it is not *the* good, or that it tends to accompany what is good. (It is, for example, pleasant to be healthy.) Having given up hedonism, he seems almost ready to abandon pleasure altogether. His readiness to sever the good from pleasure suggests that he somehow believes in a good which is unconnected to pleasure, which is to say a good which has little relation to life as we experience it.

Something similar is suggested by Callicles' joining what Socrates presents as his earlier agreement with Polus. Socrates actually modifies that agreement in asking Callicles to join it. He and Polus had agreed that people do things that are themselves neither good nor bad for the sake of the good (468b). Here Socrates says: "For the sake of the good things all things are to be done, it seemed to us then. . . . And does it seem thus also to you, that the end of all actions is the good, and that it is necessary that all other things be done for the sake of that but not that [for the sake of] the others?" (499e–500a). In identifying what is done for the sake of the good, Socrates' restatement replaces actions that are themselves neither good nor bad (or are "between" good and bad) with "all" actions. This tends to separate the good from everything else, as if the good were something we pursue or to which we dedicate ourselves but which we do not actually experience. By contrast, in the earlier discussion Polus agreed with Socrates that "wisdom and health and wealth and the other such things are good" (467e). They treated good things as part of our experience. Moreover, Socrates adds "it is necessary" (δεῖν) in the restatement of his agreement with Polus, which in this context suggests a moral obligation.

I observed earlier that Callicles' non-mercenary attachment to virtue accompanies and makes possible a belief in an imaginary unmixed good. Here Callicles answers Socrates in a way that again suggests belief in a good that transcends pleasure as we know it (to say nothing of pain), and possibly an inclination toward devotion to that transcendent good.

Socrates asks if any man can distinguish what is good and bad among the pleasant things, or if this requires an artful man for each thing (500a). Callicles says an artful man. Following this reference to art, Socrates restates his earlier distinction from the exchange with Polus and Gorgias between "contrivances" which aim at pleasure, and arts which aim at the good. He exhorts Callicles "by the god of friendship" not to joke with him, nor to take what he says as if he were joking. "For you see that our speeches are about this . . . in what way one must live, whether the life to which you urge me on, doing these things of a man (τὰ τοῦ ἀνδρὸς δὴ ταῦτα πράττοντα), speaking among the people and practicing rhetoric and acting in politics in this way in which you now act in politics; or this life in philosophy; and in what respect it can be that this life differs from that one" (500a–c). Socrates proposes that they distinguish these two ways of life, "if these two lives are indeed two and distinct," and then examine their differences, and decide which of them one ought to live. Callicles says he does not know what Socrates means (500d). He may not see a reason for Socrates' linkage of the choice between the two lives to the distinction between arts which aim at the good and contrivances which aim at pleasure. Moreover, he may not see why Socrates thinks they need to distinguish the two lives, and he may be particularly puzzled by suggestion that it is uncertain they are in fact "two and distinct."

That surprising suggestion seems to mean something like the following. Callicles and Socrates have just agreed that one must pursue the good (499e–500a), so they agree about how to live in what one might consider the fundamental respect. This invites the question of how they can nonetheless have such different views of the good life, or, as Socrates says, "in what respect it can be that this life differs from that one." Perhaps the two lives do not genuinely differ in truly important respects; perhaps in this sense they are not "two and distinct." Socrates may have one or both of two quite different considerations in mind. Political life as Callicles understands it pursues a kind of virtue, a way of being noble or impressive, as Socrates indicates in describing it as "doing these things of a man." Socrates' uncertainty that the two lives are "indeed two and distinct" may indicate uncertainty that Callicles is genuinely seeking to be virtuous or noble rather than pursuing the good in an indirect (possibly confused) manner. On the other hand, Callicles has argued that the natural aim of political activity is one's own pleasure. Socrates' uncertainty that the lives are "indeed two and distinct" may indicate uncertainty that a life of pursing pleasure is truly different than a life of pursuing the good.

The latter suggestion is supported by Socrates' next question. He asks if Callicles agrees that pursuit of pleasure is different than pursuit of the good (500d–e). Callicles does. Strauss interprets this question as suggesting (to the observer or reader) that the fact that the good is different than the pleasant does not necessarily mean that pursuit of the good is different than pursuit of pleasure. One cannot pursue the pleasure arising from health, e.g., without actually pursuing health itself.[1] Thus the two lives Socrates is describing, the one pursuing pleasure and the other pursuing the good, might not be as different as he suggests. In the remainder of the *Gorgias*, Socrates offers a strikingly ascetic portrayal of philosophy, as a choice for the good instead of pleasure. Earlier in the dialogue, however, he suggested that philosophy is good and pleasant, or pleasant because good (458a). As Strauss suggests, the ascetic presentation of philosophy seems to serve a rhetorical purpose, but it also casts light on Callicles. Indeed, it serves its rhetorical purpose precisely by appealing to something in Callicles and readers of the dialogue.

As we have seen (in Chapter Four), while Callicles is thrilled by his vision of ruthless injustice or "natural justice," he does not seek to live by it, even in principle, apparently because it seems harsh and difficult. On the other hand, he is also (though less powerfully and self-consciously) drawn to an ascetic and somehow moral vision of how to live, as revealed here in his renunciation of hedonism in favor of an obligation to pursue a good which is remarkably detached from pleasure (499e–500a). Perhaps attraction to one kind of excess tends to be accompanied by attraction to its opposite. At any rate, the two ways of life that Socrates now proceeds to describe are best understood not as politics and philosophy, but as two opposing visions which both speak to something in Callicles.

Socrates presents in more detail the distinction he made earlier with Polus and Gorgias between artful practices, such as medicine, which aim at the good and have a reasoned account of how to achieve it, and other practices, such as cookery, which aim at pleasure and do not have a reasoned account, but merely experience of what works to that end. (One might wonder why there couldn't be a reasoned account of activities aiming at pleasure—as Socrates implies in stressing that these activities do not consider "the nature of pleasure or the cause" [501a].) Socrates asks if this seems true to Callicles, and if there are similar practices concerning the soul. Callicles, who has not shown great interest in the arts, answers simply, "Not I; but I grant it, so that your argument may be brought to an end and I may gratify Gorgias here" (500e–501c). Callicles' use of the word "gratify" (χαρίσωμαι) echoes the way Socrates has just characterized practices which seek nothing "other than to gratify" (ἄλλο ἢ χαρίζεσθαι). Callicles seems to be indicating a mild disdain for Gorgias' eagerness to hear the rest of the speech.

Callicles continues to participate in the discussion, though without particular eagerness. After a number of other questions about distinguishing between art and flattery, Socrates asks if tragedy aims only to gratify the spectators. If something is unpleasant but beneficial, he adds, does it "fight to say and sing this," whether the audience rejoices or not (502b). Callicles says that at least it is clear that it strives more for pleasure and gratifying the spectators; he seems not to wish to exclude the possibility that it might aim at improving them as well. Whatever his general view of the matter, when it comes to particular activities such as tragedy, Callicles apparently considers it better to try to benefit others than merely to gratify them.

CALLICLES' POLITICS REVISITED

Socrates then turns to a matter closer to Callicles' heart, rhetoric directed toward citizens in political assemblies. "Do the rhetors in your opinion always speak with a view to the best, aiming at this, that because of their speeches the citizens shall be as good as possible? Or do these men too strive for gratifying the citizens and, for the sake of their own private interest, make light of the common interest, and associate with the peoples as if with children, trying only to gratify them, and giving no heed to whether they will be better or worse because of these things?" (502e–503a). Callicles says that what Socrates is asking is not simple, since some say what they say "caring about the citizens," while others are as Socrates says. His answer suggests that Callicles distinguishes between rhetors who seek only their own good and those who care about the citizens; he does not precisely address Socrates' insistence that to pursue the common good means striving to make the citizens as good as possible. He does not seem to notice or take seriously this part of what Socrates says. Socrates replies that if the practice is double, then one part of it is flattery and shameful popular speaking, while the other is noble, "making preparations for the citizens' souls to be as good as possible and fighting to say the best things, whether they will be more pleasant or more unpleasant to the hearers. But this rhetoric you have never yet seen; or if you can mention one of the rhetors as such, why haven't you declared to me too who he is?" (503a–b).

Callicles replies with some vehemence, "But by Zeus I cannot mention anyone to you—not of the current rhetors, at any rate." Socrates asks if Callicles can mention "one of the ancients" through whose popular speaking the Athenians became better. Callicles says, "What? Do you not hear that Themistocles was a good man, and Cimon, and Miltiades, and Pericles himself, who recently came to his end, whom you too have heard?" (503b–c). Callicles clearly admires these men; he admires political men who cared for the Athenians. As I noted earlier, this is the clearest indication of the discrepancy between his radical selfish principles and his more conventional and moral views when he considers actual politics. However, he does not model his own political activity on that of the men he admires. He seems to view their goodness as belonging to a lost era. He probably thinks (perhaps correctly) that he himself would be lost if he tried to pursue the good of the Athenians with as little regard for his own good as these men demonstrated, for Athens is more corrupt than it was in their time.

Callicles' answer is revealing in other respects as well. The four men he mentions were all generals as well as rhetors; in fact, other than Pericles, they were all more famous and successful as generals than as public speakers.[2] Of course many prominent Athenian statesmen were also prominent generals; but some were not, such as Cleisthenes.[3] Though he himself seeks to be a speaker rather than a warrior and does not seem very interested in military matters (as we saw above in his selective quote from the *Iliad*), Callicles nonetheless particularly admires men who gained great victories for Athens. He finds their activity nobler than that of statesmen who were not generals. This may be because war involves risking one's life, which indubitably requires both courage and caring for the city rather than oneself; or it may be because a general fights for the whole city against foreigners, rather than championing one part of it against another. Perhaps both considerations matter for Callicles. Be that as it may, his admiration of generals underscores how much his views change when he turns from confronting fundamental questions to responding to his actual surroundings. One might view the general who successfully leads his people in battle as the very opposite of the tyrant who exploits them.

I also note a conspicuous omission, a prominent Athenian statesman and general who worked with Cimon and was probably more celebrated in Callicles' time: Aristides. Aristides was surnamed "the Just," and although Callicles admires the public-spiritedness of the four men he mentions, his selfish principles probably prevent him from admiring Aristides. His inconsistency regarding public-spiritedness remains, but is less glaring than it would be if he praised Aristides. The statesmen Callicles admires remembered their own good as well as that of Athens, which is not as obvious in the case of Aristides, who remained a poor man even when admired by all of Greece.[4] By contrast, Cimon grew wealthy as a statesman, though he shared his wealth in a manner which was widely praised and appreciated.[5] Themistocles grew wealthy in a more questionable manner.[6] Miltiades convinced the Athenians to undertake an expedition against Paros by promising to enrich the city, but according to Herodotus his true motive was the desire to satisfy a private vendetta.[7] (Herodotus is not invariably reliable, but it seems probable that Callicles did not view Miltiades in the same light as Aristides.) Pericles was wealthy before entering politics,[8] and is thought not to have enriched himself as a statesman;[9] but his harsh treatment of political opponents,[10] and his desire for personal glory,[11] show him to be less purely public-spirited than Aristides. Indeed, as Socrates indicates, many Athenians doubted that Pericles had actually benefited the city (515e). By contrast, Socrates himself mentions Aristides favorably in the final myth at 526b, even though he is no less susceptible than the other four to the criticism Socrates offers, that their difficulties with the Athenian people prove they were incompetent (515e–516e). Aristides was famously ostracized by the Athenians and sentenced to ten years' banishment, only three of which he served due to the Persian invasion prior to the battle of Salamis, at which time the Athenians invited all ostracized persons to come to the aid of the city.[12]

There may also be another reason why Callicles does not mention Aristides. The other four statesmen differed from him not only in thinking of their own good, but also in a willingness to treat other Greek cities harshly. I have mentioned Miltiades' behavior toward Paros; the case of Pericles needs no elaboration; Themistocles misled the Spartans in order to enable Athens to build her walls; and Cimon welcomed the desire of the allied cities to send money instead of ships, which paved the way for their eventual submission, not to say enslavement, to Athens. To put it another way, these four men (or at least three of them—the case of Miltiades is less clear) seemed ready to put the good of Athens above justice, which again was not as clear of Aristides. In his more conventional, moral frame of mind, Callicles seems to embrace civic collective selfishness. This position, common and even necessary (to some extent) though it may be, tends to invite the more radical principle which he initially articulates. If one seeks the good of one's own city at the expense of other cities, then why not seek the good of oneself at the expense of one's fellow citizens? At any rate, in his public-spirited as well as his radical frame of mind, Callicles is hostile to Aristides' strictness regarding justice.

Callicles mentions men from both dominant parties or factions in Athenian politics, the one which favored aristocracy or oligarchy (and tended to be pro-Spartan), and the one which favored democracy (and tended to be anti-Spartan). Themistocles and Pericles pushed the city toward democracy, while Cimon tried to push the other way. As we shall see, Callicles seems to belong to the democratic faction; but partisanship does not overwhelm his admiration of the outstanding men of Athenian history.

Before we confront Socrates' criticism of these four men, it is worth underlining that Miltiades, Themistocles, and Cimon all gained fame through fighting Persian emperors who sought to conquer Greece. It is likely that without Miltiades, and almost certain that without Themistocles, Athens (and perhaps all of Greece) would have succumbed to Persia. So these men did not merely provide "harbors, dockyards, walls, tribute, and such drivel," as Socrates suggests at 519a; they preserved the liberty, and therefore arguably supported the virtue, of the Athenians.

Socrates replies that these men were good "if true virtue is what you were saying earlier—satisfying both one's own and others' desires" (503c). This is not what Callicles said earlier; he spoke of true virtue simply as the ability to satisfy one's own desires (492a–c). "But if it is not this, but what we were compelled to agree in the subsequent argument—to fulfill those desires that, when sated, make the human being better, but not those that make him worse . . . then I don't know how I could mention any of these as such a man"

(503c–d). As Socrates concentrates on the distinction between satisfying desires and seeking to be good, an odd thing happens. It is now Callicles who praises men who are concerned for others (a shift which Socrates conceals in claiming that Callicles is falling back upon his earlier definition of true virtue), while Socrates is vague about exactly whose goodness true virtue pursues. What he says here is consistent with the thought that the truly virtuous man seeks to make *himself* better, as distinguished from satisfying his desires.

Callicles does not seem to detect this subtlety. It is not clear that he has even noticed the contradiction between his admiration of civic-minded statesmen and his selfish principles. Moreover, the implication of selfishness in what Socrates says is concealed by his continuing to present virtue in a somewhat ascetic or devotional manner.

Socrates proposes that they examine to see if any of the statesmen Callicles mentioned is indeed a good man. Socrates asks if the good man will say what he says not at random, but "looking off toward something" (503e). He tries to explain what he means by asking if craftsmen seek to produce a certain form in their work.[13] He speaks of painters, house builders, and shipwrights, all of whom make an "arranged and ordered thing." He then says of trainers and doctors, "they order the body, I suppose (που), and arrange it together." The latter assertion is questionable, for the body of course exists before any trainer or doctor works with it, and has an order which no artisan imparts. The trainer or doctor must work with that order or form. However, Callicles agrees, without particular enthusiasm; questions about art are not really his bailiwick (503e–504a).

After concluding that there must be arrangement and order for a house or a ship to be useful, with Callicles concurring, Socrates asks if the same is true of our bodies. Callicles agrees. Socrates asks about the soul. "Will it be useful when it happens to have lack of arrangement, or arrangement and a certain order?" Callicles replies, "From what preceded, it is necessary to agree on this too" (504b). His answer suggests that he has doubts about this conclusion, but does not see a problem with the procedure that produced it. However, while a house and a ship are tools which are made for men's use, it is less clear what it means to call a soul "useful," or whose use is at issue. Socrates does not refer to the good of the soul itself. Callicles' willingness to answer this question, albeit with some uneasiness, is connected to his lack of clarity about means and ends, and particularly about whether virtue is a means or an end.

Socrates asks what comes into being in the body from arrangement and order, and Callicles answers that he probably means health and strength. Socrates agrees and asks what arises in the soul from arrangement and order. Callicles declines to answer (504b–c). He does not mention happiness.[14] This seems to reflect his view that happiness is not an arranging and ordering but rather a gratifying; not a tightening but a loosening. While Callicles admires virtuous effort, he views it not as happiness or an element of happiness, but as the thing that enables a few to achieve (or to be worthy of) a happiness of a different character. The one place in the dialogue where he mentions happiness on his own initiative is when arguing that rulers should be hedonists (492c6). He makes clear that the happiness he describes there is not available to ordinary human beings like himself; it arises only through extraordinary ability or fortune. The efforts most of us can make, such as striving for arrangement and order in body and soul, do not produce this kind of happiness, which in turn is a lesser reflection of the complete unmixed happiness which Callicles unselfconsciously feels may result from devotion to virtue. Callicles' attachment to these imaginary forms of happiness gives rise to and, more deeply, arises from dissatisfaction with the mixed and limited happiness that human beings can actually achieve.

Socrates says again that the body's arrangements have the name "the healthy," and that these arrangements produce health. After Callicles agrees, Socrates identifies the soul's arrangements and orderings as "the lawful" and "law," asserts that they make souls lawful and orderly, and adds that "these things are justice and moderation." An obviously weary Callicles replies, "Let it be" (504c–d).

Callicles becomes somewhat more engaged when Socrates asks if he says that it is better for a worthless soul to be kept from satisfying its desires. Socrates further characterizes worthless as thoughtless, intemperate, unjust, and unholy. Callicles responds, "I say so" (505b). Presumably he himself would define the worthless soul differently, but he does not object to the way Socrates does, in part because he no longer wishes to contest that point, but also perhaps because he is not sure what he thinks about intemperance now that he has given up hedonism. He then agrees when Socrates asks if keeping such a soul away from the things it desires is punishment. Socrates concludes that being punished is better for the soul than intemperance, and Callicles replies, "I don't know what you are saying, Socrates, but ask someone else" (505b–c). This is the most hostile response he gives in the dialogue.

Callicles sees that he holds conflicting opinions about whether a person can benefit by being prevented from satisfying his desires. However, he feels sure that he disagrees with Socrates on the important point, though he might not be able to say precisely what it is. Although he has given up hedonism, and is not sure what he thinks about intemperance, he still thinks that whatever the good may be, it is good for oneself; and he thinks Socrates is advocating some sort of pious selflessness. He may also feel that Socrates is advocating something unmanly: accepting being punished rather than resisting or, better yet, being the one who punishes or harms others. He does not seem to notice the tension between these objections, or his own tendency to feel that one should be manly without considering whether it is good for one.

Socrates then speaks at length with little response from Callicles; I shall skip to the next point where Callicles says something revealing. After Socrates says that one must prepare a certain power and art in order to avoid doing injustice, Callicles gives a perfunctory agreement. Socrates then asks if, in order to avoid suffering injustice as much as possible, "one must either rule in the city oneself—or even rule as tyrant—or else be a comrade of the existing regime." Callicles heartily agrees. "Do you see, Socrates, how ready I am to praise, if something you say is fine? This thing you have said is altogether fine in my opinion" (510a–b). Fine it may be, but is it true? Is this the best way to avoid suffering injustice? It is true that a being whose power is truly absolute need not fear injustice, or anything else; but no human being has such power. Considering examples such as that of Pericles, one might doubt that being a ruler is the best way to avoid suffering injustice. It is perhaps best to be a "comrade" (ἑταῖρον) or supporter of the existing regime, but not a leader, not a conspicuous target for rivals or for opponents of the regime. As I noted in Chapter Four, Callicles wants to believe that it is difficult but possible to avoid suffering injustice; this tends to make him exaggerate the extent to which the ruler does so. However, merely avoiding suffering injustice is not truly all he longs for. The hope of being in a position where one need not fear suffering injustice is connected to an unselfconscious hope of complete invulnerability.[15]

Socrates continues, "In my opinion, each man is the friend of another to the greatest possible degree, who the ancient and wise said was the friend: like to like. Doesn't it seem so to you too?" (510b). Callicles agrees. "So then," Socrates continues, "where a savage and uneducated tyrant is ruler, if someone in the city is much better than this man, the tyrant I suppose would fear him, and he could never become this man's friend with his whole mind." Callicles again agrees. They then agree that the tyrant would also be unable to be a friend of somebody much lower than himself. Socrates concludes, "As a friend of such a one, then, there remains worth speaking of only that man who, being of the same character, blaming and praising the same things, is willing to be ruled and to be submissive to the ruler. This man will have great power in the city; to this man no one will rejoice to do injustice. Isn't this how it is?" Callicles again agrees (510b–d). We might wonder whether someone of the same character as a tyrant would be willing to submit to him; someone similar to a man who risks everything in order to become a tyrant might himself be the last man to accept such submission. While Socrates' formulation seems to assume that submission follows from similarity, it could be interpreted as leaving open the possibility that these are two *separate* qualifications for friendship with the tyrant.

Socrates treats blaming and praising the same things as tantamount to having the same character. He suggests that our characters are largely constituted by blaming what we blame and praising what we praise (in that order), which seems true; no other subject absorbs so much of our conversation as blaming and praising each other. One might wonder what good all this judging does us. The chief reason why we judge so much and with so much interest seems to be that we believe there is some sort of ultimate judgment or justice. It is clear that religious believers orient themselves toward some such judgment; more striking is that people who don't consider themselves believers do so as well, as they show by the prevalence of blame and praise in their conversation. Even people in liberal societies seem to feel that justice is not merely a set of rules we should follow for the sake of other, higher ends (such as a peaceful and prosperous society), but rather the validation or even aim of our lives, an ultimate or divine judgment. We blame more than we praise in part simply because it is more pleasant to look down than up, but also because we feel there is much in people that is blameworthy, at least from the standpoint of this ultimate judgment. It isn't easy to deserve what we want or need.

The doubt that we deserve all we hope for also leads in another, almost contrary direction. Longing for something beyond what we possess or feel we truly deserve, we come to hope that it will somehow be *given* to us. We hope therefore that the fundamental principle of the universe is *giving* rather than, or in addition to, justice.[16] This may be the deepest element of our attachment to justice as a virtue, to self-sacrifice or putting something before oneself. We hope that to those who give, much will be given; and uncertain as this seems, it is a more plausible route than any other to satisfying our longings. Whatever our doubts about giving, we surely don't expect much to be given to those who *don't* give.

However that may be, Socrates has raised a powerful objection to Callicles' way of life. The surest way to be a friend of the ruler is to resemble the ruler, so if the ruler is a vicious tyrant, Callicles' emphasis on avoiding suffering injustice implies that one should strive to be vicious oneself. Callicles might have raised the possibility of *pretending* to resemble the tyrant. No doubt it is easier to appear as one is than to dissemble, but if dissembling is the only way to avoid suffering injustice while living virtuously and well, then surely it is worth considering. (Socrates later mentions the possibility of imitating without truly resembling [513b]. He denies that this can produce "something genuine in friendship," but of course the aim would be to achieve ungenuine or dissembled friendship.) Why doesn't Callicles suggest this? The chief reason seems to be that he does not believe in virtue as a way of life apart from its ability to protect one. He thinks virtue aims at security and power, so he is not sure one should cultivate it if it endangers security. More broadly, he doesn't believe very strongly that there is happiness apart from the happiness of security and power. Thus he criticizes Socrates for endangering his life through his pursuit of philosophy. As we have seen, Callicles also unselfconsciously believes in an extravagant, limitless happiness for those who are extremely virtuous. But even that happiness seems to consist primarily of security and power; it doesn't clearly have much other content, as it might if he felt greater attraction to wisdom or beauty or even moderation or courage.

Nonetheless, Callicles has some sympathy with what Socrates says about the drawbacks of befriending a vicious tyrant, and some feeling that there is more to life than mere survival, as he will reveal at 513c, and as we have also seen in other contexts. However, such feelings do not really take flight in him; security and power are what appear solid to him and capture his imagination. In *Schopenhauer as Educator*, Nietzsche asks whether men's mediocrity is primarily due to fear or laziness. His answer is laziness.[17] However this may be regarding other people, Callicles is largely shaped by something more akin to fear than laziness—distrust. He does not believe strongly in the noble things that others love or admire, at least in part because he feels that those who pursue such things make themselves vulnerable.

THE INFURIATING THING

Socrates summarizes regarding the man who resembles the tyrant as much as possible: "Then for this man, not suffering injustice and having great power, as your argument goes, in the city will have been accomplished" (510d–e). The reference to "your argument" (ὁ ὑμέτερος λόγος) suggests that Socrates does not agree, perhaps because he doubts that those who resemble the tyrant are really safe from suffering injustice (tyrants tend to be distrustful, which often does not work out well for those around them), and probably because he doubts that this sort of "power" is true power. As Polus was compelled to agree early in his exchange with Socrates, a man with the power to harm others does not necessarily have a more desirable and genuine power: the power to benefit himself (468e).

Socrates asks if this man will have accomplished not doing injustice as well as not suffering it. "Or far from it, if he is like the ruler who is unjust and if he has great power alongside this man? Wholly to the contrary . . . his preparation will be aimed at being able to do as much injustice as possible and not to pay the just penalty when he does it. Won't it?" Callicles replies, "It appears so" (510e). This is a strikingly reluctant response for someone who was earlier celebrating tyranny as natural justice shining forth.[18] When he moves from the fantasy of a godlike ruler to considering a situation more like his own, he regards doing injustice as regrettable though possibly necessary. Socrates concludes, "So then the greatest evil will befall him, when he is degenerate and maimed in his soul through imitation of the master and through power." Callicles bursts out, "I don't know how you twist the arguments up and down each time, Socrates. Or don't you know that this man who imitates will kill that one who does not imitate, if he wishes, and confiscate his property?" (511a).

Socrates responds, "I know, good Callicles, unless I'm deaf—since I hear you and just now Polus many times and almost all others in the city; but you now hear from me: that he will kill, if he wishes, but it will be a base man killing a noble and good one." Callicles gives the revealing reply which I mentioned earlier: "Isn't this exactly the infuriating thing? (Οὔκουν τοῦτο δὴ καὶ τὸ ἀγανακτητόν;)" (511b). Callicles grants the possibility of a base man killing a noble one. In other words, he grants that virtue is not a sufficient guarantee against evils. Moreover, he finds it "infuriating" when this happens, which implies that it should not happen, that it is unjust. In other words, he believes in something like "conventional" justice. Further, the base man kills unjustly; the noble and good man does not. In other words, Callicles treats (conventional) justice as part of being noble and good. Despite his outspoken immoralism, Callicles feels with part of his mind or soul that justice is a genuine virtue which deserves to prosper. (He is, as Strauss notes, "a very complicated character."[19])

I raised above the question of whether Callicles views the good man as one who can protect himself primarily because this seems to him good, a strength, while vulnerability seems bad to him; or primarily because he finds it intolerable to contemplate that a good man can be struck with impunity. In other words, does Callicles become an immoralist because he believes in justice and grows frustrated at its weakness (both the weakness of individual just men and the failure of justice itself to protect them), or simply because he feels a good man is one who can take care of himself?

The "infuriating" comment clearly points in the "frustrated" direction. Stauffer views it as the key to Callicles' character.[20] Strauss offers a similar interpretation: "Plato means that . . . if you accept this principle, this principle of moral indignation and acting on it, you arrive eventually at this tyrannic life of self-indulgence . . . you adopt the methods of the wicked, and you become wickeder and wickeder."[21] Strauss suggests that Callicles' indignation leads him to wish to punish the unjust, or, since this is not fully possible, to ensure that their injustice does not give them any advantage over the just, which means allowing the just access to whatever advantages the unjust derive from their injustice, which must ultimately include the advantage of not being limited by justice itself. For Strauss, as for Plato, the only truly satisfying alternative to going down this path is to embrace an activity which is its own reward, and which therefore need not concern itself with indignation and punishment.

Of course Callicles does not understand himself as a frustrated believer in justice. On the contrary, he thinks that a man who cannot protect himself is contemptible, a slave for whom it is better to die than to live (483b). As I noted in Chapter Four, however, this itself is a revealing exaggeration. It suggests an animus against the inability to protect oneself which is consistent with having felt that a life characterized by this disadvantage was a possibility for him. (He would not exaggerate so vehemently the disadvantages of a life of manual labor, or of actual slavery.) Moreover, the "frustrated" believer in justice also cares about being protected, or else he wouldn't grow frustrated.

It might help to distinguish two types of frustrated believer in justice. One type initially embraces justice but grows frustrated or embittered upon seeing that the just are not protected by being just, and even suffer due to it. It is unlikely that somebody like this would speak about "natural justice" the way Callicles does. Such a person would probably feel that the justice in which he once believed has nothing in common with the "natural justice" Callicles champions. His former beliefs would be inadequately repudiated, and also misrepresented and even somehow inappropriately reduced, by talking about natural justice the way Callicles does. Moreover, Callicles views the ability to protect oneself as a virtue, not merely a necessity; in his view, this ability is characteristic of a true man (ἀνδρός) (483b1). He is not so much embittered about "conventional" justice as enthusiastic about "natural justice."[22]

Another type of frustrated believer would like to believe in justice but never really has, at least consciously. However, this disposition, which does seem to characterize Callicles, also implies some sort of belief in justice, as I shall consider below.

Callicles is attracted to (conventional) justice but frustrated by its weakness; and he also feels that a good man can take care of himself. The latter feeling is not simply an effect of the former, but is strengthened by it. To put it another way, some elements of Callicles' "natural justice" are rational and natural. Who can deny that it is good to rely upon oneself, or that it is natural that those who are virtuous have more in some way? But the fact that we need others—at the very least we need them not to attack us—compels us to rely upon "conventional justice" as well. The belief that a real man can rely solely upon himself is an exaggeration or distortion which Callicles embraces due to his distrust of others. (More precisely, he focuses upon self-reliance due to his distrust of others, and does so with enthusiasm due to the normal human hope of transcending all limits.) In this way his sense of the weakness of justice, his view of how the world actually works, leads him to embrace "natural justice."

Many believers in justice (though not the frustrated ones) see that being just is difficult, but still consider it worth the effort; indeed they do not believe there is ultimately any other way to flourish. Some think that genuinely good men are tough as well as just, and that they ultimately triumph over the bad. Callicles does not share this belief, but his "infuriating" comment suggests that he might like it if he could. Though he celebrates the immoralism of the rare unfettered individual, he is much less enthusiastic about the commonplace selfishness of ordinary people like himself. Moreover, despite his enthusiasm when discussing "natural justice," he does not seem to be a very happy man. That enthusiasm does not produce the sort of enduring hopefulness about life that believers in a more generous form of justice feel.

Part of what Callicles means by "natural justice" is that genuine virtue deserves, and attains, good things. He believes in justice as a moral order or way things should be, but not as an individual virtue. However, this belief does not produce much in the way of enduring hopefulness because it is not self-consciously generous. It lacks the element that is somehow the core of justice: putting something before oneself. It is hard to believe that one will receive what one hopes for if one does not believe one is giving or sacrificing in some meaningful way. Callicles' belief in natural justice does not wholly lack this element (it appears in his enthusiasm for the imaginary tyrant of superior virtue), but it lacks the self-conscious embrace of it.

It is worth considering why Callicles doesn't believe that justice (as a virtue) is difficult but ultimately rewarding, like courage, since it seems he might like to. His discussion of natural justice indicates that he does not believe in gods who protect or reward justice. His discussion of sons of rulers shows that he thinks selfishness is rational (492b–c). These beliefs surely militate against belief in justice; yet they don't seem like beliefs he has taken deeply to heart. Both of them, for example, are somewhat at odds with his enthusiasm for the virtuous tyrant he imagines. A stronger reason is his stance toward democratic claims about justice. I noted near the end of the discussion of Thrasymachus that immoralism and hostility to democracy often appear together, particularly in times of transition to democracy or a democratic social state. One might conclude that immoralism is a somewhat twisted reaction against democracy's hostility to making distinctions. The immoralist accepts that the older ways have been refuted; he does not believe in the gods who sustained and justified those ways, and he does not wish to ally himself with the aristocrats or priests who held sway in the past. However, in part due to views and experiences inherited from that past, he is disgusted with the democratic tendency to define justice as equality without regard to virtue and vice. He is not aware of a way of understanding justice that recognizes the importance of virtue without relying upon religious or other beliefs he finds incredible. So he embraces injustice, along with the virtues that he believes accompany it (such as intelligence and courage). He fails to notice the tension between his putative rejection of justice and his half-conscious belief that the truly better people deserve better.

This portrait fits Callicles to some extent, as shown by his disdain for the many and enthusiasm for his imaginary tyrant of superior virtue; but his ambivalence about justice goes beyond hostility to democratic leveling. His attachment to "natural justice" suggests that he brought to his experience of political life in Athens, and to his encounter with philosophy (or sophistry or rhetoric), a way of approaching these matters which was influenced but not created by those experiences.

Callicles' tremendous emphasis on protecting oneself points to trust in nothing so much as strength and power. He might like to believe in a meaningful form of justice, but for the most part he doesn't—not simply because some sophist or rhetor taught him that selfishness is rational, and not simply because he thinks men make claims about justice in order to deny virtue what it deserves, but more deeply because justice doesn't seem to him to prevail in the world. To an unusual extent for a young man who is neither enslaved nor impoverished, he experiences the world as a hostile and dangerous place. The only thing he feels one can rely upon is power. These feelings interact with a normal human attraction to justice (as a principle) in forming his view of natural justice; thus a man who cannot protect himself is a slave who deserves to die (483b).

Callicles' rejection of "conventional" justice occurs against the background of, and is probably confirmed by, the fact that imperial Athens rejects it too.[23] Moreover, a desire to justify the behavior of his city may contribute to some extent to his attraction to natural justice. However, this patriotic concern must play no more than a secondary role in shaping his view of justice, which is deeply inimical to Athenian freedom and democracy. What we might call private concerns, regarding security and vulnerability, virtue and power, play a much larger role—as revealed by his contempt of the many and their laws, his longing for a tyrant to arise, his admiration of Xerxes, his criticism of Socrates' vulnerability, and even his "infuriating" comment. In fact these private concerns largely give rise to Callicles' patriotism—as such concerns do in many people. His city is by far the most powerful force of which he is actually a part, and it provides much of the security he actually enjoys. He is not free of the normal human desire to belong to something larger than himself, and this interacts with his awareness of the security Athens provides him to produce a modest but genuine patriotism.

I have distinguished between justice as a virtue, putting something before oneself, and justice as the principle that a just person puts before himself. Callicles' attachment to natural justice, which is essentially a form of deserving or of justice as a principle, is limited by his disbelief in justice as a virtue. We have seen that he unwittingly mingles devotion with selfishness in his enthusiasm for natural justice; but he does not self-consciously devote himself. Natural justice neither invites devotion nor rewards those who offer it. Natural justice makes no promise that to those who give, much will be given. Since he does not think that giving is a virtue, Callicles does not self-consciously give himself to anything, and cannot seriously hope that he will be given what he longs for by any god or moral principle. Belief in justice as a principle ultimately seems to require belief in justice or selflessness as a virtue. How can one truly believe in deserving without believing that one should devote oneself to that which is deserving? The example of Callicles shows that it is possible to believe in justice as a principle without self-consciously believing in justice as a virtue, but the belief in justice as a principle is thereby constrained and attenuated.

It may be relevant that we hear nothing throughout the dialogue of Callicles' family, not even the name of his father. With other politically minded young Athenians who figure prominently in Platonic dialogues, such as Glaucon, Adeimantus, Polemarchus, Alcibiades, Charmides, Theages, and Cleitophon, we generally learn the names of their fathers and much else about their families.[24] Callicles is somewhat older than most of these other interlocutors, but not enough to wholly explain this difference.

One might think this difference is explained simply by the fact that Callicles is a fictional character, while these other young men are actual Athenians who come from actual families. However, we are by no means certain that Callicles is a fictional character. This seems to be the prevailing view among contemporary scholars, but I myself find plausible though not dispositive the case that Dodds makes for Callicles' actual existence.[25] More importantly, though, if Plato invented Callicles, nothing prevented him from also inventing a father for him. After all, we hear of his deme (495d3) and his three closest comrades (487c).

A better explanation is that the dialogue means to suggest that Callicles is less the product of his family than other young men are. Socrates does not refer to Callicles' father or other family members simply because for the most part they have not raised him or made him what he now is. Callicles seems to have inherited wealth, which suggests that his parents are no longer alive.[26] They may have died when he was young. He may have been left to fend for himself, which may have made him less trusting than many other young men. He may have reason to doubt that even a hard-headed embrace of justice protects one in the world.

Although outspoken immoralism is not widespread in America, Callicles is nonetheless particularly relevant to us today. In (apparently) lacking a secure, protective upbringing, he resembles a growing number of young Americans. With increasing levels of divorce and birth out of wedlock in recent generations, we have moved in a "Calliclean" direction. The lack of a secure upbringing yields more than the usual degree of uncertainty that one will be taken care of. Belief in justice, as both a virtue and a principle, consists largely of belief in a common good or a decent community which watches over its members, including oneself; uncertainty that one is cared for tends to produce uncertainty about the power of justice or the existence of a moral order in the world. While this uncertainty might not produce immoralism in someone who lives in a generally decent regime, it is hard to see how it can produce confidence that just behavior will enable one to flourish.

Young Americans who do not become immoralists may yet form a relatively thin and self-serving attachment to justice or morality, a condition which may affect them both as citizens and as human beings. Moreover, something like immoralism does seem widespread in that part of our country which is sometimes called the "underclass," where the developments mentioned above are most advanced.

Indeed, if we step back, Callicles casts light on another large question. What was so unusual about Greece in general and Athens in particular during the century which saw Socrates, Thucydides, Xenophon, Plato, Aristotle, and many other outstanding individuals? Clearly it is not adequate to say that ancient Greece had especially favorable natural or genetic material, for within a century of Socrates' death, it had become vastly less impressive and interesting. The existence of a multitude of free and independent cities in various ways stimulated serious thought; but that situation did not finally change until the Roman conquest about two centuries after Socrates' death. The example of Callicles suggests that an additional factor is involved in producing impressive human beings, a delicate balance of innocence and rude vigor on the one hand and sophistication or corruption on the other. Callicles seems to have a good nature, though not an outstanding one; but it will not reach the heights it might have. He is so wary of the world that his dearest hopes are concealed from himself, driven into indirect channels, and thereby diminished. We don't know exactly how he became this way, but his upbringing seems to have been characteristic of a time in which corruption has gained the upper hand over innocence.

More broadly, as peoples leave behind the difficult conditions and stern moral codes of their early times, sophistication and individualism grow. There is a flowering of outstanding individuals, or what some call "culture." But individualism undermines itself. When parents live for themselves, their children do not become all they can be; yet when adults live for their children, or for their faith or their regime or their city or nation, they themselves do not become all they can be. Indeed, the very act of freeing oneself from an old, stern, yet rich moral code is peculiarly conducive to the flowering of exceptional individuals. So only a generation or two can live at the peak of a people's potential. This doesn't address the question of why the peak in ancient Athens seems to have been higher than any other, but it may help explain why it was short-lived.[27]

However that may be, it seems unlikely that Callicles was ever very focused on punishing the unjust, contrary to Strauss' suggestion about Callicles' "infuriating" comment. It seems more likely that at a fairly early age he accepted the power of the unjust and the futility of wishing the world were other than it is. He might have liked things to be otherwise, but he embraced living in accord with how he thought they were. What is unusual is not his being impressed by power, but his confidence that power lies with the unjust.

We all have uncertainties on this score, but most people who grow up in decent families feel that power lies at least largely with the just, which enables them to concentrate less on power and more on justice.[28] By contrast, Callicles concentrates on power, and feels it is power that shows one is in harmony with the universe, not justice or selflessness—though he then turns out to have a certain selfless devotion to power and selfishness. He is excited about "natural justice" because it seems to him to promise the coincidence of power and virtue.

However, he cannot avoid being aware that the powerful are not really the same as the virtuous. Moreover, like all (or almost all) human beings, he is also attached to justice as ordinarily understood, as giving or sacrificing of oneself. The "infuriating" comment suggests that he might like to believe it is possible to be both just and strong; but this belief seems naive to him, and the one holding it seems vulnerable. However, to feel attracted to believing something is in some way to believe it. We don't feel attracted to beliefs that seem utterly impossible, e.g., that we are gods. If it really seemed impossible to Callicles that the just might flourish and be protected, if it really seemed like saying that one plus one equals three, it is hard to see that he would feel attracted to the belief. His feeling with part of his mind or soul that it is infuriating when a base man kills a noble one suggests that in some way, to some extent, he feels the universe should smile upon the just. As I argued in Chapter Two, the belief that something should be in turn suggests a belief that some moral order or force, some power, wants it to be so; which is to say, at least in some way, that it is.

Like most of us, Callicles is divided. We might say his life moves between two poles: attraction to power and attraction to justice. The attraction to power reflects and includes a kind of belief in justice (as a principle), a belief that the powerful are worthy and their power just, but this lacks much of what we generally mean by justice. It seems likely that as he ages (if he survives), Callicles will move in the direction of "conventional" justice, and his enthusiasm at unfettered power will weaken. However, this will not fundamentally be a movement in the direction of truth. Callicles thinks philosophy, with its distinction between nature and convention, supports his unjust principles; Socrates suggests that philosophy points in the opposite direction, to the justice which Callicles thinks he rejects; but neither alternative is really philosophy. Socrates indicates at the outset of their conversation that Callicles will always be at odds with himself if he never refutes the view that doing injustice is the worst of all evils (482b). Refuting that view might make consistency possible, but it can be done only by someone who is more drawn to truth than to the charms of justice. Callicles is not such a person. The two poles between which his life moves are both forms of attraction to justice, neither of which fully satisfies him. Both consist primarily of behavior he finds worthy or deserving. Natural justice seems harsh and cannot claim to reach beyond the grave—at least not explicitly or with any plausibility. Justice in the ordinary sense promises greater satisfaction, but is for Callicles less believable. Although he leans more in the direction of power than most of us do, his being torn between these two poles, and his dissatisfaction with each of them, are by no means unique to him.

NOTES

1. Strauss, 1963 class, XI.11.
2. Plutarch is my chief source of information about Themistocles, Cimon, and Pericles. Thucydides, though of course much closer in time to these men, is less informative about internal Athenian politics. Herodotus is my chief source of information about Miltiades.
3. Victor Ehrenberg, *From Solon to Socrates: Greek History and Civilization during the Sixth and Fifth centuries B.C.* (New York: Routledge, 1996), 90–103.
4. Plutarch, *Aristides* (New York: Loeb Classical Library, 1914), 24.
5. Plutarch, *Cimon* (New York: Loeb Classical Library, 1914), 4, 10.
6. Plutarch, *Themistocles* (New York: Loeb Classical Library, 1914), 25.
7. Herodotus, *The Histories,* translated by George Rawlinson (New York: Alfred E. Knopf, 1997), VI.133–6.
8. Plutarch, *Pericles* (New York: Loeb Classical Library, 1914), 7.
9. Plutarch, *Pericles,* 15.
10. Pericles helped arrange Cimon's ostracism despite, or because of, Cimon's services to Athens. He also accused some of Cimon's friends of Spartan leanings; to clear their names, they fought bravely against Sparta and were killed (Plutarch, *Pericles,* 9–10). Years later Pericles arranged for Cimon's son Lacedaemonius to lead an expedition against Sparta with insufficient forces; he hoped not merely to remove a rival but to feed the suspicion that he was a Spartan sympathizer. The maneuver backfired, however, and harmed Pericles himself (Plutarch, *Pericles,* 29).
11. See in particular Plutarch, *Pericles,* 13.
12. Plutarch, *Aristides,* 8.
13. Strauss notes that Socrates here uses the word form (εἶδος), but does not in this dialogue articulate the view that there are eternal forms which exist apart from the particular beings that participate in them. He does not even present philosophy as grappling with the forms, but instead stresses its rigorous adherence to justice. Strauss says that in the *Gorgias* "the peak— what Plato regards as the peak—is absent, deliberately absent" (1963 class, XII.6). Nonetheless, we can learn from the dialogue's portrait of Callicles about the conditions for openness to philosophy.
14. He also does not mention virtue, probably because he thinks Socrates is thinking of something which is an end not a means (consistent with his answer to the previous question regarding the body), and he himself does not view virtue as an end (though, as we have seen, he does not simply view it as a means either). One might also think the soul's order does not produce virtue but is itself virtue.
15. The relation between these two hopes or fantasies is similar to the relation between the fantasy of satisfying all desires, which Callicles believes to be possible for rulers (492a), and the unselfconscious and still more impossible fantasy of an unmixed happiness beyond desire.
16. Shakespeare expresses a similar thought in *The Merchant of Venice*. Speaking to Shylock while disguised as a jurist, Portia says: "Though justice be thy plea, consider this: / That in the course of justice, none of us / Should see salvation. We do pray for mercy, / And that same mercy doth teach us all to render / The deeds of mercy" (William Shakespeare, *The Merchant of Venice* in *The Riverside Shakespeare* [Boston: Houghton Mifflin, 1974], IV.1.195–8).
17. Friedrich Nietzsche, *Schopenhauer as Educator* in *Untimely Meditations,* translated by R.J. Hollingdale (New York: Cambridge University Press, 1992), 127.
18. Cf. Stauffer, *The Unity of Plato's Gorgias,* 143.

19. Strauss, 1963 class, XIII.13.
20. See Stauffer, *The Unity of Plato's Gorgias*, 117–18.
21. Strauss, 1963 class, XIII.14.
22. Stauffer writes that Callicles "yearns for justice to prevail by the virtuous receiving their due," and that this yearning has been buried by his "struggle with the problem of the vulnerability of virtue" (*The Unity of Plato's Gorgias*, 121). I don't wholly disagree with this, but I also think Callicles feels that genuine virtue is able to take care of itself.
23. This rejection is reflected in the speeches as well as the deeds of the Athenians, as we see in what the Athenian envoys say to the Melian magistrates before the destruction of Melos (Thucydides, *The Peloponnesian War*, V.89, 105).
24. See *Republic*, 327a–c, *Alcibiades I*, 103a, *Charmides*, 154b, *Theages*, 128c, *Cleitophon*, 406. Socrates identifies his interlocutor as the son of his father in the first sentence of *Republic*, *Alcibiades I*, and *Cleitophon*, while Theages's father Demodocus is the first to speak in *Theages*, and Charmides's older cousin Critias introduces him to Socrates in *Charmides*.
25. Dodds gives two reasons for doubting that Callicles is purely fictional. First, "There seem to be no clear instances . . . of purely fictitious characters with personal names introduced as speakers in conversation with Socrates." Second, Plato supplies many personal details about Callicles which "would have little point if he were fictitious" (*Plato: Gorgias*, 12). I myself find the first reason somewhat persuasive, the second less so. The strongest argument on the other side, it seems to me, is the anachronistic character of the dialogue, whose dramatic date cannot be fixed (17–18). However, it is not clear why this should make us think that Callicles is fictitious when Gorgias and Polus are not. As to why we have no information about Callicles other than what Plato provides in this dialogue, Dodds points out that he may have been a victim of political turmoil in Athens before he had a chance to achieve prominence, a fate to which Plato may be alluding at 519a—or, we might add, he may have died in some other way, or merely failed to achieve prominence. We surely do not know enough of ancient Athens to establish the nonexistence of anybody whose existence is not attested by multiple sources.
26. Among other indications, Callicles says that Gorgias is staying at his house (447b). Gorgias is the sort of man who would stay with somebody who lives well and is master of his household.
27. Two other possible sources of Athenian exceptionalism in this period are the transition from aristocracy or oligarchy to democracy, and the tension between democracy and empire. Like the existence of multiple independent Greek cities, the presence within Athens of vital and truly divergent views of justice and virtue stimulated thought. Of course the transition to democracy is related to the transition to greater sophistication or corruption.
28. I don't mean to suggest that our concern for justice derives from our concern for power, but it seems somewhat less basic or essential. Those who lack food scarcely think of anything else; likewise, those who lack security, and those who grew up lacking security, tend to concern themselves with justice less than others do (at least self-consciously), but power is attractive to them, for power promises security. Justice also promises a kind of security, but it is more questionable, especially to the distrustful, though also more transcendent. To some extent we concentrate on transcendent security when we feel confident of immediate security; but the picture is more complicated, for all people long for transcendence.

Chapter Seven

Socrates Concludes

LOVE OF THE PEOPLE

While Socrates does most of the talking for the remainder of the *Gorgias*, it nonetheless reveals important things about Callicles, especially in its concluding myth.

Socrates denies that a base man killing a noble and good one is "infuriating," as Callicles has said, "for him who has intelligence, as the speech indicates" (511b). After this somewhat ambiguous denial, he asks if Callicles thinks one ought to prepare to live as long as possible and practice those arts which save us from dangers, such as rhetoric. Callicles declares, "Yes, by Zeus, and I'm counseling you correctly!" Socrates asks if the science of swimming seems "august" to him. Callicles is emphatic about this too: "By Zeus, not to me at least." Socrates points out that it too saves people from death. He then speaks at length of the art of piloting, which also saves people and their possessions as well, without assuming an "august bearing" (511c–d).

One might think that while swimming and piloting are needful in a few particular situations, rhetoric is needful in most of life. However, this does not really respond to Socrates' point. If the other saving arts are lowly, how can rhetoric be admirable on the basis of its ability to save one? The answer is that Callicles does not really view rhetoric as directed simply at saving one (at least in this life). He admires rhetoric or the power it confers because of a different kind of saving, an imaginary transcendent saving; but he is not aware of this view in himself.

After speaking of engineering, which saves whole cities but which Callicles despises, Socrates continues: "For the true man, at any rate, must let go of living any amount of time whatsoever, and must not be a lover of life"

(512d–e). He thereby reminds us that Callicles takes his bearings from a concern which does not seem especially manly, the desire for self-preservation.[1] Socrates himself does not necessarily advocate manliness, as he indicates by suggesting "turning over what concerns these things to the god and believing the women's saying that no man may escape his destiny" (512e). He says one must instead consider how to live best in the time one has. "Is it by making himself like that regime in which he lives, and should you therefore now become as much as possible like the Athenian people . . . ?" Socrates suggests that the Athenian people and the regime are the same, presumably because Athens is a democracy. "For you must be not an imitator but like these men in your very own nature, if you are to achieve something genuine in friendship with the Athenian people—and yes, by Zeus, with the son of Pyrilampes too! . . . For each group of men rejoice at speeches said in accord with their own character and are annoyed at those of an alien character—unless you say something else, dear head" (512e–513c).

Socrates speaks powerfully here, but not altogether truthfully. It is by no means clear that those who succeed best at speaking to people are those who most resemble them, as the example of Pericles demonstrates. The most successful public speakers combine seeing as their audience sees, and seeing beyond. Indeed, the point of (intentionally) imitating the *demos* is not to achieve "something genuine in friendship," but rather to make the *demos* well disposed toward oneself. More broadly, Socrates' dismissal of self-preserving rhetoric seems rhetorical. He has conceded that such rhetoric can save one's life, which means it can be very useful even if it does not belong at the center of a sensible man's life. Nonetheless, Callicles is impressed, even moved. "In some way, I don't know what, what you say seems good to me, Socrates; but I suffer the experience of the many—I am not altogether persuaded by you" (513c). Callicles likes the suggestion that there is something higher than trying to sway the *demos* in order to preserve oneself. Apparently he feels some dissatisfaction with the way of life he pursues and praises.

Socrates replies: "Yes, for love (ἔρως) of the people, Callicles, which is present in your soul, opposes me" (513c). This might seem an odd suggestion when Callicles has just indicated dissatisfaction with the need to concentrate upon the people. Moreover, throughout the conversation he has expressed fear of the people and willingness to exploit them. He himself obviously does not think he loves the people.

Nonetheless, I believe Socrates is right. For one thing, Callicles has just (somewhat uncharacteristically) put the difference between himself and Socrates in terms of having "the experience of the many (τὸ τῶν πολλῶν πάθος)" (513c5). Whatever his contempt for the many, when he looks upon Socrates, he feels closer to them than to him. He feels some attraction to the way Socrates lives, but like the many he does not wish to set aside the concern to protect himself, or more broadly the concern for his position in the city. Resembling the people in this respect is not the same as loving them; but Callicles has also decided to enter politics. One might say he has shown what he loves in deed rather than speech. The desire for power is in some sense the logical conclusion of his concern to protect himself. Nothing inspires his confidence and even admiration more than power, and nobody in Athens has more power than the people. To be sure, Callicles also fears the power of the people, but he does not try to hide from it, or quietly appease it; he tries to woo it, and wield it.

To say that Callicles loves the power of the people is not precisely the same as saying that he loves the people; but it is not so easy to separate the two. Moreover, what Callicles desires or loves most deeply is not the power the *demos* actually has, but the power he imagines it has. He would not love a madman with a dagger, the example Socrates effectively employed against Polus (469d–e). That madman would also have the power to take one's life, but his power would be passing—he could use it only once—and limited. It would not seem to reflect anything larger; but the power of the *demos* does, for Callicles. (And for many other people.) In his mind, leading or dominating the *demos* confirms that one lives in accord with higher powers in which he is only vaguely aware that he believes, such as the "justice of nature" (484b1). The *demos* is therefore a kind of link with the divine. For reasons both real and imaginary, the *demos* is the thing that counts for him, so at least in some important sense he loves it.[2] Socrates spoke at the outset of his exchange with Callicles of a feeling that he and Callicles share, being lovers (ἐρῶντε) who love two things (481c–d). Socrates indicated there that the critical thing in Callicles is love, rather than political ambition or some other passion, and that his love of the *demos* is comparable in some way to Socrates' own love of philosophy.[3]

To be sure, Callicles also fears and despises the *demos*. His feelings are mixed or conflicted. The way he views the *demos* is not in every respect different from the way he would view a madman with a dagger. Admiration of virtue encourages his contempt of the *demos*, and he longs to see a man of "sufficient nature" rise up to be its master (484a). However, he understands virtue in terms of political power, the ability to gain power and also the simple fact of having power, meaning above all power with or over the *demos*; the *demos* is in a way the aim of virtue as he understands it. We have seen that he has some enthusiasm for power bereft of virtue, or some tendency to see mere power as a virtue. He does not feel a comparable enthusiasm for virtue bereft of power. He admires and loves virtue, but the people embody something he loves even more.

Of course love generally involves finding the beloved beautiful. We see no indication that Callicles finds the *demos* beautiful, but he seems to find power noble or beautiful. We might recall his statement that the "noble and just according to nature (τὸ κατὰ φύσιν καλὸν καὶ δίκαιον)" is for a man to let his desires be as great as possible and to be "sufficient" to serve them (491e–492a). For Callicles the noble or beautiful life involves being powerful enough to satisfy unrestrained desires, which (he thinks) is possible through mastering and wielding the power of the *demos.*

Socrates later asks Callicles if the Athenians are said to have become better because of Pericles, or rather to have been corrupted by him. "For I at any rate hear these things, that Pericles made the Athenians lazy, cowardly, babbling, and money lovers." Callicles tells Socrates that he hears these things "from the ones with broken ears," by which he means people of pro-Spartan and oligarchic sympathies (515e). (Such people tended to adopt Spartan pursuits, including boxing.[4]) Evidently Callicles is on the democratic (and Periclean) side of Athenian politics, despite the disdain he has expressed for the many, notably in his first speech (483b–484b). His love of the power of the *demos* is stronger than his disdain of its vices, and he feels little love for virtues which do not lead to power, so he is not drawn to the oligarchic, allegedly aristocratic party or faction, unlike some young men (including Plato himself in his youth[5]). His comment about the ones with broken ears suggests Callicles also feels the democratic faction is the more patriotic one.

Socrates then moves from what he has heard to what "I distinctly know, and you do too" (515e). Early in his political career Pericles was treated well by the Athenians, but toward the end of his life, they condemned him for theft, and considered executing him. (Socrates does not mention that they later reconsidered and restored him to office.[6]) Callicles asks if this makes Pericles bad, without seeming to realize that Socrates' point was not the merit of the accusation, but simply the fact that it was made. "A caretaker of asses, horses, or oxen, at any rate, who was of this sort, would seem to be bad, if when he took them over, they neither kicked nor butted nor bit him, but then he brought them forth doing all these things through savageness." Callicles has nothing to say to this other than agreeing "so that I may gratify you" (515e–516b).

Socrates' comparison between engaging in politics and taming animals suggests a much lower goal for political activity than his earlier demand that Callicles tell whom he has made "noble and good" (515a).[7] Even so, Socrates still seems unrealistically demanding—as he himself suggests in the sequel, where he makes similar criticisms of the three other figures Callicles mentioned by citing similar difficulties they experienced with the Athenians (516d–e). These difficulties suggest that the Athenians were not gentle when Pericles entered political life, but rather that managing them was always a challenging and delicate matter.[8] It might be more reasonable to commend Pericles and the others for managing the Athenians as well as they did than to fault them for the difficulties they encountered. Moreover, I hardly need mention that by Socrates' standard all four of these men were superior to

Socrates himself, since none of them was actually put to death by the Athenians; yet he will soon suggest that he alone of men living practices "the true political art" (521d).[9] His treatment of the men Callicles admires is more rhetorical than enlightening, though it has the virtue of raising the question of whether they improved the Athenians.

Socrates concludes that "we know no one in this city who has become a good man in political affairs." As for the four figures mentioned by Callicles, "if these men were rhetors, they used neither the true art of rhetoric—or they would not have fallen out—nor the flattering one" (517a). Socrates indicates that there is a "true" (ἀληθινῇ) art of rhetoric which aims at the good, not solely at pleasure, and that the good it produces can be one's own. Moreover, he suggests that flattering or producing pleasure can also be a matter of art, not mere "experience." Callicles does not notice these subtleties, which is not surprising given the pace of the conversation. In his response, he seems to concede that there may be something to Socrates' criticism of the four statesmen: "But it is nevertheless far from being the case, Socrates, that anyone of those today has ever accomplished such works as anyone you wish of these men has accomplished" (517a–b). Since Callicles champions political life as a way of protecting oneself, he can't wholly resist the view that the difficulties these four men encountered constitute an objection to their political or rhetorical skill. Nonetheless, he remains impressed with what they accomplished. He admires political greatness even if it does not protect one.

Socrates responds that these men were more "skilled in service" than the politicians of the current day, but no better at improving the citizens. He adds that he and Callicles have been doing a laughable thing, repeatedly being carried to the same thing and ignoring "what we are, each of us, saying" (517b–c). Socrates goes on to spell out what it is he has been saying that Callicles has ignored, but he does not specify what Callicles has been saying that he himself has ignored. Perhaps we can infer it from what he does say: "So I think, at any rate, that you have many times agreed and understood that this occupation concerned with both the body and with the soul is indeed a certain double one, and that the one is skilled in service, by which it is possible to supply food if our bodies are hungry, drink if they are thirsty, clothing, bedding, and shoes if they are cold, and other things for which bodies come to be in a state of desire" (517c–d). Here Socrates cites as desires genuine needs of the body, not mere forms of "flattery" such as cosmetics or pastry cooking. Perhaps he means to suggest that what he has been ignoring in what Callicles has said is the necessity of the thing for the pursuit of which Callicles argues, namely self-defense.

Socrates says that when it comes to the soul, Callicles seems not to have understood the distinction between arts which serve and those which improve. To illustrate this claim, he returns to a more tendentious description of the serving arts (though he does now call them arts, at 517e7). "If so they happen to do, they fill up and fatten the bodies of human beings, are praised by them, and will also destroy their original flesh" (518c). These human beings will later blame those who happen to be serving them when the harm becomes apparent. Likewise, Callicles is extolling "human beings who feasted these ones sumptuously on the things they desired," namely the statesmen he admires. "And they say that those men made the city great; but that it is swollen and festering with sores underneath on account of these ancient men, they do not perceive. For without moderation and justice they have filled up the city with harbors, dockyards, walls, tribute, and such drivel."

I noted earlier that this description is misleading, which is not to say it has no truth. "When that access of weakness comes, they will charge the counselors then present, but will extol Themistocles, Cimon, and Pericles, the ones responsible for the evils" (518e–519a). Socrates omits Miltiades, which suggests that he is criticizing in particular the establishment of the Athenian empire. Though Themistocles and Cimon distinguished themselves above all by fighting against the Persians, they also helped establish Athenian rule over other Greek cities, a project in which Miltiades did not participate. (He died soon after the battle at Marathon.) Pericles of course guided Athens to the peak of its imperial power.

Socrates warns Callicles that "perhaps they will attack you, and my comrade Alcibiades, when they are losing to destruction, in addition to the things they acquired, the original things as well" (519a–b). Dodds surmises that this warning may foreshadow or reflect the fate actually suffered by Callicles, as it does that of Alcibiades.[10] Socrates criticizes political men who blame their cities for treating them unjustly, and compares them to sophists who claim to teach virtue but accuse their students of doing them injustice by depriving them of wages and gratitude. This seems to imply that Callicles and Alcibiades will have nobody to blame but themselves if they are harshly treated by the Athenians, which is a bit odd, since Socrates has just suggested that Themistocles, Cimon, and Pericles will be at least largely to blame. Moreover, his criticism of political men and even of sophists does not take into account the intractability of the human beings they seek to lead or teach. At any rate, Socrates invites Callicles to respond, and after some prodding he does: "And you were the one who could not speak, unless someone answered you?" (519b–d).

In response to this apt question, Socrates asks if it is irrational to find fault with those one claims to have improved. Callicles says it is in his opinion. Socrates asks if Callicles hears "those who claim to educate human beings to virtue saying such things." Callicles says he does, and adds, "But what would you say about human beings that are worth nothing?" (519e–520a). Callicles' contempt for sophistry reflects his interest in practice over theory, or more deeply his desire for and trust in power. However similar they may be, rhetoric can help one to gain political power, whereas sophistry, like philosophy, might merely lead to "whispering with three or four lads in a corner" (485e).

CALLICLES' MYTH

Callicles says little for the remainder of the dialogue. However, the dialogue ends with what Socrates calls "a rational account, which you consider a myth" (523a), and it completes the picture Plato gives us of Callicles. Let us consider first what precedes it. The penultimate time he speaks in the dialogue, Callicles asks if Socrates thinks a person is in a fine state when he is powerless to help himself in the city. Socrates replies, "If, at any rate, he has that one thing which you have agreed on many times—if he has helped himself so as neither to have said nor to have done anything unjust as regards either human beings or gods" (522c–d). Socrates claims Callicles has agreed "many times" to this proposition, but in fact he has not done so even once. For one thing, the mention of gods in this context is new, and it casts the proposition in a new light. If our ultimate fate is decided by gods who are concerned about justice, then suffering injustice at the hands of men may be a relatively trivial matter. Moreover, Callicles (reluctantly) agreed earlier that doing injustice is worse than suffering injustice, but this implies that both are bad, or that one is *not* in a fine state if one is powerless to prevent oneself from suffering injustice (cf. 508e, 509c). Nonetheless, what Callicles agreed to, however reluctantly, points in the same direction as what Socrates now claims he agreed to. Moreover, Callicles indicated without reluctance that he finds it "infuriating" when a just man suffers at the hands of an unjust one. This implies, as we have seen, that he feels (at least to some extent) that justice should be protected. The longing for justice to be protected might suggest, as its culmination, a desire for protection so complete that suffering injustice is not genuinely an evil at all.

One obvious objection to the belief that doing injustice is worse than suffering it, and *a fortiori* to the belief that suffering injustice is not genuinely bad, is the apparent finality of death. While doing injustice may well be harmful, unlike suffering injustice it does not as such entail the possibility of loss of life, which at least appears to mean the loss of any possible future benefit. Thus it is fitting that Socrates concludes the dialogue by denying the finality of death. He says that no one fears dying itself, but rather people fear doing injustice, "for to arrive in Hades with one's soul full of many unjust deeds is the ultimate of all evils." He offers to tell a "rational account that this is so," and, in the last words Callicles speaks in the dialogue, he invites Socrates to do so (522d–e).

Socrates says he will offer "a rational account (λόγου), which you consider a myth . . . but I consider it as a rational account; for I shall tell you the things I am going to tell as being true" (523a). He doesn't say the things he is going to say *are* true. He says three times that he will offer a rational account or speech. This may mean that his account is rationally required by the belief that doing injustice is worse than suffering it. In other words, the account may show what else must be true for that belief to be true.

Socrates begins by noting that Zeus, Poseidon, and Pluto divided the rule among themselves after taking it over from their father; he does not mention the manner in which Cronos' rule was traditionally said to have come to an end, through a rebellion of these three sons against their father. "Now in the time of Cronos there was the following law concerning human beings, and it exists always and still to this day among the gods, that he among human beings who went through life justly and piously, when he came to his end, would go away to the islands of the blessed to dwell in total happiness apart from evils, while he who lived unjustly and godlessly would go to the prison of retribution and judgment, which they call Tartarus" (523a–b). This law reminds us of accounts or myths which appear in other Platonic dialogues, including the *Republic* and the *Phaedo*, and elsewhere. The common element is posthumous reward of the just and punishment of the unjust, which ensure the ultimate goodness of justice regardless of how men fare in this life. (It is not immediately clear how such a law can apply among immortal gods, but Socrates does not focus on this suggestion.)

However, the law was initially imperfect, for men were judged while still alive, by other men who were also alive. Pluto and those in charge of the islands of the blessed both complained to Zeus that people who did not belong were being sent to them. Zeus promised to put a stop to this, and diagnosed the problem as due to men being judged while still alive, and clothed. Many "who have base souls are clothed in fine bodies, ancestry, and wealth, and when the trial takes place, many witnesses go with them to bear witness that they have lived justly; the judges, then, are driven out of their senses by these men, and at the same time they themselves pass judgment clothed as well, with eyes and ears and the whole body, like a screen, covering over their soul" (523b–d). Zeus apparently focused on the bad men being sent to the islands of the blessed, not on the good men being sent to the underworld.

Zeus announced a threefold solution to the problem. First, men must stop foreknowing their death. Second, they must be judged when naked and dead. Finally, they must be judged by those who are naked and dead, so the judge may "with his soul contemplate the soul itself of each man immediately upon his death, bereft of all kinsfolk and having left all that adornment behind on earth, so that the trial may be just" (523d–e).

Zeus apparently prepared the first part of this solution before receiving the complaint of Pluto and those in charge of the islands of the blessed, for he says that Prometheus has already been told to stop this foreknowledge of death (523d7–e1). By contrast, in Aeschylus' *Prometheus Bound*, Prometheus is punished by Zeus precisely for preventing mortals from foreseeing their doom.[11] There Prometheus claims that Zeus resolved to destroy human beings, and that he himself defied Zeus and saved mankind. In addition, apparently as a separate deed, he removed from people the foreknowledge of their death by giving them blind hopes (τυφλὰς . . . ἐλπίδας). For all these things Zeus punished Prometheus.[12] In Aeschylus' account, it seems that Zeus, wary and hostile toward human beings, thinks that replacement of the foreknowledge of death by blind or false hopes—hopes built upon a failure to see—will make them less fearful and submissive to the gods.

In Socrates' account, there is no question of Zeus wishing to destroy men. Socrates' Zeus presents ending men's foreknowledge of death as part of improving the process of judging men. However, it isn't clear how foreknowledge of death would prevent men from being judged justly when they are naked and dead. The problem with foreknowledge of death is that it allows people to put on their finest clothes and adornments, gather their friends and relatives, and mislead or intimidate the judges; but this won't be possible when they are naked and dead at the time of judgment. The fact that Zeus has told Prometheus to end the foreknowledge of death before he hears the complaint of Pluto and those in charge of the islands of the blessed suggests that he may have another motive, one which he is inclined to conceal. Perhaps he thinks, contrary to what Aeschylus' Zeus thinks, that people will be more just and obedient to the gods if they hope to transcend death—a false hope, of course, since they will die whether or not they foreknow the day.[13] Socrates' account suggests that this hope is a more reliable foundation for just and pious behavior than fear of death or the gods. (By contrast, one might compare Aeschylus' account to the philosophy of Thomas Hobbes.[14])

Zeus announces that he has made his sons judges—two from Asia, Minos and Rhadamanthus, and one from Europe, Aeacus. Aeacus will judge those from Europe, Rhadamanthus those from Asia, and Minos will judge when the other two are at a loss about something (523e–524a).

Socrates says these are the things he has heard, and from them he himself calculates the rest of what he says. In other words, the rest of what he says depends upon the account of the divine he has given. Death is nothing other than the separation of body from soul. If a body is large or stout when a man dies, it remains so when he is dead. Likewise, if some rascal had scars from whippings when he was alive, or if somebody's limbs were broken, these things will remain on his body "for some time when he has come to his end" (524a–c). Socrates says that the same thing seems to him to hold for the soul. "All things are manifest in the soul, when it has been stripped naked of the body—both the things of nature and the experiences that the human being had in his soul through the pursuit of each kind of business." As in the earlier part of the account, the part which Socrates heard and from which he calculates what he is now saying, the soul somehow becomes visible once it is separated from the body.

As the judge lays hold of the soul of some king or potentate, he "perceives that there is nothing healthy in the soul, but it has been severely whipped and is filled with scars from false oaths and injustice, which each action of his stamped upon his soul, and all things are crooked from lying and boasting, and there is nothing straight on account of his having been reared without truth; and he sees the soul full of asymmetry and ugliness from arrogant power, luxury, hubris, and incontinence of actions." He sends it away to endure fitting sufferings (524d–525a). We might wonder how a soul which has no body "perceives" (κατεῖδεν) another soul which has no body. One might imagine the souls communicating by pure thought, but this too is mysterious. How does the judging soul view the one it judges? How is the soul being judged compelled to participate? How is it punished? How do other souls witness the punishment? However, I do not interpret this account as Socrates' genuine belief, so it is perhaps not worth concentrating upon such questions.

This depraved king's soul resembles the body of the rascal who was scarred with whippings, though of course his body has avoided disfigurement. The judge perceives and punishes injustice and incontinence; he does not seem concerned with lack of courage or wisdom.[15] Moreover, his primary concern seems to be to punish bad qualities, not to reward good ones. Both these features are consistent with the fact that the account or myth is presented as supporting the belief that it is worse to do injustice than to suffer it.

Socrates says it is fitting for those who are "subject to retribution" either to become better, or to be an example to others, so that those others may be afraid and become better. "The examples come into being from those who have done the ultimate injustices and have become incurable through such unjust deeds; and these men are no longer profited themselves . . . but others are benefited who see these men suffering on account of their errors the greatest, most painful, and most fearful sufferings for all time" (525b–c). Such men do not benefit from their punishment, for they are no longer capable of being benefited. However, if justice is good, then punishment which harms is unjust, which is to say it is not punishment so much as exploitation. (Souls which are incurable could simply be left alone.) Socrates' use of the term "retribution" (τιμωρία) alerts us to the un-Socratic nature of the presentation of justice which follows.[16] And even if one believes in the justice of retribution, it is not clear how eternal punishment can be just. Some might consider it just to punish Adolf Hitler for six million lifetimes, but what of six million times six million lifetimes?

Moreover, we might wonder for whom these eternally punished men will act as an example. They are said to be "spectacles and admonitions to those of the unjust who are forever arriving" (525c). However, according to this account, people who arrive in Hades have already lived unjust lives, and are now to be punished for them. The admonition comes too late for them. So for whom can these tormented incurables provide a salutary spectacle? The answer must be, for people still living who hear this account or myth, people such as Callicles. In other words, the account makes sense not as a description of something actually occurring, but as a story to be told. In this way the injustice the account presents is undone, for there is no actual eternal punishment. People are made more just by a tale which is strictly speaking unjust. (Of course if people think it is a tale rather than a description of something actually occurring, or if they think it is unjust, then it will lose its improving effect—and indeed it probably has little effect on Callicles, who presumably does not believe it is true.) This also accounts for the prominence of retribution in the account, for however unjust it may be, most people need retribution to assure them that justice is truly good and injustice truly bad. Moreover, since people hope for much more from justice than they really feel they have reason to expect (who can conceive of, let alone genuinely believe he has attained, freedom from death?), their hopes need the additional weight and plausibility that are provided by accompanying fears. It is hard to believe that the lot of human beings is eternal happiness no matter what they do; but many people believe (at least to a considerable extent) that the lot of human beings is eternal happiness if they are worthy, and eternal suffering if they are not.[17]

Socrates adds that the majority of the incurables come into being from tyrants, kings, and others who engage in the affairs of the city. "These through having a free hand make the greatest and most impious errors." It is difficult and worthy of much praise when "one who has come to have a very free hand to do injustice should pass through life justly." Socrates mentions Aristides as one of the few such who have come into being (525d–526b).

When Rhadamanthus encounters a corrupt soul, he puts on him a mark which indicates whether he is curable or incurable, and sends him away to Tartarus (526b). Aeacus does the same (526c). (One might wonder how a mark can be placed upon a soul which has been separated from body; but as we have seen, the myth works as a myth, not a genuine account.) "Sometimes, beholding another soul that has lived piously and with truth—a private man's or someone else's, but mostly, as I for one assert, a philosopher's who has done his own business and not been a busybody in life—Rhadamanthus admires it and sends it away to the islands of the blessed" (526b–c). Here we see most explicitly Socrates' presentation of the philosopher as the truly pious man, just and loved by the gods. This portrayal tends to incur the contempt of Callicles and men like him, and of many people to some extent; but Socrates (or Plato) judges it safer to be allied with people's pious hopes and trust in justice than with their doubts about the gods and justice. We might contrast this judgment with that of Pericles, who makes shockingly frank statements about the tyranny the Athenians exercise and who appeals to interest as the most solid and reliable thing in people.[18] The Platonic judgment, by contrast, is that people are well disposed to a man who seems particularly pious and just, even if they despise him a little, for such a man flatters their dearest hopes. People may feel more respect for a man who offers unjust and impious counsel, but such a man runs a risk, for his counsel is at odds with their dearest hopes.

Socrates says he has been persuaded by these speeches, and that he considers how he might show as healthy a soul as possible to the one who judges. He says Callicles will be as ill-prepared before "that judge, the son of Aegina," as he himself will be if hauled into court in Athens (526d–527a). Then he adds: "Now, then, perhaps these things seem to you to be told as a myth . . . and it would not be at all amazing to despise them, if we were able to seek somewhere and find better and truer things than they." However, Callicles, Polus, and Gorgias, "the wisest of the Greeks of today," have not been able to prove that one should live any life other than this one, which is also advantageous "in that place too," meaning the judgment after death. "But among so many speeches, the others are refuted and this speech alone remains fixed: that one must beware of doing injustice more than suffering injustice," and other things they have agreed upon. This suggests that the myth is necessary because of the inability of Callicles and the others to refute the claim that doing injustice is worse than suffering it; or, to put it in the terms Socrates suggested at the beginning of the discussion with Callicles, the myth is necessary because of Callicles' (unselfconscious) belief that doing injustice is worse than suffering it. Nonetheless, in this final statement Socrates omits the most questionable claims he made earlier. He does not say that doing injustice is necessarily worse than suffering it, merely that one must be more wary of it—which may be true even if it isn't necessarily worse, since it is a much greater temptation. Likewise, it seems sensible to assert that "one must take care not to seem good but to be so," and that one must "flee from all flattery, concerning both oneself and others." One might accept even the following statement, with the proviso that the punishment must genuinely improve one (which cannot be the result if the punishment is death, unless there is an afterlife like the one Socrates describes): "If someone becomes bad in some respect, he must be punished, and this is the second good after being just—becoming so and paying the just penalty by being punished" (527a–c).

The next sentence is perhaps the most significant of the myth. "Be persuaded, then, and follow me there where . . . you will be happy both living and when you have come to your end, as your account (ὁ σὸς λόγος) indicates" (527c).[19] Socrates says that the account or myth he has given is Callicles'. It supports and is implied by beliefs which Callicles himself holds. Of course Callicles holds other beliefs as well, as Socrates indicates in the final words of the dialogue: "Let us then follow this argument, and let us urge the others on to it, not to that one which you believe in and to which you urge me on; for it is worth nothing, Callicles" (527e).

CALLICLES' CHARACTER AND WAY OF LIFE

Callicles is a complicated character, but not wholly unlike other people. He believes exceptional virtue can overcome human frailty, but he does not think he measures up to this fantastic standard. He is excited by and in some degree even (unselfconsciously) devoted to a vision of exceptional virtue coupled with exceptional selfishness and ruthlessness; but he also finds this vision harsh and isn't really drawn to imitating it. He tries to take the world as it is, without making claims about how it should be; but he also thinks that those who approach the world in this spirit should triumph over those who do not. Although he does not think (in his theoretical moments) that virtue truly includes justice or morality, his vision of virtue is largely a moral vision, a vision of something he (unselfconsciously) takes to be good in itself, worthy of devotion, and deserving of flourishing. However, since his attachment to virtue does not self-consciously include devotion or justice or giving, it does not and cannot really seem to promise what he longs for.

Like many lovers of virtue, Callicles is torn between whether it is a means or an end. Happiness as he envisages it has a different character than virtue, one of effortless enjoyment rather than bold striving. This might seem to make virtue merely a means to enjoyment or pleasure; but Callicles admires virtue too much to view it this way. Although he might not put it this way, he views pleasure unlimited by justice or moderation as the fitting or just reward for outstanding virtue. This makes him hostile to moderation, and favorably disposed toward hedonism, even though he himself is not particularly pleasure-oriented. However, he relinquishes hedonism when Socrates makes it clear to him that hedonism implies the only true measure of virtue is pleasure or the tendency to experience pleasure. Pleasure is not truly the aim or basis of virtue for Callicles, but only its reward; and even this seems to be because he has not conceived of any other fitting reward, though he also has a vague intimation that outstanding virtue produces a kind of happiness consisting of all good things, including unmixed pleasure and more.

The one thing he loves more than virtue is power. Perhaps that is not so unusual; but the extent of his doubt that power lies with justice (as usually understood) is unusual. A sense of the harshness of the world probably led Callicles as a boy or youth to rely upon intelligence and courage to the exclusion of justice as a virtue, though his natural justice is a form of justice as a principle. He probably first viewed the virtuous man as *capable* of taking what he needs or desires, but as his awareness of mortality and vulnerability grew, this came to seem like being *worthy* of, perhaps even being *allowed* to, grasp more than the normal human share.

Callicles cherishes a fantasy or even hope of a self-made tyrant who rises up to be revealed as our master. His aspiration for his own life is much more ordinary, though still characterized by a certain sense of the harshness of the world. He desires reputation and livelihood, and thinks these will provide security and comfort; but his desire for reputation is also a moral desire, a desire to be confirmed as noble and good. He does not mention honor, however; he is too wary to long for something so bound up with justice. He is attracted to Athenian political figures of the past who he thinks were public-spirited but not exclusively so. His own political activity seems unlikely to be characterized either by noteworthy justice or generosity, or by extraordinary ruthlessness or independence.

Callicles relishes hearing the exchange between Socrates and Gorgias, and later is eager to articulate his own view of justice and his criticism of philosophy. On some points, notably hedonism, he is open to reconsidering his views. But finally he seems closed. Not thinking the world has much to offer, he defiantly holds onto the most important of the somewhat contradictory views he has, and the far less than fully satisfying hopes they make possible. For a young man of some gifts, he ultimately presents a somber and sad spectacle.

NOTES

1. Cf. Strauss, 1963 class, XIII.17.
2. Stauffer offers an interpretation of Socrates' remark about Callicles' love of the *demos* according to which that love is not so much a cause as an effect of Callicles' way of life. Callicles has chosen a way of life which necessarily involves assimilation to and service of the Athenian people, and "has thus, without being fully aware of it, formed an attachment to the *demos* that can even be characterized as a form of love" (*The Unity of Plato's Gorgias*, 147). I don't disagree with that, but I don't think it correctly interprets Socrates' remark here, in which he claims to indicate what it is in Callicles' soul that "opposes (ἀντιστατεῖ)" philosophy. Callicles is young enough that if he were attracted to Socrates and to philosophy, he would be able to leave behind the derivative love of which Stauffer speaks. Moreover, Socrates' remark is meant to remind us of his earlier remark about the πάθος that he and Callicles share (481c–d), and therefore of the fundamental similarity and difference between them. Socrates is speaking not of a derivative sentiment arising from the conditions of Callicles' life, but of an enthusiasm that grips and guides him as he chooses that way of life.

3. We might wonder why Socrates characterizes himself as loving philosophy (or the love of wisdom) rather than wisdom itself (481d4). Perhaps loving philosophy is an indirect but necessary way of pursuing wisdom, since one must practice a certain way of life in order to gain and nurture so delicate a fruit as wisdom. Socrates might point to this indirectness because Callicles' love of the *demos* is also an indirect approach to something he really loves, namely power or the invulnerability that power somehow seems to him to offer or denote.

4. Dodds, *Plato: Gorgias*, 357.

5. Plato, *Epistles*, translated by Glenn R. Morrow (New York: Bobbs-Merrill, 1962), 324c–d.

6. Plutarch, *Pericles*, 35–37.

7. Stauffer, *The Unity of Plato's Gorgias*, 154.

8. Strauss, 1963 class, XIV.8. As Strauss points out, Socrates thereby undermines the conservative critique of Pericles which he himself mentioned earlier; it is not true that the Athenians were gentle and just until Pericles corrupted them.

9. Cf. Xenophon, *Symposium*, in *The Shorter Socratic Writings: Apology of Socrates to the Jury, Oeconomicus, and Symposium*, edited by Robert C. Bartlett (Ithaca: Cornell University Press, 1996), IV.5. After Antisthenes criticizes Callias for being able to make men just toward others but not toward himself, Socrates defends Callias.

10. Dodds, *Plato: Gorgias*, 13, 364.

11. Cf. Nichols, footnote 168 in Plato, *Gorgias*.

12. Aeschylus, *Prometheus Bound*, edited and translated by A.J. Podlecki (Oxford, UK: Oxbow Books, 2005), lines 226–56.

13. Strauss, 1957 class, 205.

14. Cf. Frederick Douglass, *Narrative of the Life of Frederick Douglass, an American Slave* (New York: Barnes and Noble Classics, 2003), 63. Douglass describes how as a young slave he considered killing himself and the particularly harsh master under whom he then served. He says he was prevented "by a combination of hope and fear."

15. Strauss, 1957 class, 206.

16. Stauffer, *The Unity of Plato's Gorgias*, 172.

17. In the Christian view, no human being deserves salvation, which occurs through God's grace; nonetheless, people can make themselves more or less worthy in God's eyes. As Jesus tells a sinner, "Your faith has saved you" (*The Bible*, Revised Standard Version, New York: American Bible Society, 1980, Luke 7:50).

18. Consider Thucydides, *The Peloponnesian War*, II.63.

19. There is variation in the manuscripts at this point. Dodds rejects the arresting adjective "your," following one manuscript which by his account is not in general particularly reliable (F); as he indicates, the three oldest and most reliable manuscripts (B, T, and W) all contain σὸς (*Plato: Gorgias*, 187, 385). I believe Dodds's rejection stems from a failure to appreciate the extent to which the myth, and more broadly the entire exchange between Callicles and Socrates, expose Callicles' own beliefs.

Chapter Eight

Other Tough Guys

DOSTOEVSKY'S RASKOLNIKOV

In this chapter I shall examine presentations of tough guys or immoralists by authors other than Plato in order to see whether and how the Platonic analysis applies. It is of course beyond my scope to examine all immoralists in literature or Western literature, but I have chosen a few characters who seem particularly relevant, interesting, and well known.

As perhaps the most famous murderer in modern literature, Raskolnikov of Dostoevsky's *Crime and Punishment* arguably lives his immoralism to a greater extent than Thrasymachus or Callicles. Nonetheless, the "immoralist" label only ambiguously applies to him. Raskolnikov is not merely ambivalent about justice like our Platonic immoralists, but a conscious believer in it. This is clear in an early scene in a bar where Raskolnikov hears another student tell an officer about the old woman whom Raskolnikov later murders.

> [O]n one side we have a stupid, senseless, worthless, spiteful, ailing, horrid old woman, not simply useless but doing actual mischief, who has not an idea what she is living for herself, and who will die in a day or two in any case.... On the other side, fresh young lives thrown away for want of help and by thousands, on every side! A hundred thousand good deeds could be done and helped, on that old woman's money which will be buried in a monastery!... Kill her, take her money and with the help of it devote oneself to the service of humanity and the good of all. What do you think, would not one tiny crime be wiped out by thousands of good deeds?[1]

In response to the officer's question as to whether he himself would kill the old woman, the student answers, "Of course not! I was only arguing the justice of it.... It's nothing to do with me...."[2] Raskolnikov is struck that he hears such things when "his own brain was just conceiving . . . *the very same ideas*." He considers it just to kill the old woman and steal her property, for the reasons given by the student in the bar. While it seems fitting to some extent to call him an immoralist, his immoralism is less thorough even than that of Thrasymachus or Callicles.

Despite thinking it would be just to kill the old woman, however, Raskolnikov is horrified as he contemplates doing so. He would love to find a reason to abandon his plan.[3] A peculiar sense of duty drives him to murder—not duty toward others, or even toward his own interests, but toward his pride, his sense of what he is. The key to this pride is the division he makes between ordinary and extraordinary men, a division he explains with amazing frankness to Porfiry Petrovich, the police investigator, after the murder.

> [A]n "extraordinary" man has the right . . . that is not an official right, but an inner right to decide in his own conscience to overstep . . . certain obstacles, and only in case it is essential for the practical fulfillment of his idea (sometimes, perhaps, of benefit to the whole of humanity). . . . Then, I remember, I maintain in my article that all . . . well, legislators and leaders of men, such as Lycurgus, Solon, Mahomet, Napoleon, and so on, were all without exception criminals, from the very fact that, making a new law they transgressed the ancient one, handed down from their ancestors and held sacred by the people, and they did not stop short at bloodshed either. . . . In short, I maintain that all great men or even men a little out of the common, that is to say capable of giving some new word, must from their very nature be criminals—more or less, of course.[4]

He adds that his "leading idea" consists in people being divided into two categories: "inferior (ordinary), that is, so to say, material that serves only to reproduce its kind, and men who have the gift or the talent to utter a *new word*."[5] If a member of the second category "is forced for the sake of his idea to step over a corpse or wade through blood, he can, I maintain, find within himself, in his conscience, a sanction for wading through blood. . . . It's only in that sense I speak of their right to crime in my article."[6] As he puts it elsewhere to himself, thinking of Napoleon: "The real M*aster* to whom all is permitted storms Toulon, makes a massacre in Paris, *forgets* an army in Egypt, *wastes* half a million men in the Moscow expedition and gets off with a jest at Vilna. And altars are set up to him after his death, and so *all* is permitted."[7]

The men Raskolnikov admires are of a different sort than the selfish tyrants admired by Thrasymachus and Callicles. Raskolnikov's extraordinary man breaks laws, rules over others, and sheds blood, but not for the sake of private pleasures or satisfactions. It is not clear that such a man puts others before himself, but he seems to put "his idea" before his pleasure.

It is not hard to guess, as Porfiry Petrovich does, that Raskolnikov views himself as one of these extraordinary men. (In this too he differs from Thrasymachus and Callicles, who admire bold lawbreakers from afar.) More precisely, he feels he is extraordinary, but he feels he must prove himself. This is the chief reason why he murders: If he is truly extraordinary, he will "overstep" the obstacles in his path. As he later reflects: "The old woman was a mistake perhaps, but she is not what matters! The old woman was only an illness. . . . I was in a hurry to overstep. . . . I didn't kill a human being, but a principle!"[8] The principle is obedience to the rules by which ordinary people live. The obstacles Raskolnikov faces are less important to him as obstacles than as tests or proving grounds of his ability to "overstep." We may surmise that if his circumstances were changed and he did not face the particular obstacles before him, notably poverty, he would focus on other ones, and develop other tests of himself. (This is one way in which he actually differs from the "extraordinary men" he admires. Such men do not seek out dangerous tests of their ability to do what is necessary; they simply do it.)

Raskolnikov's attraction to distinguishing between ordinary and extraordinary emerges largely from a feeling or belief that true goodness must be difficult and demanding. (The desire to make sense of the careers of men like Napoleon also plays a role.) His pride consists largely of a restless but somehow moral feeling that being ordinary is not good enough, not worthy enough. Ordinary people are scarcely human, mere "material." He murders in order to prove that he is extraordinary. He must prove this not to others but to himself, and somehow to God or the universe as a whole. He must win its favor; he must show he is one of the elect. We might even say he must devote himself to a moral order which distinguishes sharply between ordinary and extraordinary. Thus his revulsion as he contemplates murder is not sufficient to hold him back. This devotion is also part of the reason he imprudently publicizes his views. In this he resembles our Platonic immoralists, with the important difference that he feels compelled not merely to express but to act upon his views.

In distinguishing ordinary and extraordinary, Raskolnikov tells Porfiry Petrovich: "The first category is always the man of the present, the second the man of the future. The first preserve the world and people it, the second move the world and lead it to its goal. Each class has an equal right to exist . . . and *vive la guerre eternelle*—till the New Jerusalem, of course!"[9] Porfiry Petrovich is struck by this last phrase, which seems hard to reconcile with the justification for murder which Raskolnikov has just offered. In answer to Porfiry Petrovich's questions, Raskolnikov says he believes not only in the New Jerusalem, but also in God, and even in the raising of Lazarus. There seems little reason to doubt his sincerity, given the amazing frankness he has demonstrated in this conversation.

Raskolnikov's belief in God and "the New Jerusalem" has a certain logic in the context of his admiration of extraordinary men. He says such men lead mankind "to its goal." Indeed they must, if their excellence is to mean more than ability to manipulate others for their private satisfaction (which of course is what virtue means for our Platonic immoralists, at least at first glance). However, the goals of extraordinary men vary, and often conflict. If their achievements truly mean something, if their lives are more than mere acts in a pointless human comedy, then there must be some final state, some New Jerusalem, toward which extraordinary men perhaps unwittingly lead the whole of mankind; and how can there be such a thing without God?[10]

This is not the first indication in the book that Raskolnikov believes in God, at least to some extent. At one point early in the book, when he decides (temporarily) against murdering the old woman, "there was a sense of relief and peace in his soul. 'Lord,' he prayed, "show me my path—I renounce that accursed . . . dream of mine!'"[11] Later, when he is summoned to police headquarters after the murder, his first response is to pray. "He was flinging himself on his knees to pray, but broke into laughter—not at the idea of prayer, but at himself."[12] His uncertain relation to God has been severed by his deed.

Raskolnikov's complicated relation to God is a key theme, or the key theme, of the book. What may be his most scoffing remark comes shortly after one of his strongest experiences of belief. After giving money he can scarcely spare to the widowed Katerina Ivanovna, he tells her young daughter who comes to thank him: "Polenka, my name is Rodion. Pray sometimes for me, too. 'And Thy servant Rodion,'—nothing more."[13] His interaction with the bereaved family, including his unhesitating generosity toward them, briefly revives him from the tormented state into which he had fallen since the murder. Without fully articulating it to himself, he again feels that there is goodness and love and life, his own as well as that of others; he even feels that he may be worthy of God's love. As his spirit revives, however, his thoughts return to their habitual path.

> "Enough," he pronounced resolutely and triumphantly. "I've done with fancies, imaginary terrors and phantoms! Life is real! Haven't I lived just now? My life has not yet died with that old woman! The Kingdom of Heaven to her—and now enough, madam, leave me in peace! . . . and now we will see! We will try our strength!" he added defiantly, as though challenging some power of darkness. . . . "Strength, strength is what one wants, you can get nothing without it, and strength must be won by strength—that's what they don't know," he added proudly and self-confidently and he walked with flagging footsteps from the bridge.[14]

Having regained his habitual frame of mind, he recalls asking Polechka to pray for him. "'Well, that was . . . in case of emergency,' he added and laughed himself at his boyish sally."[15]

Raskolnikov thinks that strength is "won by strength," not merely possessed by strength. Strength comes from strength, not from behaving morally or even prudently. The world is amoral not only in its structure but also in its operation—not only as a noun but also as a verb. However, Raskolnikov speaks "proudly and self-confidently" because this is "what they don't know." One who does know it perhaps deserves his strength after all. At this moment Raskolnikov seems particularly akin to Callicles, and particularly far from the New Jerusalem.

Another revealing instance of Raskolnikov's wavering regarding God occurs in his first conversation with Svidrigailov. After Raskolnikov says that he does not believe in a future life, Svidrigailov ruminates about what it might be like. "We always imagine eternity as something beyond our conception, something vast, vast! But why must it be vast? Instead of all that, what if it's one little room, like a bath house in the country, black and grimy and spiders in every corner, and that's all eternity is?" Raskolnikov is appalled. "'Can it be you can imagine nothing juster and more comforting that that?' Raskolnikov cried, with a feeling of anguish."[16] Evidently he had been carrying somewhere within him hope of a more just and comforting afterlife, a hope which is painfully pierced by Svidrigailov's suggestion.

After he confesses to the police and is sent to Siberia, Raskolnikov contemplates what he has done.

> "Why does my action strike them as so horrible?" he said to himself. "Is it because it was a crime? What is meant by crime? My conscience is at rest. Of course, it was a legal crime, of course, the letter of the law was broken and blood was shed. Well, punish me for the letter of the law . . . and that's enough. Of course, in that case many of the benefactors of mankind who snatched power for themselves instead of inheriting it ought to have been punished at their first steps. But those men succeeded and so *they were right*, and I didn't, and so I had no right to have taken that step."[17]

Raskolnikov feels, or at least tells himself, that his "conscience is at rest." He does not deny, or impugn as irrational, the existence of conscience. He seems to feel there might be deeds that would cause his conscience to trouble him. He doesn't consider what those deeds might be; instead he thinks of mankind's benefactors, and insists that many of them committed deeds like his.

For Raskolnikov, benefactors of mankind are entitled, perhaps even compelled, to break the "letter of the law," a phrase which resembles Callicles' "conventional justice." Nonetheless, "*they were right*" to do so, which suggests they must be judged by a higher law or principle, one which we might compare to Callicles' "natural justice," though Raskolnikov and Callicles differ as to the dictates of this higher law. Similarly, everything is "permitted" for a man like Napoleon, which seems to imply that there is some sort of judge, one who permits.[18] Raskolnikov believes in a justice that looks to results, and to the greatness of the undertaking, rather than to fixed rules such as those laid down in the Bible. His justice sometimes seems to have an element of approval of success, even of "might makes right," which makes its beneficence somewhat ambiguous; but he also thinks that great men ultimately benefit others.

Raskolnikov's view of justice is the key to the striking absence of restraint produced by his partial belief in God. The God in whom he partly believes differs from the God of the Bible, or at least from the God who lays down Biblical law. Raskolnikov's God would not categorically tell men "Thou shalt not kill" because He would know that sometimes it is better to kill—better for humanity, not merely for the killer himself. This is not to say Raskolnikov has a clear idea of the nature of God, or even that he thinks much about it. However, insofar as he believes God exists, he assumes He is just. Indeed, how could he believe God is unjust?

Belief in God is bound up with belief in justice. As I have discussed in earlier chapters, the belief that justice *should* triumph gives plausibility to, and is in some sense tantamount to, the belief that a god supports it. On the other hand, God's support ensures that justice is more than a futile claim or principle. To be sure, many people, notably pagan Greeks, believe in gods whose justice seems questionable, even to them. Generally speaking, however, as civilization and knowledge advance, people grow increasingly, though never wholly, confident that God or the gods are just (or, better yet, merciful).[19] The superstitious terror of early peoples in the face of the mysterious forces around them slowly gives way to understanding of the world and eventually to doubt that there is any place left in it for a divine power, unless it be to answer people's longing for justice and for transcendence of their relatively secure but still frail and mortal lives.[20] Raskolnikov is closer to the end of this progression than to its beginning. It is hard for him to believe that justice and power do not ultimately coincide—which helps explain the element of "might makes right" or Calliclean "natural justice" in his view of justice. To some extent his view of justice reflects a desire to be on the winning side. In this he resembles Plato's immoralists, and many other people as well.

However, his view of justice does not prevent Raskolnikov from being horrified at what he has done. Indeed, he is horrified at the deed even before he does it. Whatever his reasoned opinion, Raskolnikov is not content with the view that "*all* is permitted," as is shown not only by his anguish after he murders, but also by his frankness with Porfiry Petrovich, which is to say his unselfconscious (or partly unselfconscious) eagerness to be caught. He wants human beings to have a different relation to each other than is suggested by the view that "*all* is permitted." Although he still feels the proud desire to stand above the world, his deeper desire is to show himself to that world (even to the police), to be part of it, to be judged by it. Perhaps the deepest part of his anguish after he murders is the profound isolation or separateness he feels; he begins to return to sanity after he tells Sonya what he has done.

Moreover, as he shows in what he says to Katerina Ivanovna's daughter, Raskolnikov wants there to be a god who cares about him personally.[21] His desire for a decent and meaningful connection to other people is part of a desire for such a connection to the whole world outside himself, to a larger moral order, and to God. Although he does not initially realize it, he longs for a god who does *not* distinguish sharply between ordinary and extraordinary men. A god whose love one must earn through being extraordinary seems forbidding and, finally, unbelievable. How can one really earn such a thing? What one longs for must ultimately be given, not earned. A god for whom "*all* is permitted," or who views any human being as a "louse," a term Raskolnikov himself uses when speaking of ordinary men,[22] cannot satisfy his desire for love, for a place in the world, a place that transcends his frailty and mortality.

A world in which "*all* is permitted" is intolerable. But if it is intolerable, in what sense can it be just? We have seen that Raskolnikov considers himself just even as he murders; however, this is obviously only part of the story. He also feels himself to be committing a horrible crime; and this feeling goes deeper than the opinion about justice which he consciously or self-consciously holds. He longs for, and ultimately believes in, a more decent or Christian understanding of justice, one in which each individual life is sacred and many things are *not* permitted. We might ask which is stronger, his belief in or his longing for this more decent world. The belief and the longing are bound up together, each supporting the other; but ultimately the longing seems stronger. He might have maintained his view that "*all* is permitted" if not for his horror at it.

Some people, including Callicles and Thrasymachus, hold views similar to those of Raskolnikov without acting on them, at least in such a decisive manner. For Raskolnikov this is not an option. He must act on the truth as he understands it. In doing so, he is testing his understanding of the truth, as well as testing himself. He is in some sense reaching out to the truth, and to God, and even asking to be shown if he is mistaken. (At one point before he murders, he prays: "Lord . . . show me my path—I renounce that accursed . . . dream of mine!"[23]) Once he has murdered, his horror at his deed makes it clear that he has misunderstood himself. Deeper than his longing to be an extraordinary man for whom "*all* is permitted" is his longing for a place in a decent world. We do not see much of what becomes of him in Siberia, but we see that he begins to move toward a more decent understanding of justice and a more Christian understanding of God.[24]

We might wonder whether Raskolnikov's Christian upbringing hinders or contributes to his need to act on his views. On the one hand, the elements of Christianity that remain in his soul make murder seem more heinous than it otherwise might; indeed, this is a large part of the story Dostoevsky tells. On the other hand, Raskolnikov grew up with an expectation or at least a hope that his longings would be satisfied. Even as he lost much or most of his faith in the God of the Bible, he retained a disposition toward expecting hopes to be realized. He was not accustomed to think, as Thrasymachus and Callicles were, that reality teaches one to suppress one's hopes. On the contrary, he was accustomed to think that truth is worthy of devotion and will set one free. However, the student whom Raskolnikov overhears in a bar likely also had a Christian upbringing, but will never act upon the views he and Raskolnikov share. While the student maintains that it would be just to kill the old woman, he does not distinguish between ordinary and extraordinary men, a distinction which comes more from Raskolnikov's pride or sense of rank than from his Christian upbringing. (To be sure, Christianity distinguishes apostles and prophets from ordinary believers; however, it more strongly emphasizes our common humanity, and the sinfulness of those who claim to rise above it.)

Callicles and Thrasymachus make a distinction similar to Raskolnikov's, but with a different effect. For Raskolnikov, distinguishing between ordinary and extraordinary leads inexorably to longing to be extraordinary, and to prove that he is—not so much to others as to himself, or to the universe or God. For Callicles and Thrasymachus, making a similar distinction confirms their immoralism without requiring any further test, and without requiring that they prove themselves extraordinary, which they do not consider themselves to be. Immoralism leads them not so much to the desire to be extraordinary as to the desire not to be a dupe or fool. They too are fascinated by men who are extraordinary, but they don't experience it as necessary (or at least not to the same extent) that they themselves become so.

Perhaps Raskolnikov's Christian upbringing leads him to focus on judging, particularly judging whether he himself is extraordinary, whereas our Platonic immoralists are somewhat more concerned with living well. (They too are concerned with judging themselves, as we have seen; but this concern is less self-conscious for them, and somewhat less dominant.) The concern to live well might seem pedestrian or low to Raskolnikov. His sense that there must be something more to life, something tremendous at stake, at least partly reflects his Christian upbringing. The student in the bar does not seem concerned to be extraordinary, as I noted; but he is interested in being just. Judging and being judged apparently remain a salient and self-conscious part of life for him. However, Raskolnikov is the only one of these four men who is eager to prove himself to be extraordinary. He has a more forceful and erotic nature than the other three, though also (or for that reason) a more immoderate and imprudent one.

Of course the way in which Raskolnikov acts on his views is brutal and repellent. Does this mean he is more brutal by nature than Thrasymachus or Callicles, or most other men? Does he lack some instinctive sympathy or decency? Is this why he acts on his views while other immoralists do not? Or is he simply more forceful and erotic than they are, and therefore doomed to drink to the dregs the folly of immoralist views? I think the answer to these questions depends largely upon whom one is comparing him to. In some ways he seems more decent and delicate than Thrasymachus (he does not curse, for example, or offer gratuitous insults), and perhaps more than Callicles. He behaves with immediate and unhesitating generosity toward Katarina Ivanovna's family. Nonetheless, he seems somewhat deficient in sympathy for others, particularly if we compare him to his friend Razumihin. He is so proud and self-absorbed that others often don't live for him as human beings—which is hardly unique and usually does not lead to murder, but it does bespeak a lack of sympathy, and perhaps of sensitivity or delicacy. He is both more forceful and erotic, and more self-absorbed, than Thrasymachus or Callicles.

Another way Raskolnikov differs from our Platonic immoralists, as we have seen, is that he is less of an immoralist. His extraordinary man seeks not to satisfy his desires, but to lead men to a goal, a goal which the extraordinary man seems to understand as beneficial to mankind. All three of our immoralists believe in a moral order which demands and rewards devotion to justice, but this belief is less submerged in Raskolnikov than in the other two, and stronger. All three also believe in an "immoral" moral order which celebrates and rewards injustice, at least as conventionally understood. Raskolnikov is more aware of his more decent beliefs partly because he is much less concerned about consistency than Thrasymachus, and maybe less so than Callicles. He often veers from one opinion or set of opinions, accompanying one mood or feeling, to another quite different one, without seeming much troubled by possible contradictions. Perhaps this difference reflects the fact that the Russia of Christianity and nihilism places less emphasis on thinking out the implications of one's opinions than the Athens of philosophy, sophistry, and rhetoric.

However, while his lesser concern for consistency plays a role, the primary cause of Raskolnikov's greater awareness of his own moral beliefs and longings is his religious background. He was raised a Christian, in a country where Christianity was the common belief. He grew up believing that God takes care of human beings and that to those who give, much will be given. Such beliefs encourage one to embrace decency and to be concerned for the good of others. Even when he turns in an immoralist direction, Raskolnikov retains elements of these beliefs and feelings, for they respond to hopes he shares with our Platonic immoralists, and perhaps with everybody. Hopes that have been consciously embraced cannot be denied or submerged in the same way as ones that someone has always doubted he can satisfy.

We cannot be sure whether Thrasymachus and Callicles grew up believing in the Greek gods, though Callicles' habit of swearing "by the gods" suggests that he might have believed in them when he was younger. However, the Greek gods' support for justice is less clear than that of the God of the Bible. The Greek gods have human passions, and seem even less restrained by justice than people do. (Indeed, their example tends to support the view of Thrasymachus and Callicles that justice is for the weak.[25]) The more ambiguous justice of the Greek gods seems to have limited the intensity and certainty with which people embraced them. The Greek gods seem never to have been quite as central to people's lives as Christianity was for several centuries. (There were no Crusades for Zeus.) To be sure, Greeks asked "Father Zeus" to support causes they believed to be just; but confidence in Zeus' support for justice was surely affected by Zeus having overthrown his own father, who in turn had overthrown his. Christianity is more in harmony with people's natural longing for justice, and for divine love and protection. Thus it takes root more deeply in people, even in those who come to doubt that it is true. Raskolnikov is less of an immoralist than Thrasymachus and Callicles because he is more conscious of his moral longings, and more under their sway. He rejects moral rules, "the letter of the law," but not morality or justice itself.

GIDE'S MICHEL

We can hardly avoid Michel of André Gide's *The Immoralist* while considering fictional portrayals of immoralists.

Although Michel does not exactly advocate injustice, it is reasonable to describe him as an immoralist. Like Raskolnikov, Michel lives in a milieu (France in the 1890s) in which Christianity has sunk deep roots, and seems to have made people stricter in their view of justice than was true in Plato's Athens.[26] Although Christianity is weakening in Michel's France, one can hardly imagine a person there openly advocating injustice.[27] Michel nonetheless approaches doing so by giving lectures in which he praises barbarism over civilization.[28] This bears some kinship to Callicles' admiration of the man who satisfies his desires without restraint.

Michel's private thoughts are more explicitly immoral. He is strongly attracted to the historic figure of a young king "plunging for a few years into a life of violent and unbridled pleasures with rude companions of his own age, and dying at eighteen, rotten and sodden with debauchery."[29] He announces to the one person with whom he feels comfortable sharing his thoughts, "I hate people of principle."[30] On his country estate he is drawn to rakes and poachers, and is particularly fascinated by a family which is said to engage in rape and incest.[31] Later, upon revisiting Tunisia after an absence of a couple of years, he is disgusted to find that most of the street urchins he knew earlier have grown into more or less respectable youths. The one who does not disappoint him has just been released from prison.[32] The novel ends with Michel having sexual relations with this youth's mistress, after which he returns to his hotel to find his wife is dying.[33] (Gide hints that Michel's transformation includes the liberation of homosexual desires which he has previously suppressed. This is never made explicit, but Michel seems much more attracted to the Tunisian youth himself than to his mistress.)

Michel's journey is in a sense the opposite of Raskolnikov's. He begins as a very respectable man, is gradually detached from morality, and ends as a kind of murderer—he is responsible for his wife's death due to insisting that they travel while she is seriously ill. However, the morality to which he is originally attached seems so thin that it is hard to take his move away from it very seriously. Early in the book he evinces no passion, no enthusiasm; he marries without love, and studies without pride or a burning desire to know.

He is a somewhat more substantial character by the end of the book; however, he never seems to feel that morality offers life real meaning. Initially he seems to experience it merely as doing what others expect of one. By the end it includes decency or concern for others as well as doing what they expect, and he rejects decency and concern for a common good in order to satisfy his desires. Those desires do not point beyond themselves to some alternative moral code, or at least not very strongly. So Michel could be taken as evidence for the view that people are for the most part simply selfish in truth or by nature.

One way in which Michel does not change is that he never believes in God, or, perhaps more precisely, he refuses to turn to God.[34] This disbelief or resistance forms the background or context in which his recovery from a life-threatening illness gradually leads him in an immoralist direction. By the end, he restlessly crosses one moral boundary after another. Unlike Raskolnikov, however, he does so apparently without believing that there is transcendent significance to what he is doing. His aim is the liberation and satisfaction of desires which he previously suppressed or did not feel.

Unlike the other characters I have examined, Michel actually is eager to satisfy immoral or illicit desire—on its own terms, not simply as a way of rising above conventional morality. (His implied homosexuality probably has something to do with this difference. Conventional moral boundaries genuinely limit and grate on him.[35]) Michel's immoralism is not chiefly or essentially a disguised moralism or attachment to justice, although it does contain this element, in a somewhat different form than for our other immoralists. Michel longs to move beyond rules and boundaries, to be free. Freedom rather than power or excellence appears to him as happiness. Pushing beyond moral boundaries seems to him courageous and somehow noble, deserving of happiness; in this he resembles our other immoralists, but with freedom rather than power or excellence as the aim and mark of true virtue. However, unlike for our other immoralists, his view of nobility seems to be more a consequence of his desires than the ground of his desires. To put it another way, he experiences the good as noble to a greater extent than he experiences the noble as good.

Like Raskolnikov, Michel finds that living as an immoralist does not satisfy him. "Take me away from here and give me some reason for living. I have none left," he declares at the end of the book. "This objectless liberty is a burden to me." He experiences disgust with merely being free to satisfy his desires, which is to say he longs for something beyond desire. He also seems haunted by what he has done, even if he does not admit it. "It is not, believe me, that I am tired of my crime—if you choose to call it that—but I must prove to myself that I have not overstepped my rights."[36] The desire to prove that he has not overstepped his rights indicates some uncertainty, if not the agony which pulls Raskolnikov back to Christianity. Concern about not overstepping rights is obviously a concern for justice, even if Michel does not recognize it as such. He seems more concerned for justice here than elsewhere in the book; indeed, this is the strongest indication that he wants something more out of life than mere living. To be sure, early in the book he seems to feel some of the hope that decent people always feel, that the world in which they seek to behave well will treat them well, but in a wan and unselfconscious form. He tramples upon this hope in order to liberate himself and satisfy his desires, but having done so, he finds life empty.

I suspect that a real person living a life similar to Michel's in the second half of the book would evince a more or less unselfconscious belief that the truly deserving are those who do not seek to be just or deserving. Perhaps something like this belief remains unselfconscious in Michel's creator. However that may be, Michel does not seem fully human at the beginning of the book, and the morality he rejects is pale and thin. Something substantial still seems to be lacking at the end of the book. Gide's treatment of his immoralist, especially in his initial moral or conventional stage, invites doubt about the adequacy of his understanding of people's attachment to morality.

As my analysis of *The Immoralist* underlines, my procedure in this book is open to an obvious objection. How can we be confident that characters in Platonic dialogues or in literature reveal the truth about human motives? Perhaps they instead reveal the assumptions or limits of their creators. My chief response to this objection is simply that it seems to me Plato's dialogues, and other great works, present human beings at least largely as they are (which is much of what makes them great works), particularly in terms of questions like those raised in the Introduction. However, I do not find *The Immoralist* to be such a work.

A critical reader might take my treatment of *The Immoralist* to mean that I embrace evidence which supports my thesis and discount evidence which does not. I offer two responses. One is that *The Immoralist* does support my thesis to some extent, in its presentation of Michel's dissatisfaction and confused self-understanding at the end of the book. More importantly, though, I cannot avoid giving more weight to work which seems to me to reflect more fully human beings as I have experienced them. We have no way of gaining unmediated access to the inner workings of human beings except possibly through self-reflection, which itself needs to be developed and informed, above all by exposure to penetrating works by penetrating authors. If a reader is not convinced that Plato and Dostoevsky are more penetrating than Gide, or not convinced by my interpretations, I can only invite that reader to consider the questions I have raised based on his or her own analysis of these and other authors.

One might think history offers truer access to human beings than philosophy or literature. History and biography deal with actual people who actually lived; nonetheless, they do not provide anything close to direct access to the inner workings of those people. I have found Plato a more helpful guide to the questions I have raised about human beings than any other author, and much more helpful than grappling directly with historical data on my own. Nonetheless, I welcome scholarly treatments of historical figures in terms of the questions I have raised, and I think Thucydides, Plutarch, and other historians offer valuable insights on those questions.

SHAKESPEARE'S RICHARD III

While not precisely history, Shakespeare's *Richard III* presents a historical figure who, at least as Shakespeare shows him to us, clearly qualifies as an immoralist or tough guy. Shakespeare's Richard is "determined to prove a villain," and he tells why in his opening monologue.

> I, that am rudely stamp'd, and want love's majesty
> To strut before a wanton ambling nymph:
> I, that am curtail'd of this fair proportion,
> Cheated of feature by dissembling Nature,
> Deform'd, unfinish'd, sent before my time
> Into this breathing world scarce half made up . . .
> Why, I, in this weak piping time of peace,
> Have no delight to pass away the time,
> Unless to see my shadow in the sun,
> And descant on mine own deformity.
> And therefore, since I cannot prove a lover

> To entertain these fair well-spoken days,
> I am determined to prove a villain,
> And hate the idle pleasures of these days.[37]

Most of the pleasures which sweeten life for others are closed to the hunchbacked Richard. For him, in peacetime, there is only the grim pleasure of deceiving and overcoming other men.

This attitude does not change when an amorous opportunity arises for Richard. He woos and wins Anne in spite of (and also perhaps because of) having killed her husband, Prince Edward.[38] Richard is elated by this triumph, and comments afterwards: "Was ever woman in this humor woo'd? / Was ever woman in this humor won? . . . I do mistake my person all this while! / Upon my life, she finds (although I cannot) / Myself to be a marv'llous proper man" (I.ii.227–54). However, there is never any question of Richard's relaxing and enjoying "the idle pleasures of these days." Having won Anne, he states, "I'll have her, but I will not keep her long" (I.ii.229). Indeed, he doesn't; he has her murdered before the end of the play.

This ugly deed shows that Richard does not truly desire, or at least is not open to pursuing, the pleasures to whose absence he attributes his villainy. Perhaps he would behave differently if he could find himself "a marv'llous proper man." However, since he "cannot," he cannot trust in and find real gratification in Anne's doing so. He has long since come to feel that love is closed to him; this belief is too deeply settled for it to be challenged by winning Anne's hand. He trusts in victory and power, not pleasure and love. Winning Anne's hand gratifies his vanity, but does not touch his heart. Thus he treats her as he treats others: as an instrument, and brutally.

The closest thing we see to friendship in Richard is his conspiratorial collaboration with his cousin the Duke of Buckingham. They seem to enjoy each other's company as they plot to put Richard on the throne, notably when they dress themselves "in rotten armor, marvelous ill-favored," in order to convince the Lord Mayor that they have foiled an attempt on their lives (III.v.1–11). However, as if to prove the adage that bad men cannot love each other, they fall out as soon as Richard is crowned. Richard asks or demands that Buckingham kill King Edward's young sons, since while they live one might doubt that he is truly king. Buckingham pretends not to understand the request, and then asks for time to consider it (IV.ii.10–26). Richard concludes privately: "The deep-revolving witty Buckingham / No more shall be the neighbor to my counsels. / Hath he so long held out with me, untired, / And stops he now for breath? Well, be it so" (IV.ii.42–45). This brief, slightly wistful reflection is the only apparently sincere expression of friendly feeling that Richard gives in the play. Afterwards Richard treats Buckingham with contempt, at which Buckingham prudently concludes that it is time for him to put distance between himself and the man he helped make king (IV.ii.120–21).

Like Callicles but to a greater extent, Richard distrusts other men, but trusts in rule over them. His feeling about kingship resembles Callicles' feeling about tyranny, with the important difference that Richard actually pursues kingship, which is of course a more plausible goal for him than tyranny would be for Callicles. Unlike Callicles, Richard has grown up in a milieu where murder, and being murdered, are distinct possibilities: The houses of York and Lancaster have been plotting and fighting throughout his life, and his father was one casualty of the struggle. (Callicles to some extent exposes himself to kindred dangers by entering politics, but probably did not face them as a boy.) No doubt this hardened him; however, he is significantly harder than his brothers, who of course grew up in the same milieu.

Richard is also, probably to a greater extent, hardened by being hunchbacked. As we have seen, he does not allow himself to hope for love, or even to enjoy it when the opportunity arises. However, he seems to despise other men as much as he envies them. (In fact he says nothing expressing envy after the opening monologue, which is not to say he doesn't feel it, at least unselfconsciously.) He believes men's pleasures and the ease of their lives lull them into foolish decency and complacency. He deceives his brother King Edward, who he says is "true and just," while he himself is "subtle, false, and treacherous" (I.i.36–37). He also deceives his other brother, "simple, plain Clarence," who believes Richard is his chief defender (I.i.118). When Richard thinks he has convinced Queen Elizabeth to let him marry her daughter Elizabeth, he observes caustically: "Relenting fool, and shallow, changing woman" (IV.iv.431). Richard's contempt for the "true and just" might well remind us of Thrasymachus, but of course Richard practices treachery instead of preaching it.

Notwithstanding his falseness and treachery, Richard is a proud man. He takes genuine pride in his family and his birth (which of course make rule a salient possibility for him, unlike for our other immoralists). As he haughtily tells Dorset, a son of Queen Elizabeth from an earlier marriage, "I was born so high / Our aery buildeth in the cedar's top / And dallies with the wind and scorns the sun" (I.iii.262–64). Indeed, he seems excessively proud, for of course humans and eagles alike depend upon the sun.

Richard also admires courage, as he shows by his eagerness to fight in battle. He is happiest on the battlefield, where he kills five men disguised as Richmond before encountering the real one (V.iv.11–2). There he forgets his hunched back and his devious ways, and feels himself a true man. After he utters the famous line, "A horse, a horse! My kingdom for a horse," one of his supporters, worried about the danger to the King of fighting without a horse, urges him to withdraw. "Slave," Richard replies, "I have set my life upon a cast, / And I will stand the hazard of the die" (V.iv.7–10).

As we have seen, Callicles also admires courage.[39] Both Richard and Callicles experience the display of courage, including risking one's life, as prompted by pride rather than devotion or selflessness. But how can it be anything other than selfless to risk one's life (unless of course one must do so in order to protect one's life)? Both Richard and Callicles experience revulsion at the thought of being ruled by fear. They feel, and think, that a man who is ruled by fear is contemptible. They experience cowardice as ignoble and therefore bad. This goes deeper than their critique of justice or their embrace of selfishness. More or less unselfconsciously, they put being courageous before pursuing their own good.[40] Our other immoralists may feel similarly, though we see less evidence of it. Raskolnikov's actions bespeak boldness and admiration of boldness, along with a degree of brutality. Michel admires the fearless animal spirits of the poachers and rakes he meets once he leaves his books behind. Thrasymachus says little about courage, but he calls prudent and good those who are "able to be completely unjust, and able to subjugate both cities and races of men."[41] It is hard to see how somebody could accomplish this without a healthy dose of courage. I note also Thrasymachus' bold or imprudent candor, and his distaste for hypocrisy.

Why don't our immoralists subject courage to the same criticism to which they subject justice? They experience courage as noble and good, whereas (at least to some extent) they experience justice as foolish or narrow. Moreover, as I noted, the attachment to courage presents itself as concern for one's own dignity rather than the good of others, so it does not seem selfless or questionable to them. Indeed, many men who are not immoralists feel less ambivalence about courage than about justice. Many men feel that courage is *the* virtue that makes a man, while justice is good but not so indispensable. Perhaps there is an element or intimation of reality in this feeling. Courage is necessary for us to live well, arguably even more necessary than justice. A person who is wholly dominated by fears he cannot master (if there is such a person) is miserable. One particularly needs courage if one is to see with one's own eyes, as our immoralists strive to do, rather than trust what others tell one.

Nonetheless, one still might wonder why, with so much at stake and given their rejection of sacrificing for others, our immoralists do not consider more carefully whether courage, or the display of courage, is truly good. To put it another way, one might wonder why they fail to distinguish courage simply, remaining master of oneself in the face of dangers, from civic or conventional courage, risking one's life for one's city or country. The chief reason seems to be the intensity of their feelings and beliefs about courage. Their belief in the dignity of courage, and still more in the contemptibility of cowardice, is so strong that they will tolerate no doubt on this score. They recoil from the mere thought or possibility of being ruled by fear. (This is by no means true only of immoralists.) These beliefs and feelings have a moral aspect which our immoralists presumably have not consciously considered:

The coward strikes them as contemptible first and miserable second, not the other way around.

Our immoralists' reluctance to question the goodness of courage points us again to a notion of giving. They somehow want to make an effort, even a sacrifice, for courage. They feel one must be ready to give something, or risk something, in order to be courageous, and worthy as the courageous are. Even Richard, who is less obviously attached to justice than Raskolnikov or our Platonic immoralists, wishes to "stand the hazard of the die." He insists on risking his life for courage; it does not seem excessive to say he is devoted to courage. Although they don't recognize it as such, our immoralists' attachment to courage is also an attachment to justice, both as a principle (a view of deserving) and, more subtly, as a virtue (putting something before oneself, namely courage itself). Important elements of justice are missing, namely self-conscious devotion and concern for other people; however, the similarity seems greater than the difference.

In one respect Richard resembles Michel more closely than he resembles our other immoralists: He is genuinely eager to satisfy an immoral or illicit desire, namely the desire to be king. His murders of Hastings and of King Edward's sons are not tests of his repudiation of conventional morality (like Raskolnikov's murder of the old woman), but simply ways of gaining and securing the throne. He does not need to prove his immorality to himself, or to argue for it with others. He is more of a doer, and less of a thinker and talker, than our other immoralists. His hunched back is at least largely responsible for this difference. As he indicates in the opening monologue, he has long assumed that the pleasures other men enjoy are closed to him, and that he must be treacherous and ruthless in order to flourish. He feels little kinship with other men, and little need to share his thoughts.

Richard is fortunate in his pursuit of the crown. The assistance of Buckingham is critical to him, as are King Edward's suspicion of their brother Clarence, Edward's early death, and the unpopularity of Queen Elizabeth's family—to say nothing of his being born so close to the throne. Richard's behavior often has a harsh and violent edge which might have prevented his becoming king if he had faced more formidable competitors. (It is impossible to imagine him ascending to the throne in the manner of Henry IV or Richmond, later Henry VII.) For example, at the moment when he informs King Edward and other family members of Clarence's death, he seems both brutal and insincere (II.i.78–81). Later he is shockingly harsh to the genial Hastings, and he clearly does not expect anybody present to believe that Hastings is a traitor (III.iv.67–79).

Nonetheless, Richard makes some effort to limit and disguise his brutality, and for the most part he follows a sensible policy in pursuing the crown. Once he is crowned, however, he unleashes his brutality, and his policy markedly deteriorates. He openly prepares to murder King Edward's sons

(IV.ii.14–20), and, still more shockingly, his own wife Anne (IV.ii.50–9). He not only pulls away from but publicly insults Buckingham when the latter is reluctant to manage the murder of the young princes (IV.ii.88–118). Later he abuses even his faithful servants (IV.iv.445–46), and strikes a messenger bearing news he expects to be bad (IV.iv.507). We do not see him giving his followers much reason to follow him. He gives them no reason to think he is good or just, or that following him will make them good.

Richard seems to feel he depends on nobody now that he is king. To be sure, he knows that as long as Edward's sons live, people might doubt that he truly is king; indeed, he himself doubts it to some extent (IV.ii.14–16). He quite reasonably wonders if his "glories" will "last" (IV.ii.5–6). However, the only threat he considers is that posed by his relatives of royal blood. He does not view occupying the throne as an inherently uncertain if not perilous situation—one that will become more uncertain and perilous for him if he murders his nephews. (He is right that his throne will be insecure as long as they live; he does not see that it will be still more insecure if he murders them.) He seems to feel that the death of Edward's sons, and his marriage to Edward's daughter, will make him invincible, both as king and (to some extent) as a man. Although he seems to be an atheist (he never speaks privately of God until he is seized by remorse near the play's end, but he privately delights in brutal and treacherous plots, and in sanguinary witticisms[42]), he also seems to feel that being anointed confers something like divine protection. The only person who initially stands between him and the throne whom he does not plot to kill is the sitting king, his brother Edward IV. He seems to have a certain restraining reverence for kingship.[43]

Richard's entire life has been lived in a milieu of striving and plotting for the crown. It is not surprising that the crown seems to him to bear transcendent significance; he feels that its possessor is as such in a different realm than other men. This belief, which resembles the belief Callicles and Thrasymachus have in the happiness of the tyrant, is not fundamentally shaken by his becoming king himself, or even by the manner in which he does so. Informed that Richmond is crossing the English Channel, he responds: "Is the chair empty? Is the sword unsway'd? / Is the King dead? The empire unpossess'd? / What heir of York is there alive but we? / And who is England's King but great York's heir?" (IV.iv.469–72). This response might not be surprising in one who ascended to the throne peacefully and legitimately, but it is surprising in one who plotted his brother's demise and murdered his nephews. Instead of doubting the transcendent significance of kingship in light of his having made himself king, Richard asks whether he truly is king. To be sure, the question is rhetorical, but it nonetheless reveals an uneasy sense that his occupancy of the throne is questionable. (By contrast, Richard II speaks in a similar vein only after losing an army to Bolingbroke, soon to be Henry IV.[44])

Like Raskolnikov, though not quite to the same extent, Richard gradually comes unhinged. He grows distracted, inattentive, and increasingly irritable (IV.iv.454–62). He resents the people around him for distracting him from ruminating on his kingship and on his desire for a decisive determination of his fate. This is striking since his subjects are the ones who will determine his fate. His rule depends not simply on killing Edward's sons or overcoming Richmond, but on the feeling he inspires in the people of England. Richard seems not to feel this, once he is king. He does not see the king as someone who must serve and appeal to other people. This of course reflects his belief in the transcendent power and significance of kingship or legitimate kingship; he broods not over having murdered his close kin in order to become king, but over whether he truly is and will remain king.

Eventually, however, he is struck with guilt for what he has done. We see that even in this brutal man, belief in justice and belief in God uneasily coexist with immoralism, impiety, and contempt for decency. Waking in the middle of the night in a cold sweat from a nightmare the night before his battle with Richmond, he asks himself if he loves himself. "Wherefore? For any good / That I myself have done unto myself? / O no! Alas, I rather hate myself / For hateful deeds committed by myself" (V.iii.187–90). In his nightmare, the ghosts of those he has murdered appear to him. Interestingly, they promise not divine vengeance but rather that Richard's awareness of his wrongs will overwhelm him with guilty despair on the battlefield. (In the event, he does not despair, but boldly confronts "the hazard of the die." However, the fact that he thinks little about prudent measures he might take to preserve his crown and his life suggests that he is possibly affected by his conscience.) One might hesitate before concluding that this reveals suppressed piety; however, the ghosts also assure Richmond that "good angels" are guarding him. (Richmond actually seems to share this part of the dream [V.iii.230–31].) Moreover, upon waking Richard cries, "Have mercy, Jesu!" (V.iii.178). While his piety is not comparable to Raskolnikov's, Richard is more pious than he has realized. I have suggested that piety is an aspect or consequence of belief in justice or morality, a belief even Richard shares whether or not he realizes it.

NOTES

1. Fyodor Dostoevsky, *Crime and Punishment,* translated by Constance Garnett (New York: P.F. Collier & Son, 1917), 65.
2. Dostoevsky, *Crime and Punishment*, 66. Ellipses in original.
3. Dostoevsky, *Crime and Punishment*, 60.
4. Dostoevsky, *Crime and Punishment*, 263–64.
5. Dostoevsky, *Crime and Punishment*, 264.
6. Dostoevsky, *Crime and Punishment*, 264–65.
7. Dostoevsky, *Crime and Punishment*, 278.

8. Dostoevsky, *Crime and Punishment*, 278–79. Ellipses in original.
9. Dostoevsky, *Crime and Punishment*, 265.
10. To be sure, some thinkers have argued for a progressive historical process; however, divine guidance, if it exists, would seem a more reliable basis for leading humanity "to its goal" than the unconscious workings of history or dialectical materialism. At any rate, this seems to be how Raskolnikov views it.
11. Dostoevsky, *Crime and Punishment*, 60. Ellipses in original.
12. Dostoevsky, *Crime and Punishment*, 94.
13. Dostoevsky, *Crime and Punishment*, 191.
14. Dostoevsky, *Crime and Punishment*, 191–92.
15. Dostoevsky, *Crime and Punishment*, 192. Ellipses in original.
16. Dostoevsky, *Crime and Punishment*, 293.
17. Dostoevsky, *Crime and Punishment*, 552. Ellipses in original.
18. Dostoevsky, *Crime and Punishment*, 278.
19. People long to attain security and some sort of transcendence through being worthy or through a god who is just. However, since it doesn't seem possible to "deserve" freedom from frailty and death, people also hope it will be *given* by a god who is merciful and loving. One might understand the (at least numerical) triumph of Christianity over both Roman paganism and orthodox Judaism in light of its greater emphasis on mercy and love. As life grew increasingly comfortable and peaceful, people increasingly longed for, or became increasingly conscious of longing for, *more* than they felt they deserved. (To be sure, mercy plays a role in Judaism as well, but is not as central as in Christianity.)
20. Consider Paul Tillich, *Systematic Theology, Volume I* (Chicago: The University of Chicago Press, 1973), 129–30: "For the physicist the revelatory knowledge of creation neither adds to nor subtracts from his scientific description of the natural structure of things. For the historian the revelatory interpretation of history as the history of revelation neither confirms nor negates any of his statements about documents, traditions, and the interdependence of historical events. For the psychologist no revelatory truth about the destiny of man can influence his analysis of the dynamics of the human soul. If revealed knowledge did interfere with ordinary knowledge, it would destroy scientific honesty and methodological humility. . . . Knowledge of revelation cannot interfere with ordinary knowledge. Likewise, ordinary knowledge cannot interfere with knowledge of revelation. . . . It is disastrous for theology if theologians prefer one scientific view to others on theological grounds. And it was humiliating for theology when theologians were afraid of new theories for religious reasons, trying to resist them as long as possible, and finally giving in when resistance had become impossible."
21. Dostoevsky, *Crime and Punishment*, 191.
22. Dostoevsky, *Crime and Punishment*, 425.
23. Dostoevsky, *Crime and Punishment*, 60.
24. Dostoevsky, *Crime and Punishment*, 558.
25. Cf. Thucydides, *The Peloponnesian War,* V.105, where the Athenian envoys to Melos declare that the behavior of imperial Athens is not in any way contrary to that of the gods.
26. Michel's contemporaries seem gentler and more decent, but also more narrow, than people in either Plato's Athens or Raskolnikov's Russia. This is perhaps because the French are both Christian unlike the Athenians, and more civilized than the Russians.
27. France was officially de-Christianized a century earlier, during the French Revolution. This episode was short-lived, but had some lasting effect. During the Commune in 1871, Paris was again briefly ruled by people hostile to Christianity.
28. André Gide, *The Immoralist,* translated by Dorothy Bussy (New York: Vintage Books, 1954), 71.
29. Gide, *The Immoralist*, 55.
30. Gide, *The Immoralist*, 90.
31. Gide, *The Immoralist*, 108–9.
32. Gide, *The Immoralist*, 137.
33. Gide, *The Immoralist*, 141–43.
34. Gide, *The Immoralist*, 26.

35. Cf. Allan Bloom, *The Closing of the American Mind* (New York: Simon and Schuster, 1987), 232.

36. Gide, *The Immoralist*, 145.

37. William Shakespeare, *The Tragedy of Richard III* in *The Riverside Shakespeare* (Boston: Houghton Mifflin, 1974), I.i.16–31. Henceforth citations from this work will be given with their location in the play in parentheses.

38. Anne speaks as if Richard alone killed Edward, but in *The Third Part of Henry VI* Shakespeare shows Edward stabbed by, in order, King Edward IV, Richard, and Clarence (William Shakespeare, *The Third Part of Henry VI* in *The Riverside Shakespeare* [Boston: Houghton Mifflin, 1974], V.v.38–40). *Richard III* alludes to this only briefly, when Clarence dreams of an unnamed ghost who cries, "Clarence is come—false, fleeting, perjur'd Clarence, / That stabb'd me in the field by Tewksbury" (I.iv.55–56). Perhaps Shakespeare wishes to emphasize Richard's wickedness in the play named for him. I note also that while both plays show Richard plotting to manipulate Edward IV into killing Clarence, Holinshed, who was likely one of Shakespeare's sources, does not mention Richard in this context (Raphaell Holinshed, *Chronicles of England, Scotland, and Ireland*, Volume III [London: G. Woodfall, 1807], 346). Thomas More, who was probably another source for Shakespeare, raises the possibility that Richard plotted against Clarence, but concludes that there is "no certainty; and whoso divineth upon conjectures may as well shoot too far as too short" (Thomas More, *The History of King Richard the Third*, edited by George M. Logan [Bloomington: Indiana University Press, 2005], 12).

39. Plato, *Gorgias*, 491b–c, 492a–b.

40. Cf. Plato, *Alcibiades I*, 115d, where Alcibiades says, "I wouldn't choose to live if I were a coward" (Plato, *Alcibiades I* in Thomas L. Pangle, editor, *The Roots of Political Philosophy: Ten Forgotten Socratic Dialogues* [Ithaca: Cornell University Press, 1987]).

41. Plato, *Republic*, 348d.

42. See, for example, III.i.79.

43. It is true that he killed Henry VI, Edward IV's predecessor, before the action of *Richard III*; however, he seems genuinely to believe in the Yorkist claim to the throne, and to view the Lancastrians as impostors (IV.iv.469–72).

44. William Shakespeare, *The Tragedy of King Richard II* in *The Riverside Shakespeare* (Boston: Houghton Mifflin, 1974), III.2.83–89.

Conclusion

One salient difference between the Platonic and the non-Platonic immoralists I have examined is that the latter actually commit crimes, while the former, as far as we know, merely praise others who do so. In other dialogues, Plato presents men who are arguably political criminals, notably Critias and Alcibiades; however, they have not committed the crimes which later make them notorious at the time of the conversations Plato presents. Plato does not present active criminals like Raskolnikov or Richard III. Socrates might avoid criminals because it is dangerous to associate with them, as well as hazardous to one's reputation. (He faces these risks to some extent through having associated with Critias and Alcibiades.[1]) However, if he had considered it worthwhile to do so, Plato could have shown Socrates speaking with a criminal while he was awaiting execution after being sentenced to death (the situation in which Socrates speaks with Crito in Plato's *Crito*). Perhaps Plato thinks the more interesting immoralists are those who remain immoralists only in speech, or at least those who have not yet moved from speech to deed. At any rate, his focus in portraying Thrasymachus and Callicles is of course not their deeds but their complicated and contradictory opinions and hopes.

I began by raising the question of whether people are truly selfish. I turned to Plato's immoralists to see if they actually live in accord with their repudiation of justice. I found that they are much more attached to justice than they realize, and even unselfconsciously inclined toward something like devotion. Something similar is true of the non-Platonic immoralists I have examined as well.

One might ask whether the immoralists I examined are typical in this respect. Keeping in mind the considerable differences among them, are the characters I examined representative of immoralists and tough guys generally, or are they merely a few individuals?

I believe they are representative. We may surmise that outspoken immoralism is generally accompanied by unselfconscious attachment to justice or morality. Given how dangerous outspoken immoralism is in a world where most people at least claim to believe in justice, the position seems to undermine itself, and to demand as an explanation a hidden moral attachment to immoralism itself.

As the example of Richard III shows, however, not all tough guys or immoralists are outspoken. Before becoming king, Richard mostly keeps such views to himself. Nonetheless, we might ask of all immoralists, including those who keep their views to themselves: Why embrace injustice? Behaving justly is manifestly beneficial in many ways. It helps make possible security, love, friendship, reputation, and other goods. Embracing injustice as a general principle requires ignoring or forgetting these benefits. It is explicable only as a confused or ambivalent attraction to a moral principle. All immoralists resemble our immoralists in this respect.

I hope my book has cast some light on the ways in which people are and are not truly selfish. I will conclude by stressing one point. Our immoralists suggest that popular doctrines that assume people are fundamentally selfish (such as the liberalism on which our country was founded) don't necessarily lead to self-knowledge. Something may be gained in this respect, but more seems to be lost. Self-knowledge on this point is elusive and difficult, but may be possible through embracing one's most generous impulses, experiencing them in all their beauty and hope. Casual selfishness, such as that fostered by a regime that encourages focusing on rights rather than duties, prevents people from recognizing the high-minded and hopeful voice within. It remains there, to be sure; but distorted of form and harder of access. In Chapter 6, I briefly discussed the "Calliclean" direction in which American society generally seems to be moving. For the sake of self-knowledge and living a full human life, Americans today especially need to examine great treatments of tough guys or immoralists, above all Plato's.

NOTE

1. Regarding the risk to his life, see Plato, *Apology of Socrates*, in Plato and Aristophanes, *Four Texts on Socrates*, translated by Thomas G. West and Grace Starry West (Ithaca: Cornell University Press, 1984), 32c.

Bibliography

Aeschylus. *Prometheus Bound*, edited and translated by A.J. Podlecki. Oxford, UK: Oxbow Books, 2005.
Annas, Julia. *An Introduction to Plato's Republic.* New York: Oxford University Press, 1992.
Aristotle. *Nicomachean Ethics.* Loeb edition. Cambridge, MA: Harvard University Press, 1982.
Aristotle. *The Politics.* Translated by Carnes Lord. Chicago: The University of Chicago Press, 1985.
Armour, Robert A. *Gods and Myths of Ancient Egypt.* New York: The American University in Cairo Press, 2001.
Austen, Jane. *The Complete Novels of Jane Austen.* New York: Random House.
Bailly, Jacques A. *Plato's Euthyphro & Clitophon.* Newburyport, MA: Focus Publishing, 2003.
Benardete, Seth. *Socrates' Second Sailing: On Plato's Republic.* Chicago: The University of Chicago Press, 1999.
Berns, Walter. *For Capital Punishment: Crime and the Morality of the Death Penalty.* New York: Basic Books, 1979.
The Bible. Revised Standard Version. New York: American Bible Society, 1980.
Bloom, Allan. *The Closing of the American Mind.* New York: Simon and Schuster, 1987.
Bloom, Allan. *The Republic of Plato.* Translated with Notes, an Interpretive Essay, and a New Introduction. New York: Basic Books, 1991.
Bolotin, David. "Socrates' Critique of Hedonism: A Reading of the *Philebus.*" *Interpretation* 13/1 (January 1985): 1–13.
Bruell, Christopher. *On the Socratic Education.* Lanham, MD: Rowman & Littlefield, 1999.
Butler, Samuel. *The Way of All Flesh.* New York: Rinehart & Co., 1948.
Churchill, Winston S. *The Gathering Storm.* New York: Houghton Mifflin Company, 1948.
Dodds, E.R. *Plato: Gorgias: A Revised Text with Introduction and Commentary.* Oxford: Oxford University Press, 2001.
Dostoevsky, Fyodor. *Crime and Punishment.* Translated by Constance Garnett. New York: P.F. Collier & Son, 1917.
Douglass, Frederick. *Narrative of the Life of Frederick Douglass, an American Slave.* New York: Barnes and Noble Classics, 2003.
Dworkin, Ronald. *Taking Rights Seriously.* Cambridge, MA: Harvard University Press, 1978.
Ehrenberg, Victor. *From Solon to Socrates: Greek History and Civilization during the Sixth and Fifth centuries B.C.* New York: Routledge, 1996.
Eliot, George. *Daniel Deronda.* New York: Oxford University Press, 1988.
Freud, Sigmund. *The Interpretation of Dreams.* Translated by James Strachey. New York: Basic Books, 2010.
Gide, André. *The Immoralist.* Translated by Dorothy Bussy. New York: Vintage Books, 1954.

Hansen, Peter J. "Thrasymachus and His Attachment to Justice." *Polis* 32 (2015), 344–68.
Herodotus, *The Histories*. Translated by George Rawlinson. New York: Alfred E. Knopf, 1997.
Holinshed, Raphaell. *Chronicles of England, Scotland, and Ireland*, Volume III. London: G. Woodfall, 1807.
Homer. *The Iliad*. Loeb edition. Cambridge, MA: Harvard University Press, 1999.
Kahneman, Daniel. *Thinking, Fast and Slow*. New York: Farrar, Straus and Giroux, 2011.
Kant, Immanuel. *Groundwork of the Metaphysics of Morals*. Translated and edited by Mary Gregor. Cambridge, United Kingdom, UK: Cambridge University Press, 1999.
Leibowitz, David. "Thrasymachus's Blush" in *Recovering Reason: Essays in Honor of Thomas L. Pangle*, edited by Timothy Burns. Lanham, MD: Rowman & Littlefield, 2010.
Machiavelli, Niccolò. *The Prince*. Translated by Harvey C. Mansfield, Jr. Chicago: The University of Chicago Press, 1985.
Macaulay, Thomas Babington. *The History of England from the Accession of James II*. London: The Folio Press, 1985.
Maguire, J. P. "Thrasymachus . . . or Plato?" *Phronesis* 16 (1971): 142–63.
More, Thomas. *The History of King Richard the Third*. Edited by George M. Logan. Bloomington: Indiana University Press, 2005.
Nicholson, P.P. "Unravelling Thrasymachus' Arguments in the *Republic*." *Phronesis* 19 (1974): 210–32.
Nietzsche, Friedrich. *Beyond Good and Evil*. Translated by Walter Kaufmann. New York: Random House, 1966.
Nietzsche, Friedrich. *The Gay Science*. Translated by Walter Kaufmann. New York: Random House, 1974.
Nietzsche, Friedrich. *Schopenhauer as Educator* in *Untimely Meditations*, translated by R.J. Hollingdale. New York: Cambridge University Press, 1992.
Nozick, Robert. *Anarchy, State, and Utopia*. New York: Basic Books, 1974.
Pangle, Thomas L., editor. *The Roots of Political Philosophy: Ten Forgotten Socratic Dialogues*. Ithaca: Cornell University Press, 1987.
Pangle, Thomas L., and Burns, Timothy W. *The Key Texts of Political Philosophy: An Introduction*. New York: Cambridge University Press, 2015.
Plato. *Charmides*. Translated by Thomas G. West and Grace Starry West. Indianapolis: Hackett Publishing Company, 1986.
Plato. *Epistles*. Translated by Glenn R. Morrow. New York: Bobbs-Merrill, 1962.
Plato. *Gorgias*. Translated with Introduction, Notes, and Interpretive Essay by James H. Nichols, Jr. Ithaca: Cornell University Press, 1998.
Plato. *Opera*, Tomus IV. Edited by Ioannes Burnet. New York: Oxford University Press, 1978.
Plato. *Phaedo*. Translated by Eva Brann, Peter Kalkavage, and Eric Salem. Newburyport, MA: Focus Publishing, 1998.
Plato. *Phaedrus*. Translated with Introduction, Notes, and Interpretive Essay by James H. Nichols, Jr. Ithaca: Cornell University Press, 1998.
Plato. *Philebus*. Translated by Seth Benardete. In *The Tragedy and Comedy of Life: Plato's "Philebus,"* by Seth Benardete. Chicago: The University of Chicago Press, 1993.
Plato. *Protagoras and Meno*. Translated by Robert C. Bartlett. Ithaca: Cornell University Press, 2004.
Plato. *Symposium*. Translated by Seth Benardete. Chicago: The University of Chicago Press, 2001.
Plato and Aristophanes. *Four Texts on Socrates*. Translated by Thomas G. West and Grace Starry West. Ithaca: Cornell University Press, 1984.
Plutarch. *Aristides*. New York: Loeb Classical Library, 1914.
Plutarch. *Cimon*. New York: Loeb Classical Library, 1914.
Plutarch. *Pericles*. New York: Loeb Classical Library, 1914.
Plutarch. *Themistocles*. New York: Loeb Classical Library, 1914.
Rand, Ayn. *Atlas Shrugged*. New York: New American Library, 1996.
Rand, Ayn. *The Virtue of Selfishness*. New York: New American Library, 1964.
Rosen, Stanley. *Plato's Republic: A Study*. New Haven: Yale University Press, 2005.
Shakespeare, William. *The Riverside Shakespeare*. Boston: Houghton Mifflin, 1974.

Stauffer, Devin. *Plato's Introduction to the Question of Justice*. Albany: State University Press of New York, 2001.
Stauffer, Devin. "Thrasymachus' Attachment to Justice?" *Polis* 26 (2009): 1–10.
Stauffer, Devin. *The Unity of Plato's Gorgias*. New York: Cambridge University Press, 2006.
Strauss, Leo. *The City and Man*. Chicago: The University of Chicago Press, 1964.
Strauss, Leo. *Natural Right and History*. Chicago: The University of Chicago Press, 1953.
Strauss, Leo. *On Tyranny*. Ithaca: Cornell University Press, 1975.
Strauss, Leo. Unpublished transcript of class taught on *Gorgias* (1957). A transcript of this class is available online through the Leo Strauss Center.
Strauss, Leo. Unpublished transcript of class taught on *Gorgias* (1963). A transcript of this class is available online through the Leo Strauss Center.
Tacitus. *The Annals*. Translated by Alfred John Church and William Jackson Brodbribb. Chicago: Encyclopedia Britannica, 1952.
Tarnopolsky, Christina. *Prudes, Perverts, and Tyrants: Plato's Gorgias and the Politics of Shame*. Princeton: Princeton University Press, 2010.
Tarnopolsky, Christina. "Shame and Moral Truth in Plato's *Gorgias*: The Refutation of Gorgias and Callicles." Paper presented to the University of Chicago Political Theory Workshop, April 3, 2000. Available online.
Thucydides. *The Peloponnesian War*. Translated by Richard Crawley. New York: Random House, 1982.
Tillich, Paul. *Systematic Theology, Volume I*. Chicago: The University of Chicago Press, 1973.
Tocqueville, Alexis de. *De la Démocratie en Amérique*. Paris: Garnier-Flammarion, 1981.
Vlastos, Gregory. *Socrates: Ironist and Moral Philosopher*. Ithaca: Cornell University Press, 1991.
Xenophon. *The Shorter Socratic Writings: Apology of Socrates to the Jury, Oeconomicus, and Symposium*. Edited by Robert C. Bartlett. Ithaca: Cornell University Press, 1996.
Zuckert, Catherine. "Why Socrates and Thrasymachus Become Friends." *Philosophy and Rhetoric* 43 (2010): 163–85.

Index

Achilles, 76
Adeimantus, 14, 54, 135
Aeacus, 149, 151–152
Aeschylus, 149
Alcibiades, 61, 79, 86n3, 135, 146, 177n40, 179
Amphion, 78, 80, 87n25
Annas, Julia, 1–3, 55n7
Anubis, 63
Anytus, 73–74, 77
Aristides, 124–125
Aristophanes, 79, 87n27
Aristotle, 20, 21, 34n31, 68, 136
Armour, Robert A., 86n7
Asclepius, 43
Austen, Jane, 55

Bailly, Jacques A., 56n15
Benardete, Seth, 30
Berns, Walter, 32n8
Bloom, Allan, 8, 38, 56n16, 177n35
Bolotin, David, 117n32
Bruell, Christopher, 32n13
Buckingham, Duke of, 170, 173
Burns, Timothy W., xv, 33n15, 33n20, 33n24, 34n26, 56n13
Butler, Samuel, 78

Caligula, 35n46
Callicles, xiv–xv, xvi, 4–5, 6, 8, 31, 47, 59–85, 86n1–87n30, 89–115, 116n1–118n35, 119–137, 138n1–139n28, 141–154, 154n1–155n19, 157, 158–159, 161, 162, 163–166, 167, 171, 173, 174, 179, 180
Cephalus, 5, 37
Chaerephon, 59, 60
Charmides, 135, 139n24
Churchill, Winston S., xiii
Cimon, 123–125, 126, 138n2, 138n10, 144–146
Cleisthenes, 124
Cleitophon, 11–12, 17, 32n4, 32n13, 54, 135
Critias, 179
Crito, 179
Cronos, 148

Darius, 68, 69–70, 71, 77, 96
Demos, 61, 104, 141
Dodds, E. R., 9n9–9n10, 86n3, 86n14, 87n26, 87n28, 87n30, 107, 135, 139n25, 146, 155n19
Dostoevsky, Fyodor, xv, 157–166, 175n1–176n24
Douglass, Frederick, 155n14
Dworkin, Ronald, xii, xviin10–xviin11

Ehrenberg, Victor, 138n3
Eliot, George, xiii
Er, 35n37

Index

Euripides, 74, 78, 82, 87n25, 87n28, 99, 100

Freud, Sigmund, 34n30

Gibert, John, 87n25
Gide, Andre, xv, 166–169, 176n26–177n36
Glaucon, 11, 14, 30, 31, 35n45, 39, 54, 135
Gorgias, 26, 59, 61, 63–64, 79, 90, 100, 105, 106, 111, 118n35, 120, 139n25–139n26, 152, 154
Gyges, 54

Hansen, Peter J., 33n15
Heracles, 72
Herodicus, 43
Herodotus, 124, 138n2
Hippocrates, 45
Hitler, Adolf, 150
Hobbes, Thomas, xi, xii, xiii, xvin4, xvin6, xviin16
Holinshed, Raphaell, 177n38
Homer, 76

Jesus, 60, 86n1, 155n17

Kahneman, Daniel, xii
Kant, Immanuel, 55n8

Leibowitz, David, xv, 33n15, 35n38, 55n3, 55n10, 56n16
Locke, John, xi

Macaulay, Thomas Babington, xviin17
Maguire, J. P., 9n1
Mao Zedong, 28
Michel, xv, 166–169, 171, 173, 176n26
Miltiades, 123–125, 126, 138n2, 144–146
Minos, 149
More, Thomas, 177n38

Napoleon, 158, 159, 161
Nero, 35n46
Neville, Lady Anne, 170, 173, 177n38
Nichols, James H., Jr., 9n9, 69, 87n28, 116n5, 155n11
Nicholson, P. P., 34n33
Nietzsche, Friedrich, xviin15, 87n17, 130

Nozick, Robert, xii

Pangle, Thomas L., xv, 33n15, 33n20, 33n24, 34n26, 56n13
Peleus, 76
Pericles, 66, 87n16, 123–125, 126, 128, 138n2, 138n10, 142, 144–146, 151
Petrovich, Porfiry, 158, 159, 162
Phoinix, 76
Pindar, xviin24, 72–73, 78
Plato: *Alcibiades I*, 79, 139n24, 177n40; *Apology of Socrates*, 87n27, 180n1; *Charmides*, 86n6, 139n24; *Cleitophon*, 32n4, 32n13, 139n24; *Crito*, 179; *Epistles*, 155n5; *Gorgias*, 4–5, 6, 9n9, 31, 40, 47, 55n6, 59–85, 86n1–87n30, 89–115, 116n1–118n35, 119–137, 138n1–139n28, 141–154, 154n1–155n19, 177n39; *Laches*, 57n19; *Lysis*, 86n6; *Meno*, 57n19, 73–74; *Phaedo*, 86n6, 117n28, 148; *Phaedrus*, 32n2; *Philebus*, 102, 103, 117n29, 117n32; *Republic*, xiv–xv, xvi, xviin13, xviin21, 6, 7–8, 9n3, 11–14, 15–31, 32n1–32n5, 32n11–33n22, 33n24–35n39, 35n42–35n45, 37–55, 55n1–57n21, 61, 67, 68, 78, 82, 86n6, 86n12, 91, 92, 106, 117n29, 133, 139n24, 148, 177n41; *Symposium*, 79, 86n3, 117n31; *Theages*, 139n24
Plutarch, 138n2, 169
Pluto, 148, 149
Polemarchus, 11, 12, 13, 14, 30, 33n18, 37, 54, 86n1, 135
Polus, 40, 60, 61, 62, 63–64, 79, 90, 106, 118n35, 119, 120, 130, 139n25, 152
Portia, 138n16
Poseidon, 148
Prometheus, 149
Protagoras, 26
Protarchus, 102, 103

Rand, Ayn, xiv
Raskolnikov, xv, 157–166, 167–168, 171, 173, 175, 176n10, 179
Rawls, John, xi
Rhadamanthus, 149, 151
Richard II, 174

Richard III, xv, 169–175, 177n38, 177n42–177n43, 179, 180
Rosen, Stanley, 17, 33n19, 33n21

Shakespeare, William, xv, 138n16, 169–175, 177n37–177n38, 177n42–177n44
Stalin, Joseph, 28, 62
Stauffer, Devin, xv, 13, 21, 25, 32n11, 33n18, 35n39, 38, 43, 55n2, 55n10, 56n16, 86n10, 116n2, 116n5, 116n9, 116n15, 117n24, 117n33, 118n35, 131, 138n18, 139n20, 139n22, 154n2
Strauss, Leo, xviin24, 7, 8, 34n26, 48, 56n12, 56n17, 86n8–86n9, 105–106, 116n1, 116n8, 116n11, 117n27, 131, 136, 138n13, 154n1, 155n8
Svidrigailov, 161

Tacitus, 35n46
Tarnopolsky, Christina, 3, 104
Theages, 78, 135, 139n24
Themistocles, 123–125, 126, 138n2, 144–146

Thrasymachus, xiv–xv, xvi, 2–3, 6, 7–8, 9n3, 11–14, 15–31, 32n1–32n4, 32n11, 32n13–33n22, 33n24–35n39, 35n42–35n45, 37–55, 55n1–57n21, 59, 61, 67, 68, 70, 72, 82, 91, 92, 106, 113, 133, 157, 158–159, 163–166, 167, 171, 173, 174, 179
Thucydides, xviin24, 87n16, 136, 138n2, 139n23, 155n18, 169, 176n25
Tiberius, 35n46
Tillich, Paul, 176n20
Tocqueville, Alexis de, xiii
Tversky, Amos, xii

Vlastos, Gregory, 3, 4, 5, 6–7

Xenophon, 35n44, 136, 155n9
Xerxes, 68, 69–70, 71, 72, 77, 96, 134

Zethus, 78, 80, 87n25
Zeus, 69, 148–149, 166
Zuckert, Catherine, 44

About the Author

Peter J. Hansen earned his A.B. from Harvard College and his PhD from the Committee on Social Thought at the University of Chicago. He is a lecturer at MIT, where he teaches ethics to engineers. This is his first book, but he has written on philosophy, politics, and finance for popular and scholarly publications.

Ingram Content Group UK Ltd.
Milton Keynes UK
UKHW040717170423
420292UK00004B/226